# INSIDE FAMILY THERAPY

# INSIDE FAMILY THERAPY

## A Case Study
## in Family Healing

**Michael P. Nichols**
*College of William & Mary*

**Allyn and Bacon**
Boston • London • Toronto • Sydney • Tokyo • Singapore

*Editor-in-Chief, Social Sciences:* Karen Hanson
*Series Editor:* Judy Fifer
*Series Editorial Assistant:* Susan Hutchinson
*Marketing Manager:* Susan E. Brown
*Sr. Editorial Production Administrator:* Susan McIntyre
*Editorial Production Service:* Ruttle, Shaw & Wetherill, Inc.
*Composition Buyer:* Linda Cox
*Manufacturing Buyer:* Megan Cochran
*Cover Administrator:* Jenny Hart
*Electronic Composition:* Publishers' Design and Production Services, Inc.

Previous editions were published under the titles *The Power of Family: Mastering the Hidden Dance of Family Relationships*, copyright © 1988 by Simon & Schuster/Fireside Press, and *The Power of Family Therapy*, copyright © 1992 by Michael P. Nichols.

**Library of Congress Cataloging-in-Publication Data**

Nichols, Michael P.
    Inside family therapy : a case study in family healing / Michael
P. Nichols.
      p.    cm.
    Rev. ed. of: Power of family therapy. c1992.
    Includes index.
    ISBN 0-205-28412-4
    1. Family psychotherapy—United States—Case studies.  2. Family—
United States—Psychological aspects.  I. Nichols, Michael P.
Power of family therapy.  II. Title.
RC488.5.N5345  1998
616.89'156—DC21                      98-14393
                                           CIP

Printed in the United States of America
10 9 8 7 6 5 4 3        04 03

*To the girl in the pool hall who recommended Psych 101
and stuck around to be my girl, for thirty-five years
and counting.*

# CONTENTS

# PREFACE

The story of family therapy is usually told in a particular way. The subject is families, but the point of view is the therapist's. This perspective allows us to narrow our focus to essential dynamics—complementarity, triangles, cross-generational coalitions—and to emphasize therapeutic techniques. Face to face with a family in pain, it can be hard to see past their griefs and complaints to the underlying dynamics. So if therapists sometimes reduce the complexities of human relationships to categories they can deal with, they do so for a good reason. But, inevitably, something is lost.

The story you're about to read is told somewhat differently. Instead of speaking to you from the lectern, *Inside Family Therapy* brings you into the consulting room to see for yourself what goes on. Many cases are described, but the emphasis is on the details of one family's therapy. This story also takes you deep into the experience of the family in treatment.

The actions and interactions of family members in therapy are so compelling that it's easy to forget that they must have an inner life as well. We hear about untamed offspring and partners who don't cooperate. Family members tell us the truth as they know it, but not the whole truth. The full story of any family is about consolation, security, tenderness, affection, desire, betrayal, heartbreak, revenge, promises, lying, risk, duty, drudgery, parents, children, excitement, entrapment, jealousy, peace, humiliation, compromise, respect, and routine.

When I first met the Salazars (as I shall call them), they were a couple at their wits' end, futilely remonstrating with their son, Jason, who alternated between ignoring and defying them. We will see how social constructions of masculinity and femininity shaped the Salazars into a polarized partnership between a man absorbed in his own agenda and a woman defining herself through others. Beginning with the initial phone call for help, I will trace the family's treatment from beginning to end, providing detailed accounts of actual clinical sessions and enriching these accounts with the personal experiences of the participants.

Instead of seeing family members primarily as objects of professional attention, by looking deeper into their hearts and minds perhaps we will be able to think of them not so much as characters in the therapist's drama, but as heroes of their own stories. My hope is that these stories will also provoke readers to reflect on their own experience. Clients aren't the only ones who get caught up in the blind, dominating power of habit.

The shift from impositional to collaborative therapy calls for a greater recognition of the fact that we're all in the same boat. Therefore, just as I do in therapy, I will occasionally offer advice about coping with various family problems. These suggestions may be especially welcome to readers who aren't clinicians, but I hope that therapists, too, will find these comments useful—in their own lives as well as in developing greater empathy for what their clients are going through.

Some of the friends who were generous enough to read and comment on various chapters were Michael LaSala, Joe Eron, Tom Lund, James Donovan, and Richard Kagan. I am especially grateful to Johnna Paratore for extremely insightful suggestions.

# INSIDE FAMILY THERAPY

# 1

# DISTURBING THE PEACE

## "Can You Help Us?"

I was just leaving my office at the medical center when the phone rang. *Let it ring*, I thought, *I want to get home*. But have you ever noticed how insistent a phone gets when you try not to answer it?

"Hello, this is Doctor Nichols."

The voice on the other end sounded distraught, near tears. Most callers are polite and a little hesitant; I could tell this woman was upset because she just launched into her story.

"This is Sharon Salazar, Doctor. I'm calling about my son, Jason. He's been giving us more and more trouble; lately he's become totally unmanageable. He's defiant and he's rude. He does what he wants, when he wants. He has absolutely no respect for his father or me. He used to be an excellent student, but this year he's barely passing any of his subjects. Last Saturday night he came home at two o'clock in the morning, and he smelled like a brewery. So we grounded him for a month. He went crazy and screamed obscenities at us, then he ran out the door. He stayed out all night. We know where he went—to his friend Kevin's house—but we just don't know what to do anymore. Can you help us?"

"It sounds like you're having a pretty rough time," I said. "How is this affecting other members of the family?"

This was my opening gambit in an attempt to broaden the definition of the problem. When families are having difficulties with "unmanageable" children, they want someone to step in and take charge. As a family therapist, I wanted to find out why they hadn't been able to take charge themselves.

"The problems with Jason have created quite a strain between my husband and me. Stewart's not home much, and when he is, he wants things quiet. So sometimes he ignores Jason and sometimes he cracks down on him too hard. It was his idea to ground Jason for a month. I thought that was a bit much. Our little girl, Heather—well, she's not so little anymore, she's in the ninth grade—she's the opposite of her brother. She doesn't misbehave at all. But I don't want her getting ideas from Jason."

"It seems like a good idea that you called," I said. "What I'd like to do is set up a meeting with the family and find out more about what's going on, so I can see if I can help."

"You want to see all four of us?"

"Yes. It sounds like Jason's problems are affecting the whole family, so I'll need to see everybody to get as much information as possible."

"Well I don't know. I doubt if my husband can come. He's a professor at the university and his job keeps him pretty busy."

"I understand. But it's essential that I hear from everyone, to get as many points of view as possible. I'll tell you what. I have an opening next Saturday at nine. Why don't you tell your husband that I said I have to see everybody, at least for an evaluation, and then call back to confirm that you'll be able to make it."

"Okay," she said, but she didn't sound very happy about it. I went home wondering if I would hear from her.

The following afternoon I returned to my office from a faculty meeting with just enough time for a cup of coffee before driving downtown to meet with a group of therapists I supervise at a low-cost clinic. By habit, I checked my messages and found one from Mrs. Salazar. She'd called to say they'd be at my office Saturday morning at nine.

I suppose I should have been pleased, but I'm never completely comfortable seeing families with teenagers. Whatever problems there are have usually gotten pretty bad. Even though this is how I make my living, Mrs. Salazar's call stirred a lot of uneasy feeling—about the family's pain, the inevitable struggle over the conditions of treatment, and the pressure on me to deliver. It's so much easier with younger children.

## Looking for Leverage

When I walked into the waiting room at nine o'clock on Saturday, the Salazars were sitting there. I consider that a good sign. People who come late or don't bring the whole family always have reasons ("The parking was terrible," "Ginger has a cold"), but the ones who have trouble organizing themselves to get there on time often seem to have trouble making a success of therapy.

I introduced myself, and Mr. Salazar stood up. He was tall and slender. His long, graying blond hair was slicked back and he wore wire-rimmed glasses. "Hi, I'm Stewart Salazar. This is my wife, Sharon. This is Heather; and that's Jason."

Sharon Salazar shook my hand but didn't smile. This was serious and she looked it. Her face was tight, set in an angry look; her dark hair, streaked with white, made her look all the more severe.

Heather stood up and nodded. Like her father she was slender, and she had his coloring. Her hair, worn long and loose, was the reddish blond of a golden retriever. She was kind of pretty but she didn't seem to know it yet.

Jason slouched in a chair in the corner. It was easy to see who was the bad guy.

"Please come in," I said and watched them file into my office. Jason was the last one in. Shoulders hunched, hands thrust in the pockets of his torn blue jeans, head down, hair in his eyes—that adolescent walk.

My consulting room is furnished with plain, functional furniture. At one end, near a window, is a large oak desk. Along one wall is a small brown sofa, along the other wall are four tired-looking easy chairs. One of the chairs wobbles unsteadily. I keep planning to get it fixed, but most of the people who sit on it are too preoccupied to notice.

This morning I had the chairs and sofa arranged in a semicircle, with a chair for myself slightly outside the semicircle. That way I could address the family—be with them, but not quite one of them.

As the Salazars arranged themselves around the room, they began to drop the guarded formality of the waiting room and settle into more familiar roles. The change was most noticeable in Mr. Salazar. The man who greeted me in the waiting room was direct and businesslike. Even though it was Saturday, he had dressed up in a light gray herringbone sports jacket and dark gray slacks. He looked directly at me and spoke with assurance, one professional to another. But the man who sat down with his family was transformed. No longer was he Professor Salazar, a person of authority used to dealing with professionals on an equal footing; now he was a husband and father, and the difference in his demeanor was striking. He looked older, worried, and not at all sure of his authority.

Heather sat on the sofa with her mother. Jason sat in the corner, as far away as he could manage.

"So," I said gently, "who would like to begin?"

Mr. Salazar looked at his wife and said, "Why don't you start?"

"Okay," she said and then launched into a litany of complaints. "Like I told you on the phone, it's Jason. He's totally disrespectful. He thinks he can do whatever he wants, whenever he wants, and he pays no attention to anything we tell him. He's *constantly* getting into trouble. I didn't want to tell you over the phone, but the latest thing he's gotten into is pornography. A few weeks ago I found some of those filthy magazines under his mattress. I was disgusted! I threw them out, but this week I found more in his closet."

Her tone was hard, mean. I was surprised. Such old-fashioned intolerance from a well-educated woman? My first instinct was to challenge her—"What's so unusual about a teenage boy looking at pictures of naked women?" But her angry determination warned me that this would only disqualify me as an expert and relegate me to the status of yet another person against her.

I glanced at Jason to see how much this was embarrassing him. All I could see was a sneer. Bravado? I could prod him to answer his mother, but this wasn't the time. First I needed to hear from each of them, to build an alliance of understanding, before getting into the battles to come. I turned to Mr. Salazar and asked, "What do you think?"

"Sharon's right. Jason has always been a problem. He's been willful and stubborn since he was little, and now that he's getting older he thinks he can do whatever he wants. I agree with Sharon, only . . . maybe sometimes she worries too much. This business with the magazines, I don't know if that's so abnormal for a boy his age."

"I suppose *you* think it's all right for him to fill our house with that trash! *You* don't care what happens to the boy. Suppose he becomes addicted to pornography?"

"Okay, hold on," I said. "Let's come back to this point. But first I want to hear from everybody."

First interviews are so difficult. At some point it's important to allow or even provoke family members to have their usual fights, so you can see what happens: who attacks, who withdraws, who sides with whom. But to them it may feel like the same old thing—the hateful, frustrating conflict they came to get away from. I want them to have their fights, but later—and with a difference. I'll want them to see how the argument between two people fits into the whole pattern of the family, and I'll want to have enough leverage to push the participants past the usual unproductive wrangling that leads nowhere.

❖

What's going on so far? First we hear about an "uncontrollable adolescent." Then Mrs. Salazar's complaints become a harangue and attack, first on the boy, then on her husband. Maybe she's an "overcontrolling mother." Blaming the mother is an easy trap to fall into. One of the hardest members of a family for most people to empathize with is an angry mother. But maybe the problem is Mr. Salazar: he doesn't support his wife. However, nothing is gained by shifting the blame from one family member to another. It's hard to get away from blaming, and hard, very hard, to get beyond the view of people as separate selves in conflict. But the secret of family therapy is to discover how disparate problems and private quarrels fit into the overall structure of the family.

❖

Next I turned to Jason. "What do you have to say about your parents' complaints?" (I said "parents' " deliberately because I didn't want to expose the split between them prematurely. That might turn out to be a significant problem, but it's not what they had come for, and whatever else I did, I wanted them to come back next week.)

"She's *always* on my case. *Nothing* I do makes her happy. So what's the use of trying? I don't see how coming here is going to do any good."

Although the parents, as architects of the family, have the most power to decide whether or not to return and give therapy a chance, it is nevertheless important to establish rapport with every member of the family. The trouble was, in this family it was going to be hard to sympathize with any one of them without alienating the others. I did my best. "I see. You think your parents are too hard on you, and you don't really feel like being here. Maybe it seems like you have nothing to gain by changing the way things are at home. . . ." And then, without waiting for an argument: "So, Heather, where are you when all this arguing goes on around the house?"

"I don't know." Heather took her lower lip between her teeth and stared at the rug, not used to being asked, or used to not answering. Maybe I was too direct.

"What grade are you in, Heather?"

"Ninth," she said, eyes on the floor.

"Do you go to the same school as Jason?"

"Yes. Only I don't see him much. He hangs around with the older kids."

"Heather, does it bother you, all the arguing between Jason and your parents?" This not-so-innocent question was my attempt to find out whose side she was on.

"Yes. He's always getting into some kind of trouble. I don't see why he doesn't do what he's supposed to." So, here was my answer: Mrs. Salazar was in control and Heather was still in line. "Only. . ."

Mrs. Salazar finished for her daughter: "Heather doesn't like all the noise. She's quiet. She likes to read."

" 'Only,' what?" I asked, trying to catch Heather's eye.

"What?" her mother tried to coax her.

Heather shook her head. As I was to discover, she could go stubborn like that. Silence was her power, her only power.

❖

Now I'd heard from each of them. I could see that Mrs. Salazar was in charge, an angry, domineering woman—or someone driven to act like one—and I could see that Jason was the only one who fought with her openly. Mr. Salazar claimed to be on his wife's side, but he wasn't very convincing. If he supported her at all, it was only grudgingly. And Heather seemed the picture of the good girl, only. . . only, I didn't know what. What I couldn't yet be certain of was how accurate these impressions were, or how they all fit together.

## Dialogue: Setting the System in Motion

Now I was ready to let them talk, to see how the family functioned to air grievances and solve problems. I was interested less in what they said, though, than in who said what to whom, and how. And I wanted to see how far dialogues would be allowed to go before a third person stepped in.

One thing I wasn't interested in, however, was getting into endless, fruitless debates of the kind Jason and his mother were expert at. I wanted to probe the flexibility of the family's organization by trying to activate the two less central figures, Heather and Mr. Salazar.

"Tell me, Mr. Salazar, what does Jason do that bothers *you* the most?"

Mr. Salazar glanced at his wife, then back at me. "I don't know. I guess it's his arrogance. I work hard to support this family. We have a nice house, they have everything they want, but they take it all for granted. These kids don't know how lucky they are."

Jason muttered under his breath, "Sure, Dad, tell us about the good old days."

"What did you say?" I asked.

"Nothing," Jason muttered.

"See? That's what I mean. He's so damned snotty, you just can't talk to him."

"That seems like a shame. If a man can't talk to his son, there's no way for the two of them to understand each other. You don't feel like he respects you; and he, well, I'm not sure what he feels. Why don't you ask him? Try talking with him now."

"You heard the doctor, Jason. You've got to learn to respect me; I *am* your father, you know. Why don't you ever—"

"Don't be so critical, Stewart!" Mrs. Salazar interjected. "The doctor said *you* should try to understand how *Jason* feels."

"That's interesting," I said. "You don't think your husband can do it by himself, so you come in. Is that the way it happens at home?"

"Ha! That's a laugh," said Mrs. Salazar. "He *never* talks to the boy; it's always up to me."

It was striking the way she called her son "the boy." She didn't use his name, as though he weren't "Jason," not a separate person, only her son. It was a peculiar distancing mechanism.

Mr. Salazar tried to answer his wife's complaint. "You never give me a chance. You're always criticizing me for not paying enough attention to him, yet whenever I do say anything, you take *his* side. What's the use?"

I interrupted. "You said over the phone that Jason is pulling you apart. Kids certainly know how to divide and conquer. It seems that you and your husband have slightly different ideas about how to handle your son. Perhaps the two of you could talk about that."

❖

This would be a turning point in the interview. This kind of invitation can be very threatening. Mr. and Mrs. Salazar hadn't come to air their disagreements; they came hoping I would do something about Jason. Unfortunately, the something I was doing was probing the conflict between the two of them. Nine times out of ten, when a child misbehaves, the parents are pulling in different directions.

❖

Mrs. Salazar felt vulnerable, exposed. She had expected therapy to be a dialogue, but hoped the dialogue would be with an outsider, an expert, someone who would take her side, someone who would help, not push her to do what she didn't know how to do. She paid careful attention to my suggestion, just like a cat does when you tell him not to chase birds. Instead of talking to her husband, she turned on Jason. "You never do anything I ask. And you lie!"

"I never—" But he didn't get to finish. Most families are more reserved, but these two were on each other like a shot. She reviled him with pent-up rage, and although he tried to fight back, in the end he was no match for her—at least not verbally.

Their acid tones shouldn't obscure the fact that these two were intensely preoccupied with each other. The connection might be conflictual, but it was as strong as Krazy Glue. Regardless of who else was speaking, these two addressed themselves to each other. When I asked a question, they responded with barbed comments and rhetorical questions, expertly baiting one another. They fought, but it was a little like the play-fighting of puppies: snarling and growling and nipping, but no real biting. Perhaps the conflict between Jason and his mother served to diffuse a more pernicious conflict between the parents and, at the same time, was made worse by the parents' inability to form a united front. I wanted to see the pattern and test its elasticity with an enactment.

Once again I interrupted. "I don't think you're going to get anywhere with Jason unless you two parents talk over your differences and come up with a strategy for dealing with him. And I don't think you can do that by letting Jason interrupt you. Talk to your husband. What do you want him to do? Talk to your wife. You two need to work together."

This time they complied.

Mr. Salazar crossed his left leg over his right, clasped his hands around his knee, and held on. I looked where he looked. I noticed the puffiness under Sharon Salazar's eyes. Tired eyes. It was a pretty face—large brown eyes; a full mouth; thick, wavy, dark hair—a face in that long transition between young and middle-aged. The signs of strain and complaint showed around the eyes and mouth, and some isolated strands of gray—white, really—appeared in her hair. It was a nice face, but she tightened it when she turned to glare at her husband.

"You don't care about us. All you care about is that precious job of yours. For years I've tried to get you to be more involved with this family, but you're always too busy. Even when you are around, you're so grouchy you make the rest of us nervous. All these years you've left everything to me. Who drives the children everywhere? Who waits up till all hours when Jason's out late? Not you. You have to have your precious sleep. Do you know what Jason's midterm report card looks like? No. You haven't even looked at it."

"I didn't see the report card. Where was it?"

"I put it in your hand last Sunday night. 'Not now,' you said." Her tone was mocking. "It's always 'later' with you. With you, later never comes."

Mr. Salazar's cheeks reddened. He looked away and lapsed into silence.

I wasn't ready to let it end this way. Sometimes my job is no more complicated (and no easier) than refereeing a boxing match. You just have to keep the spectators from entering the fray and prevent the combatants from leaving the ring before they finish the fight. "Can you answer her?"

"No," he said, glaring at me. "She doesn't want my opinion. She just wants everything done her way."

"Tell *her*," I urged.

"What's the use? She complains that I'm not more involved. Maybe that's true. But maybe it's not because I'm some kind of selfish monster. Maybe I'm just sick and tired of her constant criticism. If you want to know what I think, I think that when the children upset her she takes it out on me."

"That's not fair," she said, starting to cry. "Nothing's *ever* your fault. You're *so* innocent. Poor you. It's got to be me. I'm always wrong." Now she was sobbing.

"I'm sorry, honey. I don't mean that I'm all right and you're all wrong. You know that. It's just . . . I mean, sometimes I can't take all the criticism." He leaned forward and reached for her hand, but she pushed him away.

## It Must Be a Marital Problem

Another false conclusion we might draw is that the real difficulty in the Salazar family was a marital problem: The parents don't get along, and the boy's misbehavior is a product of that conflict. This is true, but it's only a partial truth.

Jason's rebelliousness was due in part to his mother's possessiveness, which was a product of his father's distance. When family members sense these or similar connections, they think in terms of simple cause-and-effect and look for someone to blame. This type of thinking mistakenly casts each of them in inflexible roles—the rebellious teenager, the managerial mother, the disengaged father—and obscures the rich interconnections among all the members of the family.

## Linear versus Circular Causality

In *linear causality*, A causes B. This works fine for some things. If your favorite geranium turns yellow (effect), go ahead and look for a simple cause. Not enough sunlight or too much water may turn out to be the direct cause of your plant's unhappiness.

Human unhappiness is a bit more complicated. From the perspective of *circular causality*, behavior is seen as a series of moves and countermoves in a repeating cycle. The illusion of unilateral influence tempts each member of the Salazar family to believe that there is one cause (A) for every effect (B). Jason believes that his mother's excessive demands make him disobey ("If she were more reasonable, I'd do what she wants"). She, on the other hand, thinks that if he would just do what she asked, she wouldn't have to be on his case all the time. Each of them is convinced that if only the other one would change, things would be better. Once things become stuck in a recurring cycle like this, change rarely occurs, because instead of breaking the dysfunctional pattern, the participants simply act it out more forcefully.

Replacing the usual habit of thinking linearly and beginning to think in terms of reciprocal influence helps us approach relationship problems with a new and more productive outlook. You don't get along with your supervisor? Instead of worrying about whose fault it is or who started what, consider the relationship as a series of moves and countermoves that go around in a circle. He calls you into his office to discuss a new assessment form, lecturing you about the need to operationalize goals in behavioral terms and to follow *DSM-IV* guidelines. You listen respectfully but with growing annoyance that he cares more about paperwork than about people. You agree with him, sort of, but put in a word or two about chart writing taking up too much time. He gets irritated and tells you to do it his way. The meeting ends with both of you unhappy and each of you knowing why.

Circular thinking means figuring out that when he does X, you do Y, and he does more X, and you do more Y, and so on. Remember, if Y is what you do, Y is all you can change. This doesn't mean that he's right and you're wrong, or even that you have to give in to him. For example, one possible change in the cycle is to agree with him, and then do what you wanted to do in the first place. This may or may not solve the problem. It probably will if his real agenda is wanting to tell you what to do and have you agree with him; it probably won't if he really wants to monitor exactly what you do (most bosses don't).

To understand the circular process in the Salazar family it's necessary to recognize that the cycle is *triangular*, not bilateral. This is true of most family problems, as we shall see. Because Jason's relationship to Sharon is related to her relationship with Stewart (and his relationship to Jason is related to Jason's relationship with Sharon), change in any one of these links will reverberate to the others. In plain English, getting Sharon to back off from Jason requires getting Stewart more involved with her (or getting her more involved with friends or other adult outlets). You don't change one side of a triangle without affecting the others. In the triangle involving Jason and his parents I wanted to see three changes: (1) Jason and his mother more separate, (2) Stewart and Sharon closer, and (3) Stewart more involved with Jason. Remember that all three changes are interrelated.

The easiest place to start is often the most dormant relationship, the one least entrenched in conflict. So, I decided to see if I could get Mr. Salazar more involved with his son. Later, I would tackle the more difficult jobs of getting him more involved with his wife and of pulling her away from Jason. Unless I found a way to accomplish this, Mrs. Salazar's attempts to dominate her son might very well drive a basically normal adolescent into ever more extreme acts of rebellion.

❖

"Mrs. Salazar, you seem pretty discouraged. Do you sometimes feel like nothing you do or say matters? That things just never seem to improve?"

"Yes," she said quietly.

"Would you be willing to pull back a little and let your husband take a more active role in disciplining Jason?"

"*Willing?* Yes, of course, that's what I've been trying to tell you."

"So, Mr. Salazar, would you agree to take a bit more of an active role with Jason?"

"Sure, I guess so," he said without conviction.

"Which is it, 'sure' or 'I guess so'?"

"I said I would."

"Okay, fine. Why don't you begin by talking with Jason about one area where you'd like him to improve this week. Just pick one thing and try to come to a clear agreement about that."

"All right, Jason, you heard the doctor. What about starting with your homework? No going out or watching TV until you finish your homework."

Jason looked at his father absently, looked at me absently, spotted his mother's look and said to her: "What business is it of you guys *when* I do my homework? As long as I get decent grades, I think it should be up to me. Besides, I can do half of it in homeroom and the rest in study hall."

Mrs. Salazar lit into him with a fury. "You lie! That's the worst thing about you. You say that you do your homework but you don't. It's gotten so that we can't trust a thing you say. You've become a rotten, spoiled brat!"

All the cockiness went out of Jason's face. She blistered him. When she was done, both father and son just looked at me. Their eyes said, *See what I have to put up with?*

The ensuing silence lasted several tense minutes.

❖

Transactions in families routinely occur within familiar limits, defined by habit, that maintain *homeostasis*—a balanced steady state of predictable routine. The therapist's job is to increase the intensity to force them to go beyond the threshold. You have to speak loud enough to be heard, but not so loud as to make them back off.

❖

"Mrs. Salazar, do you really want Jason to grow up? Because what you're doing isn't helpful."

Jason broke in: "She doesn't control me! *I'm* an individual."

"Sure you are, but your individuality is affected by the way you feel you have to rebel against your parents' authority. It's as though you think that you can only be a man by defying them."

Then I turned to Mr. Salazar. "Your staying outside keeps your wife overburdened. Why do you do that? You must have a very good reason."

"It's that precious job of his," Mrs. Salazar blurted out. "He thinks that's the only thing in the world that matters."

I tried to goad him into fighting back. "There you are again! She's on your back again. How do you do it?"

"I didn't say a word!"

"Exactly."

"You said that I should try to talk to Jason. Well, I tried. You saw what happened. She won't let me."

"What I see, Mr. Salazar, is that every time you pull back, your wife takes over. And, Mrs. Salazar, every time you criticize his way of handling Jason, he pulls back. Is there some way you can help your wife feel that she doesn't need to take over? Is there some way you can let your husband get involved other than by nagging him?"

"I guess I could pull back, take a rest as you say, and give Stewart more of a chance to take over."

"That's good, but Jason won't let you. He's hooked on dragging you in. He knows he can get around you. He's not so sure about his father. How are you going to respond when Jason baits you by behaving like a stubborn thirteen-year-old? Are you always going to take the bait?"

❖

I thought, *If Jason could learn to talk to his father, he would be less tied to his mother.* I said, "Jason, I doubt this will make any sense to you, but if you don't learn to relate to your father, you may always have trouble relating to men. Mr. Salazar, your son is growing up without you two knowing each other. Why don't you talk to him now, explain your point of view. Shouldn't a father and son understand each other?"

"I don't think he wants to hear it," Mr. Salazar answered. "He doesn't care what I think." They exchanged looks.

"Give it a try," I said.

Cheek muscles tense, frowning with the unaccustomed effort of instructing his son about life, Mr. Salazar told Jason that a man has to learn to do what he's supposed to do. It starts in the home but extends into your career. There are important things to do. Much to accomplish. It was a ponderous lecture, filled with words like "respect" and "self-discipline." Stewart Salazar didn't have much practice talking to his son, and he wasn't very good at it. I could see how much trouble he had understanding what Jason was feeling. I wanted to teach him how to get through to his son, but I held back from commenting because I wanted to push them to try harder, not interrupt to tell them that they were doing it wrong. I wanted to get Mr. Salazar more involved, not add to the weight of criticism in this family. Nagging is nagging.

I took my cue from Jason's monosyllabic responses. "Jason has taught you to ask what's on his mind in such a way that he only has to give short answers. Can you speak to him in such a way that he can talk more like an adult—so that he can begin to grow up?"

My goal wasn't just discipline—or distance—but to establish a hierarchy, which meant putting the parents in charge. To do that I would have to break the pattern where one parent did all the childrearing while the other remained on the periphery. They wanted to throw me the problem of Jason's behavior like a hot potato. I threw it back to them.

These two parents had probably been distant for years. Why? She attacks and he withdraws—or, when he withdraws, she attacks. Who started it? *It doesn't matter.* Either one of them could stop it. But their distance left a void in their lives. Mr. Salazar filled the empty space with work; his wife filled it with the children. This worked when the children were small, but now it didn't work so well.

Jason had grown to a point where his mother's control provoked him to rebel. The more he struggled to get free, the more she tightened her grip. Now Jason was trained to rebel—not only to maintain autonomy in the face of his mother's control, but also to fill a missing role in the family: to be the man in his mother's life.

Jason thinks his problems will be over once he gets out of his parents' house. (Didn't we all?) He's wrong. The patterns with which we relate to our parents become etched in our character.

If Jason continues to define his autonomy as opposition, he'll do so into manhood. Who knows, maybe twenty years from now he'll be on some therapist's couch trying to resolve a "problem with authority." If so, life will provide him with a series of trials. Dealing with his mother would be the final exam. He could put it off indefinitely or, with my help, learn to pass it now.

To complicate things further, Jason's mother's relentless criticism had undermined his self-esteem. The pornography and masturbation were one way of dealing with his hurt pride. These things may seem like a predictable part of adolescent sexual experimentation, but Jason overdid it. He retreated to his room and soothed his wounded ego with teenage fantasies. Unless he curtailed this habit soon, it might have a detrimental effect on his social life, and it might perpetuate the age-old male tendency to think of women as either domineering mothers or sexual playthings.

❖

Although I'd broadened the focus of problems in Jason's family to include his parents, I had neglected his sister. It was easy to do because she was so quiet. But if there's one thing you'll learn, it's that trying to do family therapy without drawing in all members of the family can be a big mistake.

In subduing her own nature to conform to her mother's rule, Heather had become inward, a shy girl with a good reputation but few friends. I made another effort with her.

"Heather, are you always this quiet?"

"I don't know. I don't really have anything to say."

"What effect does the tension at home have on your social life? Do you try to get out of the house more? Do you hesitate to have friends over?"

"No."

I felt challenged by Heather's timid truculence, but I wasn't about to cajole her to open up. Failure would make me appear impotent and allow Heather to continue to lose by winning. Success, unlikely as that was, might show up her parents—timid daughter opens up to sensitive therapist. No, better to get them to talk with their daughter.

"I don't seem to be getting anywhere. You two are the parents; can you get Heather to talk about how she feels about all of this?"

Mrs. Salazar said she knew exactly what Heather felt, and Heather nodded. I said, "That sensitivity is very important when children are young; it's what makes you such a good mother. But now they're beginning to grow up." And then, to Heather, "Does it sometimes bother you that Mom speaks for you?" Finally, to Mr. Salazar, "Can you help Heather speak to your wife about this, because your wife is too strong for her."

Just then I happened to notice the clock on the wall above Mrs. Salazar's head. It was 10:15. We were well over the hour. "Well I'm afraid we're out of time. There's a lot more to talk about, and I'd like to see you again next Saturday at this time." I didn't make it sound like a question.

Mrs. Salazar looked at her husband. He said, "Okay, we'll be here."

They didn't talk on the way out. Each of them was absorbed in private thought.

Jason was probably thinking, *I'm outta here! This therapy business is going to be just like I thought it was—a lot of pointless arguing, all designed to get me to be a goody-goody wimp, like precious Heather.*

Heather most likely didn't want to come back either, but she wished Jason would quit causing trouble. Sometimes she hated him.

Mrs. Salazar had a mixed reaction. She seemed to like me; though she thought I was somewhat oblique, she apparently felt that I knew what I was doing. What I was doing, she sensed, was putting pressure on the family to handle a problem they had already tried in vain to solve. She had hoped that I would take a more active role. Why must everything fall to her?

Mr. Salazar doubtless resented being there. One thing he was sure of was that he didn't want to open up old feelings about the marriage. But maybe coming here would be enough to make Sharon stop worrying so much and always picking on Jason. If she backed off, maybe Jason would stop being so defiant. Why couldn't this psychologist just tell her that? Why did he have to stir up the whole family?

❖

The consultation with the Salazars was the beginning of a new approach to their problems with Jason. Instead of focusing on Jason's behavior in isolation, I would focus on his interactions within the family. Therapy based on this framework isn't directed at a collection of individuals but at the organization of the family. When the organizational pattern of the family is transformed, the lives of every family member are altered accordingly.

To say that people are products of their families isn't news. Surprisingly, however, treating whole families together hasn't become as common as you might think. (It's so much easier to talk with people one at a time.) What's more, seeing that families have an overall organizational structure that shapes the lives of their members is less common still. As we shall see, discovering these patterns in a family is like turning on a light in a dark room.

# 2

# THE MAKING OF A
# FAMILY THERAPIST

One thing we rarely doubt is our selfhood. Even if we spend much of our energy focused outward, toward making our way and getting along with others, we do so with a sense of being separate and distinct, self-contained personalities. This is what gives continuity to our lives: There is a coherent unity, "myself," as an organizing center of our existence.

Under duress, we retreat even further into selfhood. Some beleaguered individuals withdraw to lick their wounds, others strike back, some reach out for help. When people seek professional assistance, they tend to go alone. What do they seek? Healing? Yes, but also sanctuary, refuge from troubled and troubling relationships.

In family therapy, however, people are no longer isolated from emotional sources of conflict; instead, problems are addressed at their source.

❖

In the 1950s, family therapists were bold pioneers, busy opening new territory and staking their claims against unfriendly elements in the mental health establishment. While they were struggling for legitimacy, family clinicians tended to emphasize their common beliefs and downplay their differences. Troubles, they all agreed, came in families. Moreover, families weren't simply groups of individuals; they were complex social units, organized to maintain the balance of the collective entity—even, in some unhappy cases, at the expense of some individuals.

Not only were families sometimes inimicable to individual development, they could at times actively resist change, developmental or therapeutic. Thus, there was an invidious undercurrent to the discovery of family therapy—a sense that not only is the family an organic whole but also that this organism sometimes swallows individuals. Maybe it was this exaggerated attention to the family's homeostatic aspects that sometimes made family therapists a little combative.

We fought with the psychiatric establishment to win a place for family therapy, we fought with each other to carve up the new-won territory, and, regrettably, we sometimes fought with families to rescue scapegoated "identified patients." Looking back with 20/20 hindsight, our tendency to be a little impatient and aggressive with families probably stemmed from an exaggerated optimism about what we could accomplish.

Later we discovered that we'd gotten a little carried away. Unlike individual therapy, which can be quiet and contemplative, family therapy does call for an energetic approach. But the truth is that when any member of a system overfunctions, including a therapist, other members are prone to passivity. So we've learned to be more collaborative. We've learned, too, to recognize the profound role of gender in shaping human experience and family relationships.

Some of us were slower than others to come to this recognition. It wasn't until my forties that I would begin to appreciate how my understanding of gender was shaped by my own privileged experience and that I was never really free of bias or blindness. And, like many of my colleagues who grew up with this field, I've only lately begun to appreciate the limits of my ability to understand the experience of people of other cultures, colors, and sexual orientations.

Family therapy grew up a lot in the 1970s and 1980s. Today it is a mature field, sure of itself but no longer cocky. Thirty years ago it was a whole new way of thinking.

❖

One of the first patients I saw in my early training was Tito Ramirez, a five-year-old boy brought to the child psychiatry clinic after he set a fire in the closet of the apartment where he lived with his mother and sister. The note I received from the intake interviewer said little other than this, except that his mother said, "He acts kind of strange and doesn't play much with other kids."

Fire-setting, along with running away and cruelty to animals, is an ominous symptom in a small child, so I wondered if this little boy might be psychotic. I saw him, as was the custom then, individually, in a room equipped with toys designed to let him express his feelings in play. Naturally, his mother was excluded from these sessions, lest her presence inhibit him.

For three weeks Tito played quietly while I watched and made encouraging comments. The only thing remarkable about his play was that he was rather listless. He liked to play with stuffed animals and look at pictures in old copies of *The Ladies' Home Journal*. Unlike other boys his age, he never reached for the dart gun or water pistol, and although he was interested in the big Bozo doll, he never punched or wrestled with it. Tito was quiet but he didn't seem particularly strange, certainly not psychotic.

When I decided to invite his family in, it was more out of confusion than conviction. What I saw cleared up the confusion.

Ms. Ramirez, Marina, was twenty but seemed very young. Dressed in a striped tank top with a short skirt, she looked more like a teenager ready for a date than like a mother coming to the doctor's office. She seemed totally out of her element as a parent. Ramona, her three-year-old, was a handful. No quiet toys for her! She ran around the room, grabbing one toy then another. She banged, yelled, threw things, and generally did a pretty good imitation of a roomful of kindergartners when the teacher steps out. I waited for Ms. Ramirez to quiet her daughter down. I had a long wait.

Tito seemed utterly lost. Instead of becoming more adventurous with his mother present, he seemed even more shy. He sat next to her, hanging on to her arm, and once or twice tried to climb onto her lap. His mother ignored him. She also ignored Ramona, as though Ramona's rambunctiousness was nothing out of the ordinary. All she wanted to talk about was her boyfriend, Leon, and all the troubles they were having.

Things started to fall into place. Tito, the little fire-setter, was not a disturbed youngster. He was a lonely little boy, poorly supervised and starved for attention. Nor was his mother some kind of cruel or neurotic parent. She was a not-quite-grown-up young woman, too preoccupied with her own problems to pay much attention to her children. It only took a minute to see.

Although I had no special knowledge of family dynamics, I did have enough common sense to realize that the number-one priority in Marina Ramirez's life was working things out with her boyfriend. Once she did that, and had some security and a little love in her life, she was able to turn her attention to her children. That and a little counseling about empathy and discipline was really all it took to make a big improvement in Tito—in all of them.

❖

I was elated. A whole new world of possibilities opened up. Instead of seeing separate individuals acting and reacting to each other, I began to see patterns that tied families together. Misbehaving children, for example, usually turned out to have a couple of parents pulling in opposite directions. How is some six-year-old going to get away with leaving dirty dishes around the house, biting her baby brother, or sassing her parents unless they let her? But why? Parents aren't stupid. The problem usually turned out to be that they undercut each other's authority, either because one was strict and the other lenient, or because they were angry and fought through the children. I was amazed at how many times a parent would complain about something in a child that was remarkably similar to what the other parent did.

Still, something was missing. I could see certain patterns and I began to see the family acting as a group, but nothing I had learned prepared me to understand the family's underlying organization. Most of the family concepts taught in graduate school were *dyadic*,—that is, they referred to something going on between two people. As I was to learn later, what goes on between two people is often a function of what goes on between them and a third (a woman overinvolved with her mother isn't likely to be fully engaged with her husband) or other activities (a workaholic husband probably won't be close to his wife, while a man who's merely putting in time at a boring job may require more togetherness than his busy wife can tolerate). Our courses emphasized discreet processes—marital schism and skew, conflict-avoidance, scapegoating—rather than how to understand a family's overall organization.

I learned the lingo—"pseudomutuality," "splits" and "alignments," "identified patient," and so on. But even though I got As on my exams, I was just doing C work with my patient families. About a third of the people who come to a therapist are in a crisis that will resolve itself unless the therapist does something really stupid (like prescribe antidepressant medication for someone mourning a loss). Another third will get better merely through the process of talking things over with the whole family. That leaves one more third, those people whose complaints are due to ingrained problems in the family. These problems won't clear up just by talking things out. Some problems require basic changes in the way a family is structured—changes that the average person may not understand how to bring about, and about which I, as a young family therapist, didn't have a clue.

## Behind the One-Way Mirror

After completing my Ph.D., I took a job as an assistant professor to pass on my wisdom to the next generation of students. I was a certified expert in family therapy. My diploma declared it. My license confirmed it. For a while, I even believed it.

I knew enough to keep most of my students awake in class most of the time, and I continued my two-out-of-three success rate with patients. It wasn't long, however, before that other third really started to bother me.

One of the myths of professional education is that completing your doctorate or master's degree prepares you to be a competent clinician. It doesn't. Or at least it didn't for me. In graduate school, I'd learned a little about a lot of things—psychological testing, research, behavior therapy, Gestalt therapy, group therapy, psychoanalytic therapy, family therapy—and I'd learned to be a little skeptical about all of them. Most graduate programs are indoctrinations in agnosticism.

What separates most really good therapists from their colleagues is some form of advanced training. Reading books, watching videotapes, and attending conferences and workshops are all very useful, but they don't substitute for a period of sustained immersion in a therapeutic training program. In my case it was studying with Salvador Minuchin that made me feel for the first time that I really knew what I was doing. I probably could have learned the basics of the structural approach at a workshop or two, but nothing had as powerful an impact on my understanding as those months of observing and being observed behind the one-way mirror.

What the telescope is to astronomy, the one-way mirror is to family therapy. When a patient is interviewed alone in a consulting room, it's natural to conceive of him or her as the locus of problems. But when patients are observed interacting with their families, it's impossible to see only one person as the problem.

❖

Trying to discern the underlying rhythms of a family while interviewing them is like trying to catch the drift of a new dance while you're caught up in the noise and excitement of a crowded nightclub. Remember the session with the Salazar family described in the first chapter? Once they dropped their polite formality, they started arguing and interrupting whenever a hot subject came up. I'd ask Mr. Salazar a question; he'd say something, innocently undercutting his wife; she'd feel the unspoken hostility and snap at him; he'd shut up and sulk; and then Jason would say something provocative. When things heated up, the session got pretty chaotic. That the chaos in families is patterned chaos is something that takes a little practice to see.

When I first met the Salazars in the waiting room, I saw no family, no system. Only four individuals. Even after years of studying family patterns, even though my intention was to figure out how they interacted, I still responded automatically to them as individuals. I was struck by the two faces of Mr. Salazar—the self-confident professional and the self-effacing husband. I had a little trouble seeing past Mrs. Salazar's anger to the hurt and disappointment underneath. I thought Jason's adolescent bravado was less well-practiced than many I've seen. And I wondered about Heather. Was she merely shy, or was she depressed? It takes deliberate effort to get past this preoccupation with individual personalities.

The great French neurologist Jean Martin Charcot once advised Freud to look at things again and again, until they themselves begin to speak. If we can observe from behind the one-way mirror—or in some other way removed from the pressures of interaction and response—things do begin to speak for themselves. With a little emotional distance, we can observe family life and concentrate not on personalities but on patterns: who says what to whom, and how; and then what?

Freed of the necessity to respond, we direct our attention to recurring sequences in the family's muddled whirl. We can simplify and abstract the confusing welter of data. We can discover a patterned dance, where family members, the dancers, see only private struggles and occasional collisions.

Sitting behind the mirror, therapists begin to see the same patterns repeated over and over again. The muddles of life are endlessly diverse, but the number of basic stories of family life are relatively few. Let me illustrate.

❖

I was recently asked to consult with a therapist who was treating "an extremely complex situation." The family consisted of two deaf and mute parents and two daughters, a thirteen-year-old deaf child, also mute, and an eleven-year-old hearing child who could speak. The parents wanted the therapist to explain to the girls the importance of obeying their parents and the need to take on more responsibility for household chores. The reason the parents felt they needed professional help was that their deafness made it difficult for them to explain all this adequately to their children.

What made the sessions so confusing were all the complications introduced by the various combinations of deafness and hearing. The therapist could speak directly to the younger daughter but had to address the parents and older daughter through an interpreter. So, in order to ask the older daughter to explain her feelings to her parents it was necessary to ask the interpreter to translate the request to the daughter and then wait for the explanation and the answer to be translated.

But when all is said and done, the story of this family was simple. This was a family in which the parents didn't exert their authority over two spirited and precocious daughters on the verge of adolescence. Sitting in the room, having to cope with all the complications, this was much harder for the therapist to see than it was for the consultant sitting safely behind the one-way mirror.

❖

How do we learn to see the self-defeating patterns in family lives? Some lessons can be drawn from the one-way mirror. One lesson is that we see events better when we are not active participants.

Suppose, for example, a mother complains about how hard it is to get her kindergartner off to school in the morning. Both you and she have some idea of what the problem is and what form the solution should take, but remember the lesson of the mirror: Try to remove the filter of biased consciousness; focus on what actually happens, not on what you know or assume. Here's what you might discover.

At 6:30, she wakes him up and says blah-blah. Then she goes downstairs and cooks breakfast. Half an hour later, she goes up again and says blah-blah, blah-blah. Both of them get upset. He comes downstairs, half dressed, and eats his breakfast. She says blah-blah and goes upstairs to fetch his shoes and socks. Then she says blah-blah-blah while she finishes dressing him. Finally, with more upset, she gets him to the corner and onto the school bus. Once a week, there's more blah-blah and more upset, and he misses the bus. On these occasions, she drives him to school.

Not only have I picked a simple (though, believe me, common) example, I have also described it in such a way as to make the process obvious: The mother takes too much responsibility for the child; she says blah-blah, instead of making him do what she expects. Above all, the example is inadequate because it includes only one segment of the family. "But, but . . ." her husband may be thinking, "it has nothing to do with me; it's my wife's problem." Wrong. The family is a system, one whole entity. Even when some family members aren't actively participating, they are involved. In the example above, a complete description of how the system works is: The mother nags the boy to get ready, and when he dawdles she nags more, and if he misses the bus she drives him to school, *and* her husband looks on critically.

This scenario, simple as it is, is an example of how a system works. (The best way to see how a system works is to keep it simple. Don't leave anyone out, but keep it simple.) The most effective way to introduce change is to alter the basic pattern. Create a new pattern, not by tinkering with the old one—the wife nagging harder, or the husband telling her that she's doing it all wrong—but by trying something novel, something discontinuous with the old pattern. What can you come up with? Almost any change in the basic pattern will work. The real secret isn't finding specific solutions for individual problems, but discovering the direction the system is going, and then changing it.

❖

Descriptions of therapy sometimes imply that change is easy. All you have to do is focus on solutions, or externalize problems, or find a clever way to reframe unhelpful points of view. Why not? This satisfies the human urge for simple answers to hard problems—and it sells books.

In the remainder of this book you will discover a variety of concepts for understanding how family systems work. Some of them may be so strikingly applicable to situations you're dealing with that things will suddenly fall into place and change will occur almost easily. Almost.

❖

The family is a social unit that faces a series of developmental tasks. Each new stage of development requires a shift in the family's organization. One of the keys to successful living is recognizing the need to reorganize and having the flexibility to do so.

In the following chapters I will describe some of the tasks involved in normal family development, and we will see how the relative successes and failures of the Salazars led them to the point where we met them—in a therapist's office.

What you won't find is a cookbook approach to technique. I will, in fact, have a lot to say about the practice of family therapy, and you will find a number of examples of useful interventions. But the real heroes of this book are the Salazars, not me. In reading the story of their lives, in and out of therapy, I hope you will discover that coming to a deeper understanding of people is a lot more important than any set of techniques for changing them.

# 3

## LOVE'S YOUNG DREAM

Sharon and Stewart didn't talk much after the first family session. She liked the therapist. He seemed to know what he was doing, but she thought it best not to say much to Stewart about it. Stewart wasn't sure what to think. It would be nice to have an ally, to not always be the bad guy, but he didn't really want to get involved right now. He had too many other things on his mind.

The following Monday night Stewart was driving home from work late. The snow was sloppy, gray slush. He still remembered how lovely it had been in the morning: pure and white, soft and lovely.

When he finally got home the driveway wasn't plowed, so he had to park on the street and trudge through the snow to get to the front door. By the time he got into the house his feet were cold and wet and he was ready for an argument.

"Did you have any trouble getting home?" Sharon wanted to know.

"No, the streets were pretty clear," Stewart said on the way to getting himself a glass of wine.

"Dinner's almost ready. Come and sit down."

"Where are the kids?" he asked.

"Jason's out, I'm not sure where, and Heather's up in her room. Please come to the table."

"Can't you wait five minutes until I've had a drink and a chance to relax?"

Now Sharon was mad. She hadn't said a word about his being so late, and here he was snapping at her. "Can't you just sit down and be with me, without having something to drink first?"

*Can't you leave me alone for one minute? Just because your father doesn't drink doesn't mean the rest of us can't.* This is what Stewart thought but didn't say. Instead he just got quiet. They ate dinner in silence. It wasn't pleasant. Afterward, to make up, he started clearing the dishes.

"Don't do me any favors!" Sharon snapped. "You still haven't said a word about our meeting with Dr. Nichols, and I'm afraid to bring it up. Anything I say, you just tune me out. The least little thing, and boom! Up goes that wall you hide behind." Then she stormed into the bedroom and slammed the door.

His annoyance was drowned in fear. If she was this hot over his silence, what would she do if he said what he really felt? It never dawned on him that he could walk away. Or that he could shout just as loud as she could. She had him afraid, and that only made him more ashamed, fanning his secret anger. In the house he was paying for, she had him afraid.

If the marriage lasted another twenty years there would be graduations, vacations, many of them happy, a father who cried at weddings, grandchildren, and more. But now there was only this awful fight. He hated her.

A faint sound of sobbing came from the bedroom. Many nights this, her surrender, had been for him the final weapon of defeat. Not tonight. He'd be damned if he was going to go in there and make up. Let *her* apologize. *Just once* let her say, "I'm sorry." Fat chance.

Later, after the eleven o'clock news, tiredness overcame him and he tiptoed into the bedroom. He slipped off his clothes, then climbed into bed, making as little noise as possible. It was too dark to see, but he knew she was awake. This knowledge banished sleep.

They both lay still in the darkness, straining to be silent, invisible to each other. It was as though if there were no noise, they weren't there together. Some nights she seemed to make noise just to irritate him, to punish him for not paying attention. Not tonight. Tonight she was like a wild creature, still and noiseless, not wanting to be discovered. *She must really be mad,* he thought, and his stomach gurgled.

After a long while, Sharon's breathing became more regular and then took on the rhythm of sleep. But for Stewart sleep didn't come. He went over their argument, all the reasons he was right and she was wrong. *What did I do? She's such a bitch.*

As he lay there thinking, or rather brooding, he was distracted by the swish of Sharon's nightgown when she rolled over. Memory ambushed him. He recalled a rather different occasion when his heart had been slaughtered by just the rustle of her dress.

## "We'll Sing in the Sunshine"

Sharon and Stewart met in Nantucket. He was working as a busboy at the Snooty Fox in the summer between his junior and senior years in college. One night at about ten o'clock Sharon walked in with her parents. She looked familiar, like someone he'd seen at school, but he couldn't be sure. Girls didn't dress like that in college. She was wearing a red silk dress and a strand of pearls around her neck. He guessed they were real. She sat with her parents in the corner across from where he was clearing up. Long dark hair, a full mouth, and large dark eyes—she certainly looked familiar, but more like Sophia Loren than the girl he'd seen on campus.

To his surprise, she came over to him. His heart thumped hard. "Don't you go to Hartwick?" she asked.

"Yes, I do, and you're . . .?"

"Sharon, Sharon Nathan."

"Have you been here before?" he heard himself saying. He was flustered. She looked so sophisticated. Her perfume drifted over him.

Then he heard her say, "Well, I guess I'd better be getting back to my parents. We're taking the ferry back in the morning. Maybe I'll see you on campus."

"Sure," he said. *Yes!* he thought. As she walked away the pleated skirt of her dress swayed back and forth, swishing softly against her stockings.

Back at school Stewart was on the lookout for Sharon. He had to see her again. She was so gorgeous, he didn't have the nerve to ask her out. Instead, he asked about her. Sharon Nathan, he found out, was from New York—that explained why she'd seemed so at home in the Snooty Fox—and she'd been going with a senior who broke up with her last spring when he graduated.

The first time Stewart ran into Sharon he was too nervous to do anything but make small talk. How was your summer? What classes are you taking? What surprised him was that she seemed so friendly. She must just be a nice person, he thought.

He kept finding excuses to talk to her. Nothing they talked about was very profound. Stewart was embarrassed by his inability to speak a single interesting word to her. Sharon was disconcerted by her inability to draw him out. He saw her beauty as exotic and mysterious. She was "the other," someone strange, different— someone who stood for all the things he felt were missing from his life. He couldn't have told you what these things were; in fact, Sharon's "otherness" was something he only barely apprehended.

Feminists argue that "otherness" implies difference, implies inferiority— women as "the second sex." But to Stewart, Sharon's differentness exerted a magnetic pull. She found him different, too. He was more serious than the other boys she'd known. And he seemed to give her enough room to relax and be herself. She was used to boys crowding her, pressing in on her. Stewart was different, and funny too. It was refreshing.

Unsure of himself, Stewart fell back on his sense of humor. He was so good at wisecracking and imitating certain professors' mannerisms that not too many people saw his compulsive joking as a distancing mechanism. When a person makes jokes and puns in a social situation—no matter how clever the joke and its author— the joker has momentarily drawn back, making connections that he wouldn't think of if he were fully involved in the social moment. But Sharon didn't seem to mind. Not yet, anyway. And the fact that she laughed at his jokes made him feel that she liked him.

Stewart's heart was no longer his own, but the step from chatting to asking Sharon out was too big. Like the gulf between the poor and the rich, it seemed unbridgeable.

Finally, in the middle of the fall, he got up the nerve to ask her out. To him it was a momentous occasion; to her it was a date to the movies. Later, on the steps of her dorm, he asked if he could kiss her. She said no and walked in. He was crushed. Later she told him, "You should have just done it. Why don't you have more self-confidence?"

Stewart was hurt. It had taken nerve to ask Sharon for a kiss, and her "No" hurt. In his mind it was more than "No, I don't want to kiss you; it was "No, I don't really like you; no, there's no chance we can have a relationship; no, you aren't in my league." So Stewart did what would become a pattern in their relationship. He withdrew to lick his wounds in self-pity. He avoided her. And he rehearsed in his mind how he would never give anyone a chance to hurt him again. He day-dreamed of becoming a monk—he'd be alone and pure and safe. It was only a day-dream, but he spent the next few days living out an imitation of it. He avoided people. He got up early, studied hard, and went on long, solitary walks.

Stewart found a certain solace in this monk's pose. He didn't need anyone, he told himself. Sometimes, however, he found himself imagining that he was an ob-ject of great interest to the people he was avoiding. They would see him as strong, mysterious, lonely. And Sharon, Sharon might guess how hurt he was. Maybe she'd be sorry for what she'd done. Maybe . . . oh, forget it. He wasn't going to let himself think about it.

Sharon did notice. Not that she thought of him as a mysterious monk, though—more like a boy whose feelings were too easily hurt. At first she was an-noyed that he was so sensitive, but then she decided it was rather sweet. One night she saw him in the library and waited to talk to him. It was 10:30 when he finally left. Sharon caught up to him on the steps outside, and walked beside him in the darkness. "Hi!" she said and tried to take his hand.

Stewart jerked his hand away and said, "What do you want?"

"Don't be mad. I missed you."

Stewart was confused. This was what he wanted to hear, but he wasn't sure he was finished punishing her yet.

Sharon cleared up the confusion. "Come here," she said, and she put her hands on his face, drawing his mouth down to hers. As their lips met, her mouth opened, all warm and wet. Oh, it was thrilling! Now he didn't ask a thing. He slid his hands underneath her sweater, and Sharon arched her back slightly. The soft brush of his fingers felt so good. But then she thought about where they were, and gently took his hands in her own and put them around her back. Still plastered up against him, she said, "We can't do this here. Can I see you tomorrow?"

"Yes."

Stewart met Sharon the following night outside her dorm at 7:30. She took him into the big sitting room off the front lobby. There weren't any lights on, but Stew-art could hear rustling noises from one or two other couples. Sharon led him over to a leather couch in the corner and started kissing him again. It was like before, only better. Her mouth was hot and wet. They kissed until their mouths ached.

Sharon's heart was racing, her breath was fast and shallow. She felt Stewart's hands trembling as he unbuttoned her blouse. Sharon leaned back with dreamy eyes, hoping to absorb all the pleasure she could.

They started seeing each other almost every day. They went to meals together. He walked her to class. They studied together. Sharon watched him at soccer prac-tice, and she came to all the home games. They were a couple. After supper they went into town to the movies or drank beer and listened to music at the Chicken

Shack. At the end of the evening they usually ended up on the couch in Sharon's dorm. Sometimes they even went there right after supper.

They didn't go all the way, but Stewart didn't care. He was crazy for her. This must be love.

Sharon was in like with Stewart. He had brains and ambition. He cared about serious things. Someday he'd be somebody. If only he had more self-confidence, she thought. Given time, she could fix that. He really did have a lot of potential.

The rest of the year went by in a hurry. The leaves changed color and fell, the snow came and went, and then it was spring, time for Stewart to decide what to do in the fall. He'd planned to go to graduate school in English. Iowa, maybe, or Berkeley. But now he didn't want to be so far from Sharon. So he applied to Cornell. Ithaca wasn't far from Hartwick, or from New York for that matter.

They talked about marriage as if it were a game. Sharon said they should live in Switzerland, in a chalet on the side of a mountain. Stewart said they should have four children, all looking like little Sharons. But Sharon made it clear that she couldn't marry someone who wasn't Jewish. Stewart wasn't at all sure he was ready to get married anyway. As a token of this understanding, Sharon said that "We'll Sing in the Sunshine" was "our song."

The following year, Sharon's senior year, she saw Stewart every other weekend. Once or twice she drove to Ithaca, but mostly he came back to Hartwick. Then there were weekends in New York. Sharon went home a lot, and Stewart loved to visit her in the big city. It was nice to go back to Oneonta and Hartwick, but those weekends in the city were magic.

Their time together was when he truly came out of himself. The rest of the time he was a watcher. He watched people on the street and even in classes when he got bored. Of some he approved. He admired most of his professors and people who seemed at ease and self-sufficient. But of many more he disapproved. So many people were frivolous, crude, loud, gum-chewing slobs. Not Sharon. With her, he talked about the things he cared about—how the great writers knew so much more than psychologists about the human condition, and how people wasted their lives getting and spending money. Here was someone with whom he could talk about anything, all the serious ideas and opinions he'd been storing up for years. Sharon took it all in.

Their weekends were compact, high-energy periods with no letdown. Sunday afternoons ended at the Greyhound Bus station. They'd sit talking, waiting for the bus, ill-at-ease in those awkward predeparture moments. It was hard to talk in the bus station and hard not to. They'd kiss hard and then he'd climb aboard. She always waited and watched him pull away. He never loved her more.

Once he was in his seat and the bus was moving, all the tension that relationships bring flowed out of him. He usually read for a while and then looked out the window, watching the trees and houses roll by. Solitude crooned to him. Later, the loneliness hit. It was a gentle loneliness. He almost enjoyed it.

Sharon finished her senior year without enthusiasm. She had no plans for the future, and with Stewart away she felt that her present was just going through the motions.

After Christmas, Stewart bought a car, a faded green Volvo 122-S with 40,000 miles clearly showing on its exterior. Not too pretty, but only $600, and it ran just fine. The fact that having a Volvo made Stewart feel a little unconventional didn't hurt either.

Things were falling into place for Stewart. He was settling into graduate school, doing better than he thought he would. But by late winter he started to get lonely. He realized that he didn't want to be without Sharon. Suddenly the idea of getting married seemed like the best idea in the world. Thinking about having her with him all the time, in his apartment, in his bed at night, he forgot his earlier doubts.

It was 2:00 A.M. when the telephone in Sharon's bedroom rang. "What's wrong?" she said when she heard Stewart's voice.

"Nothing. I'm lonely. I want to see you."

"Okay, come this weekend."

"I'll be at your place around noon."

"I'll be waiting," she said.

"Good night. I love you."

"Me too."

He wasn't going to hit her with it right away. They would have the whole weekend, then if everything was okay he would ask her on Sunday. He drove down on Saturday and they had dinner with her parents. Sharon's mother put all the food on the table and everybody helped themselves. Family style. It was very different from what he was used to. At his house things were more formal. Sunday, Stewart and Sharon went out for brunch. Afterwards, walking in Central Park, he asked her.

"Sharon—I want to spend the rest of my life with you. Will you marry me?"

Sharon was shocked. He had asked her before, sort of kidding. She'd smiled and said, "Let's wait. See what happens." They dropped it. But this is what happened. Sharon's eyes filled with tears. She put her face in his sweater. Trembling, she said yes.

It was late when Stewart finally got into his car for the long drive back. Out on the highway the snow was beginning to stick and the right lane was filling up with cars slowing down. On the radio, Frankie Lyman was singing, "Why Do Fools Fall in Love?" Stewart didn't pay any attention to the words; he just kept driving and listening to the beat. He didn't care about the snow; he sped along in the fast lane, drunk on happiness.

## Why Do Fools Fall in Love?

It's no secret that getting married is among the most important and least rational decisions a person ever makes. The point isn't that people really are fools, or that getting married itself is irrational, but that the decision is usually too clouded with a romantic haze for us to see clearly who we're marrying or what marriage is all about.

Usually, love comes first; friendship comes later, if at all. Too bad it isn't the other way around.

Sharon and Stewart were very much in love. He revealed to her secret hopes and ambitions that he would never entrust to anyone else. She let down her guard and showed him her little-girl side. He loved it when she talked baby talk. It made her seem so sweet and vulnerable—and made him feel securely protective. How could he not love her?

Still, there was plenty they didn't know about each other. Some aspects of their personalities they deliberately held back, and other traits simply wouldn't surface until later, after they were married. Most of us suppress childish parts of ourselves when we leave home. Teachers and bosses and friends and lovers won't put up with the same crap our parents did. But later, after we marry and are once again part of a family, most of us regress and begin to react to stress and frustration like adolescents. That's why the first few months of marriage can be so trying.

The question of why people fall in love and get married interests no one less than young couples in love. That's what makes going into the reasons—unconscious wishes, idealized fantasies, life histories, relationships with parents, values, aspirations, and so on—seem a little superfluous. Most people aren't interested when it counts.

Premarital counseling used to be one of my favorite professional duties. What could be more rewarding than helping two people along the road to Happily Ever After by giving them a few well-chosen words of wisdom. Ha! Most couples who've sought me out for premarital counseling have had serious problems getting along. I'd often recommend that they postpone the decision to marry until they found out if they could work out their difficulties. There's no sense marrying someone you can't get along with, right?

It didn't seem to matter how poorly matched these couples were, or how unsuccessful they were at resolving their problems. Their minds were made up. Plans were made. What could be worse than having to cancel a wedding?

❖

Sharon and Stewart thought they knew each other pretty well, and the little they didn't like, they thought would improve with time. Beneath the surface of conscious considerations, they were propelled by powerful yearnings and pulled together by a deep, instinctive urgency.

As a child, Sharon had been obedient but indulged. She was admired for being pretty but never quite taken seriously. Her future, it was assumed, was family. Just that. Sharon had aspirations but she was programmed for domesticity. Petted at home and allowed to get by on promise at school, she lacked the self-discipline and drive for personal achievement that propels people into professions. By the time she met Stewart she had already accepted defeat in the realm of personal ambition. Thirty years ago this wasn't unusual.

Stewart was a young man, deeply insecure, driven to achievement and uneasy with intimacy. Sharon was equally insecure, but rather than exercising independent initiative, she was driven toward merging with someone stronger. Stewart's proposal made everything right, for that moment canceling every trace of unhappiness in her life. She had wanted to end the confusion of emotions that had made her adolescence so miserable. When Stewart spoke the magic words "I love you," he conjured up all the fantasies of falling in love.

Notice the term "falling" in love—a passive drop into happiness. It sounds automatic, like presents on your birthday or that last-day-of-school feeling in June. There seems to be no limit to the human hope for happiness served up on a plate.

Stewart's fear of weakness masqueraded as strength. He avoided small talk, and the eyes in Sharon's heart saw strength of character. Sharon was a girl afraid of being on her own, who took on the guise of a perfect companion. Naturally they fell in love—with each other's projected image.

## "I Do"

Sharon never imagined how much there was to be done to arrange a wedding. There were caterers, flowers, a band to pick, what music to play, who to invite, choosing the invitations, who should sit where ("You can't put Aunt Adele at *that* table!" her mother said), and on and on. Weddings were supposed to be romantic. This was turning into a chore.

The night after the rehearsal, Sharon's father staged a big family dinner at the Empire Room. While everyone was eating and drinking and laughing and making toasts, Sharon watched Stewart. He was smiling and talking but he seemed out of place, uncomfortable with all these people—her family. *It's a mistake*, she thought. *I don't love him. He's just a boy.*

The day of the wedding Sharon woke up at 6:00 A.M. She was nervous, sick to her stomach. She went with her mother to Vidal Sassoon's, where they both had their hair done. All that money and it still didn't turn out very well. And naturally, her face broke out. Today of all days. But she didn't let it get her down. Besides, she was too caught up in all there was to do to spend much time thinking.

Stewart spent most of the day alone. He had breakfast with his friend Roger, who'd flown all the way from California for the wedding, and lunch with his parents. Mostly, though, he wanted to be alone. He did a lot of walking. Up Broadway, over to Riverside Church, and then all the way down to a terraced garden he'd seen with Sharon on the east side of Central Park. Walking and thinking. He didn't think about the wedding or the marriage, or even Sharon. He deliberately avoided these subjects, and concentrated instead on "bigger" things: what he wanted to do with his life, how fleeting everything is. And he worked hard at noticing things: the dark, swirling color of the Hudson, rushing toward the sea; the wide-eyed fascination on the faces of shoppers gazing at the glittering array of elegant objects in store windows. Material lust, he thought. Stewart was preparing for the wedding in the same way he prepared to take an exam or give a lecture: keeping his anxiety at bay by walking and looking and thinking.

Sharon and her family were late getting to the synagogue. Her father was nervous. He was quiet, tense, short with people. She'd never seen him like this. As soon as she walked into the temple and saw Stewart, she felt fine, calm. He smiled. Everything was okay.

The bridal room was packed with people. Her dress wasn't quite what she wanted. But when she put it on, everyone *ooh*ed and *aah*ed. She was excited, a little bit out of it.

The wedding itself went by so fast that neither Sharon nor Stewart had time to focus on anything other than a few stray details. Despite her attempts to cover them with makeup, Sharon was painfully aware of the two red blotches on her chin. She noticed the tears that filled her father's eyes just as they were about to walk down the aisle. *He really loves me*, she thought. The ceremony was a blur. There was the rabbi, and Stewart, and behind her everyone who loved her, and then she heard herself say, "I do." And it was done.

Stewart was aggravated by all the picture-taking. Every time he tried to talk with somebody or have some champagne, the photographer was dragging him away. "Okay, let's have the bride and groom and the bride's parents." *Whose wedding is this?* Stewart thought. But he knew the answer. It was Sharon's family's wedding. So he allowed himself to be pushed along like a leaf in the wind.

Once Stewart stood next to Sharon under the canopy of flowers, everything stopped. All the noise, all the pushing and pulling, all the foolishness. It was quiet. His heart was full. The rabbi's words sounded right. Sharon was beautiful. She looked like a woman and a little girl all at the same time. "Do you . . . ?" "Yes, I do!" he said with all his mind. Then the spell was broken, and the rest of the night was back to bedlam.

They went back to Nantucket for their honeymoon. It seemed fitting. The first day on the island Sharon had her period and she was constipated. That put a crimp in Stewart's fantasies. He felt resentful, cheated, as though she were holding out on him. (*Now, of all times*, he thought). Sharon felt lousy. She hadn't planned on this either. She felt a little guilty, and a lot annoyed that Stewart wasn't more sympathetic.

Still, they managed to have a good time. The summer season doesn't really get started until the Fourth of July, so they had the beauty of the island without the crowds of summer.

Walking along the beach, they met an older couple, Bill and Emily Robinson, who'd been coming to the island every summer for twenty years. They ended up spending a lot of time with Bill and Emily. It was fun being with them.

Bill knew someone with a yacht, and one night they went for a cruise in the moonlight. Sitting close on the deck chairs, sipping wine—this was what they had wanted. Sharon snuggled up to Stewart and slipped her hand inside his shirt. She whispered, "I love you." They were happy.

# 4

# THE PROGRESS OF LOVE

The honeymoon didn't last long. They couldn't afford to stay in Nantucket for more than four days. Besides, Stewart had to get back to start work as a teaching assistant for the summer session.

The apartment he'd found for them to start married life was inexpensive but cozy. The living room, bedroom, bathroom, and kitchen had seemed roomy enough to Stewart. He couldn't wait to have Sharon there with him. But when they filled it up with furniture the apartment seemed more than a little crowded. Sharon said it was charming, but he heard her tell her mother over the phone that the kitchen was the size of a phone booth. That was just like her, he thought, always exaggerating.

For the first few weeks it was like dating, only without anyone watching over them. This closeness made it possible for them to relax into themselves—to be less on their best behavior and more open to their full natures, not just the sanitized versions they wore on the surface. Being married made Stewart feel more sure of himself. Now he had a wife—a beautiful and intelligent woman—for everyone to see. It was a reassuring reflection of his own worth.

At home with Sharon he felt safe enough to let down his defenses and give in to his needs. Sharon gave Stewart lessons in how to enjoy himself. She liked cooking for him and she got a kick out of buying things for him—special deserts, expensive shirts, an enormous red bath towel. "You spoil me," he said. "Yes, and you love it," was her knowing reply.

It made Sharon happy when Stewart needed her. All she asked was a little appreciation.

Stewart drew Sharon into the circle of his friends in the English department. They started having frequent parties, and their little apartment became a kind of emotional headquarters for single graduate students. It was at one of their parties that the dean of students told Sharon that she could use some part-time help advising freshmen. The job worked out fine. Sharon took pleasure in mothering the students, and the extra money came in handy.

❖

In marriage, buried aspects of our personalities are disinterred.[1] We leave home, most of us, in the midst of growing up. Then we step out into the wide world, putting our best foot forward. Marriage re-creates family, and family is the place where we become who we are. Marriage is also a thrust toward completion and integration of the self. Mates are chosen not only on the basis of compatibility, but also out of longing for completion.

When courtship begins, we trot out our best selves. *Maybe she'll like this one.* Later we show our partners a few more selves, testing for commitment. While they were dating, Sharon had gotten to know several Stewarts—the serious student, the ardent suitor, the boy who played soccer with such abandon. She thought she was marrying two or three of these guys: the one who made her laugh, the one who was so self-disciplined, and the one who occasionally made her feel safe enough to let go. Secretly (even from herself) she hoped she was marrying a series of possible selves to complement the various selves in her own character. When she felt like being Grace Kelly, he would be Cary Grant; when she was scared, he would be brave; and when she needed to be held, he would be there.

Unfortunately, not all of these compatible pairings last for long.

❖

After her first day of work in the dean's office, Sharon walked into the living room where Stewart was sitting on the couch.

"How was your day?" he asked.

"Fine, thanks." But she couldn't relax in his embrace without him starting to grope. Why couldn't he just hold her? His restless hands were all over her. He was never still, and she was never relaxed.

Where had these other Stewarts come from—the one who was always pawing her, the one who knew how to talk but not listen? It was a strain always having to listen to the intrigues of the English department. Some of it was interesting, but he never talked about anything else. Sharon had things on her mind, too. Didn't he care?

Oh, well. You marry everything, like it or not. It took Sharon a few months to realize this and a few more to accept it. Well, accept the idea anyway.

## "Why Are You So Mean to Me?"

Yes, opposites attract, but they may have trouble living together. It's like visiting an exotic foreign country. People pay a lot of money to visit faraway places. Living there, however, may prove difficult. That's why, unromantic as it may sound, similarity of background is one of the most powerful predictors of marital satisfaction.

❖

[1]By *marriage* I mean a commited union between two people. To avoid implying that such unions occur only in traditional marriages, I will use terms like "intimate partnership" and "couplehood" as often as possible.

Sharon had been drawn to Stewart for many reasons, but none greater than that he seemed more serious and substantial than her family. Now she discovered the other side of that seriousness, his morose moodiness and inability to let her get too close too often. His favorite phrase seemed to be "I have to go."

The seriousness of purpose and self-discipline Sharon had admired in Stewart now made him appear rigid and unaccommodating. There was a tense deliberateness about everything he did. Little things that normally require only brief consideration—whether to go to the movies, how to spend Sunday morning—became matters of serious deliberation. Most of the time he was preoccupied with himself and his career, following the imperative "I should," as if determined to overcome some obstacle. Sharon admired him for being conscientious and hard-working; but he overdid it. He didn't forget himself or lose himself. Hence it was difficult for him to give himself over to her or their relationship. He was estranged from his own wants and desires, and, as Sharon discovered, rarely ever aware of her needs and feelings.

Some of what had fascinated Stewart about Sharon when they were dating got hard to take later. With strangers she was shy. She was no wallflower, but out to dinner with friends or at parties, she had little to say. More than once she whispered to Stewart, "Don't leave me alone; I have nothing to say to these people." He found this endearing in a girlfriend but confining in a wife.

At home she was transformed. He had seen it with her parents. Now, gradually, with him she became a chatterbox. Stewart was just the opposite. He saved up his talking for special occasions. At home, he wanted to be left alone. They were so different.

Although people didn't take her for an insecure person, Sharon was always alert for signs of rejection. She never minded taking the initiative—inviting people out, throwing parties—but once she took it into her head that someone was neglecting her, nothing Stewart said could dislodge the thought. Although neither of them realized it, these discussions could have been about their own relationship. His attempts to soothe her only made her angry. "You're on *her* side!" Sharon would say whenever he tried to suggest that some friend didn't mean to slight her. Eventually, he stopped trying. Another subject for silence.

❖

When it came to loving, they each did it in ways that were familiar. The trouble was they tried to give what they wanted for themselves. As a result, the marriage became suffused with misunderstanding and conflict.

His parents did many things that annoyed Stewart. His mother constantly criticized his father's preoccupation with his career. His father was helpless in the kitchen. His mother never talked about her feelings, or had any patience for anyone who did. His father was always gushing over people, other people. Stewart noted these things, and a few others, and decided that his marriage would be different. (Later, he would learn more about his parents by observing how they treated his own kids.) But for the most part, it never occurred to Stewart that there were other kinds of marriages.

So many things about the way his parents lived together Stewart just took for granted as "the way things are." His mother was competent and independent. She took care of most of the house, inside and out, and liked being by herself. Stewart's dad often went out for the evening with his friends and was away for weeks at a time on business. The family did some things together, like going on picnics in the nearby mountains, but more often they went off separately. Sometimes Stewart went fishing with his father for the weekend; sometimes he and his mother sat around reading while his father was off with his cronies. His parents were more independent than most, but Stewart didn't know that. They were . . . well, just parents.

Sharon was more aware of her family, and she had definitely decided there were a number of ways her marriage would be different. She didn't want to be tied to family obligation and tradition. She wanted to travel and meet interesting people. Stewart was more than different, he was going places. Sharon liked this in him, but like most of us, she never suspected that the attraction of opposites reflects a measure of unconscious self-loathing. So much of what appealed to her about Stewart had to do with disappointments in herself and in her family.

It infuriated Sharon that her parents never said directly what they wanted. Instead they implied and hinted. They gave noncommittal answers, reserving their options, trying to get what they wanted but without ever saying so. And she hated how bossy her father was. Selflessness may sound like a fine quality, but not if it means trying to run everybody else's life for them.

Notice that these attributes—bossiness, lack of candor—are personality characteristics, not patterns of relationship. Like Stewart, Sharon took much of her parents' way of relating for granted. In her case, the example was reinforced by seeing similar patterns acted out by a regiment of aunts and uncles and cousins. Sharon didn't mind that Stewart put so much energy into his career because her father had always worked hard. She was used to it. But after work, she expected the same kind of togetherness her parents shared.

Stewart, with extremely independent parents, had other expectations. Differences like these are easier to manage in courtship. In marriage two things happen: We loosen up some of our careful consideration, becoming more the people we are, and whatever differences exist begin to polarize the partners.

Some conflicts are resolved by compromise, but others are exaggerated by the inevitable polarizing effect of two people living in close quarters, both of whom feel pressure to change—the other one.

Stewart loved sports. For every season he had equipment and a regular routine of disciplining his muscles into shape. Even as an adult he played so hard that Sharon couldn't tell where play left off and work began. Sharon was a robust person, with strong, womanly muscles and absolutely no interest in sports or exercise. Stewart tried to encourage her. "Why don't you get in shape?" But he expected her to do it on her own, and she wasn't interested. When she asked him to go bicycle riding with her, he said, "You're too slow." He didn't have a clue as to how unkind he sounded.

So instead of coming together, at least on these things, they moved farther apart. As a result of polarization, conflicts within each of them became conflicts *between* them.

An ambivalent inner balance between pairs of conflicting impulses (demanding/conciliatory; tough/tender; dependent/independent) is resolved by projecting one's own motivation onto the partner. Mates begin to fight, in each other, denied and repudiated aspects of their own personalities. One partner becomes avoidant, the other a pursuer; one longs for affection, the other is cool; one is emotional, the other restrained. What appear to be personality differences may be partly based on character, but small differences are exaggerated. This projection and polarization impedes each one from integrating latent positives in the self, because these are played out by the other. The hard-driving career woman is unable to integrate her softer side to the extent that her partner acts helpless and dependent. A healthier model is the couple who can take turns being weak or strong. Unfortunately, Sharon and Stewart were better at splitting roles than taking turns.

❖

One of the forms that polarization took with Sharon and Stewart was an escalating series of arguments, terrible arguments. It usually started with Sharon feeling neglected. He'd wander away from her at parties or stay after school drinking with his friends while she waited supper for him. He never seemed to care what she was feeling. She tried not to say anything, so as not to injure that bundle of sensitivities she had married. (Was anyone ever as sensitive to criticism as Stewart?) But after a while she'd get fed up.

"You don't care about anyone but yourself!" These complaints were totally unanticipated by Stewart. For no good reason (that he could see) she'd start in on him, speaking in that special voice of hers: shrill, cruel, mean. He was defenseless before it.

The louder she shouted, the less he heard. "Yes, yes," he'd say, meaning *Please stop; I can't stand it*. But she knew he didn't hear her. So she kept at him. Eventually, he'd walk out and slam the door, leaving her alone, crying.

After a fight, they both went over it in their minds, nursing their resentments. He felt cheated, bitter, disappointed. Marriage was bringing out a meanness in her. She was like a big baby. Yet her ferocity scared him. He could think of no way out except escape. Later, when he realized that he wouldn't leave, *couldn't* leave, he felt like a coward. The real cowardice was not being able to listen or fight back. Maybe he couldn't listen until he learned to fight back.

After she cried herself out, Sharon was ready to forgive him, but that wasn't enough. Forgiveness is never enough. It means that one accepts something as done and excuses it. Forgiveness also assumes that it won't happen again, but it will. All those things we hate in our mates, the awful, annoying, and inconsiderate things they do, they will do again. Acceptance means accepting the person as she is or as he is, warts and all.

Sharon was always ready to make up before Stewart was. He'd still be sulking and she'd be trying to be nice. After a day or so he'd break down. He'd be sitting alone somewhere and start to think of her with fond detachment, loving her and pitying her, regretting all the cold space that grew up between them. Moments of affection and reconciliation were such a relief that he purchased them by giving in, falsifying the truth of his feelings. It was easy, and it became a habit. He'd bring her a present with a note expressing what he had trouble saying out loud: *I'm sorry.* She was generous with forgiveness.

❖

When needs clash, it feels like the other person is being cruel and selfish. More than once, after a fight, Sharon broke down and sobbed, *"Why are you so mean to me?"* Stewart only thought it, and never more than ten times a week.

In Stewart's opinion, Sharon's need for conversation was exorbitant. She'd blurt out whatever was on her mind, regardless of what he was doing. If they sat in the living room reading, she'd interrupt every few minutes to read some tidbit from her magazine. It broke his concentration and made him furious. But he was afraid to say anything. Instead, he just turned on the television.

As far as Sharon was concerned, Stewart appreciated her only when she was doing something for him. The rest of the time he took her for granted—or shut her out. He'd get annoyed when she tried to talk to him. Reading or watching television, his posture said, *Don't bother me, I'm busy.* His version of talking was to interrogate her, asking her complicated questions about things *he* was interested in. Why couldn't he just let her be herself?

Stewart rarely dated before he met Sharon because he feared rejection. Now he adopted a submissive attitude toward his wife. His own dependency needs and aggressive tendencies were so suppressed that he was hardly aware of their existence. All anger was banished. Sharon saw his attempts to withstand her emotional onslaughts as aloof, unfeeling. "Don't just stand there like a stone!" she'd scream at him when he wouldn't answer her complaints. He found these scenes so alarming that he perfected a whole armory of pretense and avoidance, which of course only ensured more scenes. They seemed trapped on a merry-go-round of torment.

What made it all so painful was that they'd both expected marriage to be relatively conflict-free. The way it was at home. The way they remembered it, anyway.

We evaluate events not only in comparison to past experience but also in comparison to imagined possibilities. Most of us grow up with an image of a happy marriage and family life. Not that our own families were necessarily happy, but even if our parents were at war, hot or cold, we hoped things would be different for us.

The experience of arguments is quite different when linked to the possible scenario "Marriage will be wonderful" than when linked to "Marriage will have a certain number of fights." Sharon was used to arguments. In her family people said what they felt. As a result there was plenty of conflict but also the experience of being able to air gripes and work things out. Stewart's family was just the opposite. He wasn't prepared for Sharon's outbursts. She'd never expected to marry someone who would punish her with silence just for expressing her feelings.

We should know better, but still the myth of placid normality endures, supported by two-dimensional images on television comedies. This picture of people living in harmony, coping cheerfully with the few amusing problems that do crop up, crumbles whenever anyone looks at a real family with its normal problems.

Unfortunately, the happy-family model is still fixed in our heads as a standard against which we judge our own families. A family that works isn't one without conflict; it's one in which the partners know how to settle conflicts when they do arise.

Sharon was willing to try to work things out. Unfortunately, Stewart was unprepared to tolerate her way of doing so. He felt devastated and withdrew into a den of self-pity. He came out once in a while to look around, but the slightest chill sent him scurrying right back. It was a pattern that would last for years.

❖

So what's going on here? The story is familiar enough. Two decent people doing the best they can, still they make things very difficult for each other. They meet and fall in love, and each finds the other by turns different, fascinating, and finally frustrating. Nobody gets beat up, nobody becomes bulimic or addicted to cocaine, and so the story lacks some of the drama we're accustomed to seeing on television and in the movies. And yet the quiet tragedy of two ordinary people who make each other unhappy is every bit as sad as those other, more dramatic problems. Unhappy is unhappy.

Sharon and Stewart each had their own point of view, at best sporadically sympathetic to the other one. You, the reader, may have a wider view. Sitting outside the range of hurt and blaming, perhaps you can see the unfortunate misunderstandings, the poor choices, and the inability to compromise—two young people with too great a disparity in their backgrounds to fit together easily, and too little experience to know how to work at it.

Accurate as this assessment may be, it stays well within our familiar way of thinking about families: as collections of individual personalities. When they married, Sharon and Stewart also created something new, a system, a unit, a whole entity. And this new entity had certain laws of its own.

No, the individual personalities of Sharon and Stewart didn't disappear, or even merge; nor did traits like courage, compassion, and unselfishness cease to be important. Nothing was destroyed, but something was created. Family systems function according to predictable patterns, patterns that incorporate but also transcend the characteristics of their individual members. Caught up as they are in the everyday flow of their families' lives, it's hard for our clients to see these patterns, and harder still to navigate them without experience or guidelines.

## Idealization

In our culture, love is put forward as the *summum bonum* of human relationships. Love is sacred. To analyze love implies a sacrilege, a desecration of what should be cherished rather than understood. In twenty-five years of asking couples what attracted them to each other, I have yet to hear a really thoughtful answer. Intelligent, good-hearted people can tell you a lot about many things, but very few can say much about why they fell in love.

Most of us marry a dream. Romantic love promises more than it can deliver. The passionate woman Stewart married turned out to be dependent and demanding, or so it seemed to him. Sharon's attentive lover metamorphosed into a distant and neglectful husband. When her expectations were disappointed, Sharon started to criticize Stewart. He felt wounded and withdrew. Some of her criticism was, of course, valid. But little or none was heard. Sharon didn't even have a chance to respond to Stewart's complaints; he never spoke them out loud.

At this point it may seem that I'm painting a relentlessly negative picture of married life. I don't mean to. Most people are happy when they marry; that's why they marry. Despite all their problems, Sharon and Stewart were content much of the time. The idea I wish to emphasize is that the inevitable disappointments that come into our lives can be faced and understood and can serve as the basis for constructive action. The alternative is that disappointments fester and, all too often, slowly poison a relationship.

Couples can and do struggle through dark moments and unhappy times to build a relationship with affection, happiness, and love. To do so, however, they must get past their disappointments without falling into the trap of blaming their partners for their dissatisfaction. Disappointment (and blame) is magnified the more the relationship is based on fantasy and wishes. Sadly, most couples discover this only after they're already married. For a time, "for better or worse" feels like for worse.

People react to frustrated expectations in various ways. Some become grievance collectors, hoarding slights and affronts as though they were coupons in a game that eventually entitled the bearer to a prize.

Stewart kept his eyes wide open, fixed squarely on what Sharon "should" be and how unfair it was that she wasn't. He was cursed with imaginative powers that conjured up dreams his bride couldn't live up to. For one thing, she didn't turn out to be the sex goddess of his daydreams. (Like many young married people, Stewart thought that her response to him was entirely her doing.) For another thing, she didn't seem capable of living her own life. The eager, affectionate woman he fell in love with was turning out to be a wife-child who made him responsible for making her happy. Why couldn't she live her own life? Marriage, he thought, was a tragedy of lost illusions.

❖

Perhaps this all seems to add up to something that everyone knows: "Love is blind." (Well, everyone but lovers knows.) Another adage cautions, "Keep your eyes open before marriage and half-shut afterwards." But the metaphor of blindness isn't quite right; it's strictly negative—*not* seeing. Love also works a positive distortion on our vision—we aren't so much blind as that we see what we want to see.

Sharon wanted someone kind and serious, strong enough to know what she wanted and attentive enough to love her well. And she found him—or rather, half found and half imagined him. Stewart yearned for someone who would love him completely. She would look up to him and admire him, and she would always be there for him when he needed her.

The name for this mechanism of illusion is *idealization*. Putting a name to this familiar human experience does more than call it to our attention. Idealization is a complex, motivated psychological phenomenon, which, once we understand it, tells us a great deal about the progress of love—and disenchantment.

According to Freud, idealization is based on a dual process of projecting our best hopes onto the loved one, while vigorously suppressing negative feelings.[2] Lovers project their "ego ideal"—their own concept of a perfect personality—onto the loved one. What the lover wishes to be, he or she fantasizes the beloved as being. The second part of the process is *reaction-formation*. Idealizing someone is also a way to defend against recognizing one's own aggressive feelings. People who always make a point of saying how "wonderful" their partners are may be protecting themselves from facing their own anger and resentment. In Freud's view, falling in love is an irrational reawakening of romantic yearnings of child-hood. Part of what we long for in a mate is a perfect parent.

An alternative and equally useful explanation for idealization comes from Heinz Kohut's psychology of the self.[3] Kohut believed that we develop a healthy and secure sense of self when our parents fulfill two essential needs. The first is for what Kohut called *mirroring*, the expression of appreciation by which parents nurture their children's sense of worth. The second way parents help strengthen the growing child's personality is by providing a model for *identification*. Children look up to their parents as images of what they will become when they grow up.

Thus, parental admiration and inspiration are the building blocks of the child's inner resources. Chronic or traumatic failures in either empathy or idealization weaken the child's self-esteem and leave him or her forever hungry for compensation. The child who longed in vain for praise grows to adulthood alternately suppressing the craving for attention, then letting it break through in relation to anyone who seems a likely source of admiration. Similarly, people who were painfully disillusioned about their parents' worth may always be searching for someone to look up to and lean on. In some individuals, like Sharon, this longing takes the form of open dependency. Others like Stewart, mask their longings with a show of independence and strength, yet nevertheless secretly yearn for a mentor (someone to borrow strength from) and worshipful attention (mirroring).

As you see, idealization and disillusion aren't part of an inevitable and unvarying process. The degree and nature of idealization tells us a great deal about a person. The more insecure we are, the more we look for people to idealize. We meet someone special and we fall in love with a blurry blend of that person's real qualities and our own projected longings.

The object of idealization may be flattered by being put on a pedestal—that is, until the inevitable disillusion sets in. Then the person is punished for being what he or she always was: a flesh-and-blood human being.

---

[2]Sigmund Freud, "Observations on transference love," in *Standard Edition, 12*, 157–172. London: Hogarth Press, 1958.

[3]Heinz Kohut, *The Anlaysis of the Self*. New York: International Universities Press, 1971; Heinz Kohut, *The Restoration of the Self*. New York: International Universities Press, 1977.

A therapist might draw attention to the process of idealization with a couple of questions: "Why do you think you needed him (or her) to be so wonderful? What do you suppose you might have been making up for in your own life?" This can be followed by asking, "What were your parents like?" These questions, designed to shift partners away from blaming each other for their own disappointments, are part of what Murray Bowen considered the fundamental mechanism of change in family therapy: developing self-focus.

Analytic therapists endeavor to help their patients uncover and reconsider idealized expectations. Doing so can improve a couple's relationship by enabling partners to own their own fantasies as just that and thereby to stop blaming their mates for failing to live up to some fictionalized ideal and get to know the real person.

A family therapist might, however, take a different tack. Instead of simply renouncing their idealizations of each other, couples might be helped to think of their perceptions during courtship as real—in the sense of being preferred visions of the self, the partner, and the relationship. By exploring couples' stories of what drew them together, they may be better able to locate the misguided patterns that got them off track. Thus courtship begins to speak the "truth" of the relationship more than the painful patterns of misunderstanding that often take over later. Couples don't get stuck just because they have idealized expectations. They get stuck because they don't talk about their expectations in nonblaming ways. Once again, owning one's expectations ("I had hoped . . .") rather than casting blame ("You never . . .") sets the stage for accommodation.

## Accommodation

Young people often think of marriage as a state—the state of matrimony. But intimate partnership isn't something you enter, like the state of Texas; it's something you create.

When two people in love decide to share their days and nights and futures, they must go through a period of often difficult adjustment before they complete the transition from courtship to a functional partnership. They must learn to *accommodate* each other's expectations and ways of doing things. If marriage is a union between a man who can't sleep with the window closed and a woman who can't sleep with it open, accommodation is the process of working out a compromise.

With or without the term *accommodation*, the idea that long-term relationships begin with a period of adjustment is familiar to everyone, especially everyone who's ever been in one. Usually, however, we think of this process as involving two people working out a pattern of compromise. But accommodation is also a systemic process of automatic mutual adjustment, much of which goes on outside of awareness.

A number of tasks face any couple who decide to live together but none more pressing than the need to accommodate to each other in large and small routines. Both partners expect transactions to take forms that are familiar. Both try to organize the relationship in patterns that are familiar or preferred, and press the other one to accommodate. Some things are easy. He learns to accommodate to her wish to be kissed hello and good-bye. She learns to leave him alone with his paper and morning coffee.

These little arrangements, part of the process of accommodation that cements a couple into a unit, may be accomplished easily or only after intense struggle. Each partner will have areas of relative inflexibility. Sharon and Stewart, like many newly married couples, were more or less blind to their own rigidities. Stewart was so well aware of giving in to Sharon on some big issues that he overlooked his lack of easy adaptability to the little occasions of life. He changed religions for her but he couldn't let her pick which direction to walk in, and although he asked her which restaurant she wanted to eat in, nine times out of ten he'd respond by saying, "Why don't we go somewhere else tonight?"

Sharon left her home, her family, and her friends for Stewart. She cooked for him. She put up with people she didn't like in order to please him. And yet she hardly realized how jealous she was of anything he did without her—his spending time with his friends or even just sitting quietly with a book. She pressured him into togetherness. But to her it didn't seem like pressure. It only seemed natural.

❖

Considering the emphasis I've put on the need to accommodate, some people might wonder what happens when couples *don't* learn to accommodate to each other. Does this mean the relationship will end in divorce? Not at all. Being happy isn't the only reason people stay together. Lots of people live unhappily ever after.

The two common alternatives to successful accommodation are: fighting and distancing. Enmeshed couples who fail to accommodate often resemble tired boxers in the late rounds. They're worn out but keep punching anyway. Disengaged couples develop a pattern of detached coexistence, a domestic version of the cold war.

When some clients hear about accommodation, they think the therapist is suggesting that having a harmonious relationship means giving in all the time. When they hear that letting the other person be right will resolve a lot of difficulties, they protest, "That's what I do all the time—give in."

Yes, a lot of people do give in much of the time, and yes, successful accommodation does require a good deal of compromise. But once people learn to see their relationship as a unit, they will realize that they can change the other person by changing themselves—not who they are, but what they do in relation to their partners. Not fair? Maybe not, but it puts people in charge of getting what they want.

❖

The other side of accommodating to each other is reorganizing involvements outside the relationship—work or school, friends and family. The commitment to a relationship is made at the expense of other relationships. The degree of investment in the new relationship may depend on how much is given up in old relationships. Stewart kept the same apartment and the same career. Sharon gave up her job and her friends and family to move away with Stewart. Naturally, she demanded more from the relationship.

## Boundaries

One sweltering afternoon in July Sharon came home from work, took a cold shower, and sat outside in the shade to wait for Stewart. When he finally got home, he looked like someone coming out of a steamroom fully dressed. "Hi," he said, limply. Sharon watched him go inside. She waited for him to come back and talk to her. She had a long wait.

Stewart was halfway through his second gin and tonic when it hit him. His head was light. He became self-conscious. The line between mellow and muddled was thin, and he'd crossed it.

Sharon came in and started talking. He put on a look of exaggerated attentiveness, hoping to dispel any hint of the dizzy confusion he really felt. It seemed to work. Sharon talked on. It took so little to keep her talking.

"You look beat," she said.

"I am."

She told him that going to the community pool for a swim would be more refreshing than sitting around under the air conditioning.

"Okay," he said. "Just give me a few minutes."

At the pool he plunged into the cool water and took a long, slow swim. All the heat and tension went out of him. Finally, he hoisted himself up (no ladder for him) and stretched out on one of the reclining lawn chairs, letting the sun and air dry him. His eyes found the blue spaces in the trees where the sky shone through. It was the first time he felt relaxed in days. He just wanted to sit quietly for a few moments, feeling refreshed, cleansed. But then Sharon came over and started talking. She wanted to know if he could take some time off so they could visit her parents. He felt the gloom settling in again. Couldn't she leave him alone for five minutes?

❖

Stewart and Sharon were dealing with one of the most pervasive problems of intimate partnership, the drawing of personal boundaries. Boundaries exist on two levels: behavioral and emotional. Behavioral boundaries refer to the preferred amount of togetherness in a relationship. The second, emotional, level has to do with distinguishing which thoughts and feelings and wishes are within the self and which are within the partner.

According to Murray Bowen, there are two major human needs: the need to be a separate self and the need to be connected to others. Although it's possible to satisfy both needs, there is a tension between them, and most people lean either in the direction of being connected or of being independent. This *inner* tension between autonomy and intimacy is related to the *outer* pattern of togetherness and separateness that Salvador Minuchin referred to as *enmeshment* and *disengagement*.

Bowen's *fusion* and Minuchin's *enmeshment* both deal with blurred boundaries, but they aren't the same thing. Fusion, like the psychoanalytic term *individuation*, is a quality of individuals—it's a personality variable existing *within* the person. Enmeshment is strictly a social systems concept—it occurs *between* persons. In explaining different aspects of family life, I shall have occasion to use both ways of describing relationship boundaries, but before returning to the Salazars, I'd like to make one important point. As everyone knows, how we behave is related to how we feel. Those who find intimacy difficult, and become anxious if they're too close too long, naturally tend to seek their privacy. Likewise those who are uncomfortable with independence prefer togetherness. But—here's the point—we don't always have to act in accordance with our feelings.

To behave more flexibly in a relationship system, you sometimes have to act counter to what your feelings dictate. This does not mean, however, that it's necessary for people to fight with their feelings—"I shouldn't *get upset*." Let people feel what they feel, but also let them decide how they will act. Often by the way, new patterns of interaction will help people begin to feel differently.

❖

Understanding emotional boundaries, past and present, does much to clarify the difficult early months of Sharon and Stewart's marriage. By now you've already figured out the patterns of enmeshment and disengagement in their respective families of origin.

Sharon's family was enmeshed, Stewart's was disengaged. Remember that when Stewart and Sharon first met she was a college student spending her summer vacation with her parents. She also made frequent trips home for the weekend during her years at college. If we knew them better, we'd have seen additional signs of enmeshment. Bedroom doors in Sharon's family's home were always open, people in her family felt free to interrupt one another, and it was rare that her parents did anything separately.

So far we've heard less about Stewart's family. Perhaps that's one indication of their disengagement. Few of them came to the wedding; that's another example of separateness. And I described how Stewart's father often went off by himself fishing or with friends and that his wife never seemed to mind.

Reading even these brief descriptions, you may be having a personal reaction: "What's wrong with leaving doors open?" or "What's so unusual about a man going off fishing?" Boundaries stir strong feelings. We're prone to take our own built-in preferences for emotional closeness or distance as the standard. Our families' truths are embedded in us.

Remember the relief Stewart felt at the end of weekends with Sharon in New York, when he climbed aboard the bus? Even under the influence of infatuation, he could stand only so much closeness. Sharon, on the other hand, felt no relief at the end of those weekends, only longing. In fact, it gave her an uneasy feeling when she sensed that Stewart was anxious to get away.

Looking at the relationship from Stewart's point of view, it might seem unfortunate that he didn't get to know Sharon better before marriage. Perhaps if they'd spent more time together Stewart would have decided that they were just too different to get along. Her clingy dependence was hard to live with. Or if they'd spent more time together before they got married, they might have learned to work out more compromises. Stewart might have learned to argue with Sharon, before being married made him afraid to try. It wasn't accidental that Stewart proposed while they were living apart.

Stewart was the sort of person who loves best from a distance. It was his ability to get away that made intimacy possible. Their being closer longer would have been a better test of his love. He might not have passed.

Because of the long-distance courtship, Sharon didn't have to learn to become a separate self. When Stewart wasn't there she had her family.

Stewart and Sharon entered matrimony each looking for a different kind of bliss. He sought a relationship with intense moments of coming together, well spaced out by periods of time alone. When they were courting he thought only of being close to Sharon, but that's because he took his privacy for granted.

People like Stewart, who are concerned about having space, experience requests for intimacy as invasions of their inner self. Now when Sharon crowded him, he couldn't go home. He was home. Telling lies is one way of protecting your autonomy. It would be years before Stewart told Sharon deliberate falsehoods, but he learned quickly that a man can be angry about something and avoid exposing himself by not discussing it. Pressed by her demands for emotional closeness and unable to fight back openly, Stewart started holding in his feelings, shutting her out of his inner life.

Sharon expected something quite different. One of the things she loved about Stewart was his open-hearted warmth. He was so ardent when they were dating. She assumed that after they were married they'd share the same closeness, only more naturally. There would be fewer separations and less pressure to be on guard. Married, she'd be free to be herself. Why not? He loved her, didn't he?

What caused so much pain wasn't the assumption (on both their parts) that things would be like they were at home; it was the feeling that their way was the right way, and that the other person was unreasonable not to understand. How could he go off and leave her alone so often? Didn't he want to be together? How could she crowd him so much? Did she want to smother him?

❖

At this point some people might question whether or not bringing in the concept of systems and how they're regulated might be overcomplicating matters. Take boundaries, for example—aren't they really just a matter of personality? Men tend to be more distant and women want to be more intimate; isn't that just the way things are?

There is some truth to this, but not much. The element of truth is that, at least in our culture, men used to be brought up to be primarily achievement-oriented and women more oriented toward relationships. But the need to be close and the need to be distant aren't just male and female psychology. In plenty of couples it's the man who wants to be together all the time and the woman who cherishes her privacy. It's a matter of how you were brought up, not your gender.

Furthermore, even within the same couple, patterns of closeness/distance often change over the years. The reason for this is that the boundary between the couple is a function of the boundaries between them and the rest of the world. A young husband may be so attached to his job that he doesn't get very close to his wife—it's not only a matter of time but also of limited emotional energy.[4] Later, he may want to move closer to her, but perhaps by then she's learned to accommodate to his distance and has filled the empty space with other interests—friends, her own career, or children.

One way for a therapist to help break down polarization over boundaries is to detoxify pejorative accusations. When partners call each other "cold" and "selfish," or "dependent" and "smothering," asking them concretely what they mean helps transform name-calling into more neutral descriptions.

"By 'cold' do you mean that she's often busy with her own projects and doesn't like to spend as much time together as you do?" "By 'dependent' do you mean that he prefers to do things with you rather than separately?" Note the word "prefer." Asking questions about preferences is more effective than preaching tolerance. (Not as much fun, maybe, but more likely to get through.)

No task is more crucial to a couple's satisfaction than working out boundaries, and nothing is more important to accommodation. Not only is defining the boundary between them important, but also, as we shall see in Chapter 5, the boundary separating the new couple from the outside world.

## How to Succeed as a Couple by Really Trying

I thought of titling this section "Happily Ever After." It sounds so much more positive, and anyway, who wants to have to work at love? Didn't we always expect it to come naturally? Although I don't want to convey the impression that intimate partnership requires endless effort, the truth is most of us have to work hard to overcome certain habits in order to make our relationships work.

Unfortunately, most of us react badly—in predictably human but self-defeating ways—to disappointment in love. Some people turn to fantasies of escape when they feel trapped. Stewart was like this. After a fight with Sharon, he'd withdraw to lick his wounds, and brood over how awful she was, how unfair life was turning out, and what a mistake he'd made in marrying her. If only he hadn't married her, just think of all the freedom he'd have.

When couples come to me for therapy, very often one partner engages in this kind of obsessive rumination. He or she thinks endlessly about all the reasons to leave *and* all the reasons they can't. Like most obsessions, this one draws attention away from more active solutions. As another example, the adolescent girl who obsesses about binging and dieting is distracted from other things that might be more important but more scary—like fighting openly with controlling parents, say, or making friends and dating.

---

[4]It isn't only or even primarily that some people have outside interests that becomes an obstacle to intimacy. It's that they don't share these passions by talking about them with their partners.

When unhappily mated clients consult me, not knowing whether to go or stay, I often suggest they try to make it work. I call this a "trial nonseparation." If they try hard and things don't improve, that may help them decide. Besides, it only takes a minute to leave.

Another trap is the reassuring hope that fulfillment merely waits on the next step—a new love, more money, a child, or one more child. We live, most of us, aiming to the future. Things may not be so hot now, but they will be when . . .

One of those "whens" is when the other person changes. Sharon kept hoping that Stewart would change. *Maybe when he finishes graduate school and gets a job he'll settle down and spend more time with me.*

Actually, there are two traps here. The first is projecting blame for a couple's problems onto one of them—the *other* one. The second trap is slipping into the habit of thinking of a relationship in terms of two separate persons, forgetting that in the interaction a new entity, the couple, is born.

Let's consider projecting blame first. The watchword of unhappy people is: "*They* have to change for me to feel better." A related axiom, is "No matter what, I have to be right." A lot of family quarrels are maintained by two people each trying to be right. The problem is that most of us assume that for us to be right, the other person must be wrong. The truth is, we're *always* right. At least about important things. We always remember what we remember, feel what we feel, think what we think, and for the most part, we always do the best we can. So do our partners.

The instant you let your partner be right, a great many disputes will automatically clear up, or at least lose their toxicity. But you don't have to falsify your feelings in a phony show of acceptance. With a little practice you can learn to see that your partner has a legitimate position, and acknowledge it. All this may seem relatively obvious. It is. One reason intimate partners have such a proclivity for projecting blame and assigning fault is that they're still smarting from disillusioned idealization.

❖

Once partners start learning to accept that the person they're with is the person they're with, they can turn their attention to working out accommodations. When we think of accommodation as a transaction between two people, the two most important things to keep in mind are compromise and negotiation.

Compromise is easier to talk about than to bring about. New couples have a difficult task. While they're willing to learn to relate intimately, they don't want to be controlled or taken for granted. Naturally they resist giving in on certain issues; still they have to give up some things and give in to each other. It's possible to give in without a feeling of surrender.

We're most generous when our own needs are met, or we're confident that they will be. A sense of personal power helps, as does faith in the goodwill of your partner. But you don't have to limit yourself to blind faith in your partner's goodwill; you can create it by being as generous as possible, giving in on those things that are more important to your partner than to you. Much of the compromising that takes place in the early part of a relationship doesn't require much deliberation. Each of you will accommodate to some of the other person's wishes without need for discussion. Some things, however, do require negotiation.

Making demands may seem the opposite of giving in; one is selfish, the other generous. Not really. Both contribute to enlightened self-interest; successful accommodation maximizes satisfaction in a relationship. Some people are better at giving in than making demands. They make an effort to accommodate to some of their partner's wishes (usually less than they think) and then assume that the partner will automatically sense what they want in return. If they don't get what they want, they ruminate on how unfair it all is, and then turn sour.

Part of accommodation is speaking up for what's important to you. It's not quite either/or—either you win or you lose. Expressing your wants and having them acknowledged is itself a significant victory. At the very least the two of you understand each other. This may sound mawkish. But it really is so important to give and receive understanding that even unresolvable conflicts are bearable if couples can acknowledge and tolerate their differences.

❖

There were many things that Sharon and Stewart didn't talk about. He didn't say much about her family. He wished they were less intrusive but was afraid that if he said so, Sharon would never forgive him. She didn't say much about his work. She thought he used it as an excuse to avoid her, but instead of speaking up she just felt hurt. And, for sure, neither one of them talked about sex. Too bad, because sex was one of their biggest problems.

Sex is a problem with a lot of couples, most of whom imagine others have it pretty good. The sad thing is that so many people can't even talk to each other about conflicting wants and needs. Talking about differences won't necessarily resolve them—life is more complicated than that—but it certainly is a shame that men and women feel so guilty and angry that they can't at least acknowledge each other's feelings.

❖

Creating a working partnership means developing a sophisticated system of mutual aid between two parts of a single system, an organism, that minimizes the demands made on each one and avoids as much as possible the internal friction of competitiveness that exists between unjoined individuals.

A couple is more than a collaboration between two separate persons; it's the formation of a new unit, a partnership. In the mathematics of couplehood, one plus one equals one. This is a slippery concept, hard to grasp in dry abstraction and even harder to see in flesh-and-blood relationships—at least hard to see without a little practice. Perhaps a visual illustration will help. Remember the Chinese symbol for yin and yang, the male and female forces in the universe?

Notice how, together, they are complementary and occupy one space. Relationships are like that. Together two people occupy one space, the space of the relationship. Because of this, if one partner changes, the relationship changes, and *the other person will automatically change*. If a woman wants to change her mate—and they're a part of a unity—the only way to change him is to change herself. If she becomes less competent around the house, he will become more competent.

Many people intuit this principle but underestimate its force. Fear holds them back. They're afraid that if they change, the other person won't; things may not get done or, worse, their partners will stop loving them. Suppose one person gets stuck with all the shopping and cooking. Talking it over and asking the other partner to help or, better, *share* the chores may result in some change. But don't count on it; talking is overrated. If one person stops doing certain chores, their partner will start to—eventually.

That's another thing that holds people back. Change takes time. Often we give up before giving accommodation a chance to work. If you stop picking up the mail, or making the morning coffee, or getting the paper, your mate will likely take over rather soon. If on the other hand you're tired of sitting around watching television on Friday night and you start buying tickets to go out or inviting people over, it may take some time before your partner accommodates to the change. He or she may grumble and complain. Remember, it isn't talking that changes things—only changing things does that. Be sympathetic, look for areas where it is easier for your partner to be flexible (maybe movies instead of concerts). But don't change back. Hang in there.

The examples I've chosen are deliberately prosaic. Other changes may be more intimidating, but the same principle applies. For example, suppose your partner doesn't share his feelings with you. You've tried asking, you've tried criticizing, and you've tried giving up. These are only my examples. You have to consider what you've tried; this means starting to think about patterns of interaction instead of personalities. Try something different. Try accepting and acknowledging whatever feeling he *does* show. If he says, "I don't feel like talking about it," say, "Okay, you'd probably like some peace and quiet." If he says, "My boss is an asshole," let him tell you about it, don't argue or give him advice. Feelings aren't problems to be solved. They aren't quarry to be caught. Hot pursuit only chases emotion away.

If someone changes from a person who pulls for feeling and pushes for disclosure to one who is receptive and responsive, their mate will gradually start sharing more. *Nota bene,* this may take time. Changing one person's part of any relationship pattern creates space for new behavior and pressure on the other person to move into it. Can you change everything this way? No, but you can change plenty. Moreover, once people recognize the power of the relationship and their power to affect it, they will begin to feel more in charge of their lives and their relationships, and less like victims.

# 5

# IN-LAWS

If the cliché that men marry women like their mothers and women marry men like their fathers is true, someone forgot to tell Sharon and Stewart. Stewart loved and admired his mother. She was intelligent, competent, and full of energy. But she often seemed to prefer her own company to that of anyone else. Unlike Stewart's mother, Sharon was warm, outgoing, openly affectionate—and she loved to make a fuss over him, something his mother never did.

Sharon's memories of her father were happy ones. Mostly she remembered him doing things for her. Once, when they were staying at a motel by the beach, Sharon thought the tap water tasted funny, so her father went to the store to buy her a quart of bottled water. He was always doing things like that. Only as she got older did she begin to see that the other side of his attentiveness was control. There was never any doubt of his love, but he was so domineering. Nothing could be less true of Stewart. He was never outwardly demanding, and—unlike her father—he seemed to respect her as an independent person.

Another interesting parallel was that Sharon's father, like Stewart's mother, was clearly the dominant partner. Thus, both Sharon and Stewart grew up in households where the parent of the opposite sex made most of the visible decisions and demonstrated the most energy and competence around the house. The effect on their expectations should be obvious: Sharon expected her man to repair faucets, empty the garbage, and deal with bill collectors. Stewart expected Sharon to do these things. In short, they both wanted mates who made up for lacks in their parents, but who at the same time possessed all the virtues of those parents—different, yet the same.

Sharon was tied to her family by loyalty and tradition. Her relatives were a powerful network that still had a hold on her. Stewart was jealous. He couldn't accept anyone else's claim on her.

Stewart thought distance made him independent. He had no wish to be the cringing sort of person he took his father for, nor did he care to be as lonely as his mother. But—not to worry—he had moved out and moved on. He would write his own story.

❖

On his first visit to New York, Sharon's parents invited Stewart to stay for dinner, letting him know that as a friend of Sharon's he was welcome. Dinner was served family-style on a long, formal dining room table. Mrs. Nathan shuttled back and forth from the kitchen with platters of gefilte fish, challah, sweet-and-sour meatballs, oven-browned potatoes, and noodle pudding. Mr. Nathan wanted to know what Stewart was studying, and did he like the college, and what was he planning to do with his future. If the questions seemed perfunctory, so were Stewart's answers. Besides, Sharon and her mother kept interrupting, Sharon to elaborate on what Stewart was saying, her mother to urge more food on them.

It was a genial, hectic meal. As Sharon and Stewart were preparing to go out for the evening, Mrs. Nathan was still trying to get him to have another portion of noodle pudding. Stewart wouldn't have guessed that this would be his last supper at the Nathan's for quite a while.

As soon as it became clear that Stewart was more than a friend, that he and Sharon were dating, her parents became noticeably cool, an antipathy Stewart found difficult to comprehend. When Sharon told him they didn't like the idea of her dating a non-Jewish boy, Stewart could hardly believe it. It just didn't make sense.

For a while, this stupid prejudice—that's how he thought of it—puzzled more than angered him. It wasn't until later, after he and Sharon were married, that he allowed himself to feel the full weight of his anger. In the early days of his relationship with Sharon, deep down in his heart he didn't feel fully worthy to be accepted, though not for anything having to do with religion—or race, or culture, or whatever the hell it was. He was insecure and not at all sure that he deserved anyone as wonderful as Sharon.

Stewart saw so little of Sharon's parents that he learned of the next switch in their attitude from her. When they realized that Sharon was serious about Stewart, and might actually marry him, their resistance stiffened briefly—there were one or two shouting matches between Sharon and her father—then melted. Not only did they give in to the inevitable, they seemed to forget their earlier reservations and became, once again, very warm toward Stewart. He learned from Sharon that the night he proposed, her parents called up all the relatives to tell them the good news.

❖

When Stewart took Sharon home to meet his parents during Christmas vacation, he had no thought about their getting married. He just wanted to show her off to them, and them to her.

Stewart had painted such a glowing picture of his parents that Sharon was a little intimidated; she expected them to be imposing intellectuals. Actually, they were quite nice. Mr. Salazar was friendly, just short of effusive (Stewart was embarrassed), and he seemed genuinely glad to meet her. He was more like her family than Stewart had led her to expect.

Mrs. Salazar, accepting Sharon on approval, showed every courtesy. She asked about New York. Where did Sharon like to shop? What were her favorite restaurants? She was perfectly friendly, but hard to read. With her there was always something held back, a little something in reserve. Sharon wondered how much Stewart's mother really liked her. Mrs. Salazar was polite but never really engaging in conversation, and she said next to nothing about herself. Much of the time she was off in the kitchen or working on one of her many projects. It would be some time before Sharon realized that the reticence was just Mrs. Salazar's way.

Mr. and Mrs. Salazar—or "Earl" and "Nancy," as they insisted she call them—accepted Sharon right away and made her feel part of the family group celebrating Christmas. This wasn't her first contact with Christmas festivities, but this was special. She went with Stewart and Mr. Salazar—"Earl" (it was hard to get used to)—to pick out the tree, and then the four of them hung decorations taken from an old wooden box in the attic: shiny, fragile ornaments; yellowed strings of popcorn; shimmering strands of tinsel; and plastic icicles. It was fun. Christmas morning, she went with them to church and then back to the house for a big breakfast before they opened the gifts. Everything seemed to follow tradition—they all knew exactly what to expect, including Earl Salazar's mock-pompous way of passing out all the presents.

If the visit was a test, everybody passed. Sharon could tell that Mr. Salazar liked her. He wasn't one to hold back his feelings. As for Mrs. Salazar, it was harder to know what she thought. Why, for instance, did she make a point of saying what a fine people the Jews were? Sharon decided that the condescension didn't mean anything. She liked the Salazars. They were good, interesting people. There was nothing about them to arouse uneasiness in her mind about Stewart.

After he proposed, Stewart took Sharon to visit his folks again. He wanted to tell them in person. His father was thrilled. His mother was pleasant, but Sharon thought she had reservations. Nancy showed so little emotion that it was hard to know what she thought. With Sharon's parents, there was never any doubt. In fact, though, she thought very little about Stewart's family. They were okay, and that was enough. She was marrying Stewart, not his family.

## "Alone at Last"

One of the reasons people marry is to break away from their families. For Sharon, this was deliberate. She was escaping their suffocating influence, her mother's narrow, mean view of the world, and her father's bossiness. Stewart was less concerned about his family. He thought of himself as long ago emancipated from his parents. Now that he and Sharon were getting married, there would be no one to interfere. They'd be alone at last.

Remember Carl Whitaker's quip, "There's no such thing as marriage, only two scapegoats sent out by their families to perpetuate themselves"? At one time in history this was true in a very obvious and political sense. Family ties counted for a lot: lineage, political power, the control of kingdoms. Today, it's often less obvious, but usually no less true.

The first thing to realize about extended families is that they exist. They don't go away. They exist as *introjects:* internalized images of the way family life should be; and they exist as real networks of a relationship, with the potential for complicating and enriching the new couple's union.

In the case of the Salazars and the Nathans, two families who would never have pursued a social relationship were being joined by a permanent bond that neither side ever sought. Whether or not the two extended families ever had much to do with each other after the wedding, they were still joined by their influence on Sharon and Stewart.

Every intimate partnership exists within a multigenerational system. Relationships with in-laws are only the most visible tip of that enormous system. Most people are amazed to discover the complex and powerful connections between events in one generation and effects in another.

An elderly parent dies and a forty-year-old father tightens his grip on his teenage son just as the boy is trying to break away. His grandfather's death may not have seemed very important to the teenager, yet its effect of making his father more insecure and demanding may have a profound impact on the boy.

People who speak of the "joining together of two families" conjure up images of a happy union. The reality is often more like, *When Worlds Collide.*

## Invaders from Another Planet

Stewart's parents came to New York two days before the wedding, and the night before the rehearsal, Stewart's father took the two families out to dinner. Sharon felt a little strange. She couldn't quite figure out if there were two families (the Salazars and the Nathans) or three (her parents, his parents, and Stewart and her).

Mr. Salazar, who wanted to play the gracious host, insisted on taking them all to Little Italy, to a wonderful restaurant he had eaten at many years ago. He didn't remember the name, but he knew where it was. "You'll love it," he assured the Nathans. He hailed a cab, and after they all squeezed in, Mr. Salazar told the driver to take them to Little Italy. They would stroll around and then find the restaurant.

At first the walk was pleasant. The two fathers ambled ahead, each one enjoying the chance to get to know the other. From behind, it looked to Sharon as though her father was doing most of the talking and Mr. Salazar was doing most of the listening. Stewart was more interested in the mothers. What would his mother think of Mrs. Nathan?

They went down one block and up another. Mr. Salazar couldn't seem to find the restaurant. Maybe it had gone out of business. No problem. They could walk around and pick another place to eat. After all, it was a warm evening, everyone was having a good time. Why worry? Mrs. Nathan leaned over and told Mrs. Salazar that it wasn't a good idea to walk around in this neighborhood at night.

Sharon overheard and told her mother that she worried too much. They were all getting a little edgy.

Two blocks and six menus later, Mr. Salazar found a place he liked. "Ah, what atmosphere," he said, looking around the candlelit room with murals depicting scenes of Italy on the walls. Mrs. Nathan thought it was a little dark. Sharon was hungry. Mr. Salazar told the headwaiter that they were celebrating a wedding, and asked him if the food was good. Mrs. Salazar gave Stewart the kind of look conspiratorial students exchange when the teacher makes a fool of himself.

So, Sharon thought, Stewart and his mother found Mr. Salazar's open show of emotion annoying, but instead of saying anything they just got aggravated. In the years to come, Sharon would have reason to remember that look of disdain.

Mr. Nathan ordered champagne and they all drank quite a bit. Stewart could tell that his parents were nervous. They acted like themselves, only a little more so. His mother got quiet and his father got sentimental. He rose to make a toast to the young couple and to the joining of the families. It was a nice toast, but maybe a little long. Glancing in his mother's direction, Stewart saw her sitting stiffly, her fixed smile betraying nothing of what she felt. *Is she embarrassed?* he wondered. No one else seemed to mind.

Stewart hated his father's sentimentality. Other people saw him as genial; Stewart saw a relentless seeker of approbation. He didn't like it in his father and didn't see it in himself. His father reminded him of Peter Lorre sucking up to Humphrey Bogart in *Casablanca*. The Lorre character didn't really like the Bogart character, he was just a weak person currying favor. Stewart sometimes felt the same obsequious desire to please; he just didn't let it show. In fact, he tried so hard to be different from his father that he was sometimes brusque, even rude.

After a while, Stewart relaxed his anxiety about his father and began to pay more attention to Sharon's parents. He saw them more clearly now, through his mother's eyes. Sharon's father was warm and open but—as usual—a little bossy. He insisted that they order red wine with their food, even though Sharon wanted white, and at one point he told Stewart's mother that she should order veal instead of fish because they were in an Italian restaurant. Stewart could see his mother freeze up. She was pleasant, trying to like them, but the Nathans weren't really her kind of people.

Sharon's mother told a couple of jokes that Stewart thought were a little crude. He was surprised. But he wasn't surprised when she made a few pronouncements about the big event. A wedding, she told him solemnly, was a "watermark" in a person's life. Later, she said that marriage was a "sacred institute." He thought of a seminary. Stewart, in the arrogance of youth, mocked her silently. He would be making similar slips of the tongue before he was forty-five. As we shall see, one of the more painful things about growing up is discovering in ourselves flaws we thought the exclusive province of others.

It was late when they finally finished dinner and found a taxi. Sharon was tired and nervous about the rehearsal tomorrow. Stewart was remembering who said what at dinner. He was still very proud of Sharon, but about his in-laws he wasn't so sure.

❖

Sharon thought the wedding went fine. Everybody seemed to have a good time. Stewart said his mother was nervous, but Sharon didn't think so. What she did think, but didn't say, was that Stewart was a little stiff toward her family. He was civil, but he was not enthusiastic. It didn't occur to her that he would someday turn this chilly correctness on her.

At the reception, Stewart again became aware of how different the two families were. Sharon's parents were okay, but some of her aunts and uncles were pretty loud. The aunt with the cast-iron permanent showed up wearing the kind of elaborate dress he'd only seen before in Technicolor movies. It was purplish-red, and she wore a long feathered boa that didn't quite match. She wasn't a woman to let colors scare her.

All the kissing and handshakes would have tired out a politician. Stewart decided that this was Sharon's family's affair and so he just let himself go along with the flow. The first quiet moment came when he went to the bathroom. He stayed a little longer than necessary, trying to collect his thoughts.  When he returned and stood in the doorway, watching all of Sharon's people drinking and dancing and chattering away, he thought he belonged in this family like a pickle in a glass of beer. But the thought passed, and he went back in just in time for some more family pictures.

Sharon was exhausted when she and Stewart finally got ready to leave. On their way out, she overheard her mother say to her father, "At last, they're settled." It's a familiar sentiment—as though a wedding resolved something rather than coming in the middle of a complex process of changing family status.

## Accommodation and Boundary-Making with the In-Laws

When they set up housekeeping together a couple faces the task of separating from their families and changing the nature of their relationships with parents and siblings, and in-laws. Loyalties must shift. For the new couple to function effectively as a unit, the partners' primary commitment must be to the relationship. Most families understand, in principle, this need for separation. Complications take the form of unfinished emotional business with parents and conflict with the in-laws.

❖

A couple in their mid-thirties once came to see me, saying they were having terrible fights and Sheila was threatening to move out. Everything was fine in their relationship, they said, except for one thing. Sheila felt Angie was too attached to her parents, spent far too much time with them, and worried about them excessively. Angie, trying to be reasonable, said, yes, maybe she was very attached to them, but what was wrong with calling on the phone once a week or so and visiting them every two or three months? The couple had gone round and round, and were at an impasse.

Though dissension over in-laws isn't unusual, this one was unusually intense. Instead of compromising their differences, both partners kept pulling harder in opposite directions. The more contact Angie sought with her family, the more Sheila resisted. Conflicts like this one don't go away, but I helped them reduce it to manageable proportions by breaking it into three constituent elements. The first was clarifying the boundary around the couple. Did she really want to leave? I asked Sheila. No, she loved Angie. I helped her see that she needed to convince Angie of that—that her primary emotional attachment was to Angie, not to her parents. How could Angie doubt that? Sheila wondered.

The second problem was how they communicated with each other. Contrary to popular belief, human problems rarely clear up when people learn to "communicate." Clear communication doesn't dissolve conflict the way New Improved Tide destroys stains, but it does clarify the nature of the conflict. With a little help from me, Angie and Sheila were able to understand how the other one felt about their one big problem. Sheila could see that Angie just wanted to stay in touch with her parents. Angie could see that Sheila felt they didn't have enough time alone together, and she didn't want to share her. A little empathy can prevent differences from growing into major aggravations.

Once the boundary issue was clarified and the two of them were communicating better—saying what they felt, not attacking each other, *and* showing that they understood what the other was feeling—the hard part, working out compromises about what to do, got easier. The actual mechanics of deciding how often to visit, and whether both of them would go or only Angie, never got simple, but they were no longer freighted with all the extra baggage of bitterness and misunderstanding.

Incidentally, one thing that helped immensely was that Angie agreed in advance to leave her parents' when Sheila wanted to go. Once she felt some control, Sheila was much more willing to stay, and—what Angie really appreciated—Sheila stopped saying disparaging things about her family's traditions.

❖

When two people join their lives, from two separate emotional cultures comes a new one. As we've seen, the partners must decide which rituals and traditions to retain from each family, and which ones to develop for themselves. The couple's parents can help avoid conflict in this process by scrupulously avoiding criticism of their son-in-law or daughter-in-law, and their family traditions. If a parent makes the mistake of criticizing, the son or daughter can gently but firmly defend the partner. This has nothing to do with what's right or wrong; it has to do with loyalty. In matters of the heart, if you're not with me, you're against me.

❖

After Stewart and Sharon were married, she got into regular fights with her father on almost every visit. Sharon wanted to be treated like a woman and a wife. Her father paid lip service to her new status—even playfully calling her "Mrs. Salazar"—but by the second day of every visit he'd start treating her as though she were still a child, his daughter.

He was always inspecting her house, finding something to complain about. "This drawer shouldn't stick like this." "Why don't you get that screen replaced?" Another thing that annoyed her was that whenever she tried to tell him about something she or Stewart had done, he'd change the subject to someone he met five years ago or a second cousin who had done something vaguely similar. But the worst thing, the thing that really drove her crazy, was the way he baited her with ethnic jokes ("Did you hear the one about . . . ?") and conservative political remarks that even he probably didn't take seriously. If Sharon challenged him, he dismissed her opinion as though she were still a child. His favorite expression was, "When you've lived a little longer, you'll understand these things."

Half the time she tried to ignore him, and sometimes they could find a subject to discuss without arguing. Eventually Sharon, who loved him and wanted to be close, would let down her guard and open up to him. Invariably, he'd then say something mean or dismissive. When this happened the fights were terrible.

One particularly bad fight occurred when Sharon and Stewart drove her parents to the airport and then had to wait two hours because the flight was delayed. Stewart could see that Sharon was tense, her patience worn thin by her father's constant fault-finding. "These goddamned airlines never run on time." "Why don't they have a decent place to eat in this airport?" "If you'd called to find out if the plane was on time, we wouldn't have had to spend all day here."

By this time Sharon had had enough. She snapped, "Why don't you just shut up!" He flushed and said, "Don't you *dare* speak to me that way, young lady!" Sharon lost it. She flared up and started screaming at him, by now totally hysterical.

Stewart stood there, frozen, as Sharon and her father shouted at each other. Before Stewart could think of anything to say, Sharon ran off down the hall, sobbing. He was rooted, unable to move, still shocked at the fury of her outburst. She wanted him to follow her—he knew that as surely as he knew anything. But she was wrong. He stood there awkwardly, not wanting to be with her parents but unwilling to support her temper tantrum. Lamely he commented, "She sure gets upset sometimes."

After several minutes he went to find her. Too late. She was wounded and furious that he hadn't followed her. She'd needed him, and felt deserted.

❖

When two people pledge themselves to each other, wise families honor the sanctity of the new union, offering their support but keeping their distance. Ah, but how much distance?

Stewart wanted Sharon to move away from her family—but not too close to him. Her parents wanted her and Stewart to be close—to each other, maybe; to them, definitely. Caught between competing demands for her affection, Sharon couldn't get far in either direction without a crippling sense of disloyalty. So, she did what most of us do: shifted back and forth in response to her feelings.

When she felt ignored by Stewart, Sharon moved closer to her mother—shifting from one side of the triangle to the other. She looked forward to visits home, where she could bathe in the warm love of her family. When she and Stewart arrived, her family enveloped them. Sharon loved it—for about twenty-four hours. Then her parents would begin to get on her nerves, and she'd move toward Stewart. When she got fed up with her mother's gossip and her father's not listening to her, she'd suggest that she and Stewart go off alone together—something her parents found intolerable. They didn't say much, but they blamed Stewart for refusing to fit in, for taking Sharon away from them.

Sharon's connection to her family had a positive and a negative pole. The togetherness ethic was so strong in her family that whenever she ventured too far from them, physically or emotionally, guilt yanked her back like an iron leash. But it wasn't obligation alone that kept her tied to them. She also felt a positive, loving bond.

Stewart sensed, though probably could not have described, both of these pulls, and resented them equally. Obligation, he thought, was stupid. As for the still-strong bond of love, Stewart thought of it as dependency.

❖

In addition to honoring the new couple's autonomy, there is also stress on the families to open themselves up to an outsider who is now an official member of the inner circle. The more that person differs from the family's culture and tradition, the harder the accommodation.

❖

Gay and lesbian couples have to contend with parental reactions not only to their partners but also to their sexual orientation. Even sons and daughters who have long been out to their parents may be in for a shock—from disapproval to banishment—when the reality of their relationships is made public with a commitment ceremony or even just by moving in together.

Given the likelihood of parental disapproval, coupled gay men and lesbians may be particularly prone to emotional cutoffs.[1] This is unfortunate because individuals cut off from their families may harbor a high level of unmet emotional need which they project onto their partners. This places intense pressure on these relationships and increases the likelihood of dysfunction.

Gay and lesbian couples may be uniquely embattled in our homophobic culture, but their dilemma is instructive for us all. Young adults must separate from their families to couple and form new families. Ideally, intergenerational boundaries won't be so rigid as to prevent supportive and enriching contact with parents and in-laws. But it's important to keep in mind that the number one priority is protecting the integrity of the new couple.

Gays and lesbians may be especially likely to need clear boundaries to protect the sanctity of their relationships, but anyone for whom family contact is too painful may need distance to protect their havens in a hostile world. In their enthusiasm

---

[1]Michael LaSala (1997). *The Need for a Thick Skin*. Unpublished doctoral dissertation. State University of New York at Albany.

for family ties, therapists should remember that some couples and individuals may need to keep their distance from parents and in-laws to give their relationships the priority necessary for them to flourish.

❖

Once they reconciled themselves to Stewart, Sharon's parents were glad to have a new member of the family. They thought of it as an addition, like adding a spare room onto the house. Stewart had other ideas. He was marrying Sharon, not her family.

Sharon was caught in the middle. She knew that her parents would like to see more of her and Stewart, and she knew that he would like to see less of them. Consequently, there were arguments about how often to visit, and the visits themselves were always tense.

At first, Stewart and Sharon's parents, aware of their conflicting claims on Sharon, made extra efforts to be polite. Stewart tried to warm up to Sharon's dad. He prided himself on his ability to tolerate Mr. Nathan's brusqueness, and he tried to ignore the bossiness. There was only one way to fry an egg, mix concentrated orange juice, or get from one part of town to another. Stewart went along—he was good at that—but he did so at a cost. It hurt his pride, and because he was humoring Mr. Nathan, he couldn't really like him. As Stewart began to feel more sure of himself, he began to speak up more. He told them he didn't want to call them "Mom" and "Dad," and he frequently refused to go along when Mr. Nathan proposed little excursions.

Once the barriers of politeness were dropped between Stewart and his in-laws, it didn't take them long to find each other out. And what was it they found? It wasn't a rounded picture, or even the essential character of each other; it was that which made them different. Stewart found out that Mrs. Nathan was loud and shallow. With her, everything was a florid show of feeling. She was easily agitated, quick to criticize people who weren't around, and equally quick to break into raucous laughter at the slightest provocation. For her part, she thought her son-in-law was a cold fish. She greeted him effusively, though he knew she didn't mean it. Stewart aimed his kiss to one side of her mouth but she turned slightly so that their lips met. It seemed natural to her. To him it wasn't. And her laughter was jarring, like music turned up too loud. She was nothing at all like his own mother.

❖

Unlike Stewart, Sharon was drawn to her in-laws. She especially admired Nancy, whose self-possession was such a contrast to her own mother's boisterous emotionalism. Nancy was a good listener, too. She always wanted to know what Sharon was doing, how things were going—and she didn't interrupt or change the subject to talk about herself.

Nancy was easy to talk to but hard to get to know. Sharon's questions provoked discussions mainly of a meteorological nature. "How's everything down your way, Nancy?" "Oh, fine. We're having a lovely spell of warm, sunny weather."

One Christmas when Sharon and Stewart were visiting his parents, Sharon suggested that Stewart go with his father to get the tree, so that she'd have a chance to talk with Nancy.

"Good idea," Stewart said. Maybe Sharon would have more success getting close to his mother than he did.

As soon as the men left, Sharon sat down by Nancy in the living room and started talking. Not more than five minutes went by before Nancy excused herself to start cooking dinner. Sharon, who felt uncomfortable in other people's kitchens, picked up the paper and waited for Nancy to return. Half an hour went by, and things got quiet in the kitchen. Sharon got up and went to see what was happening.

There was Nancy, sitting and smoking, smoking and coughing. A half-inch-long ash hung, poised at the end of her cigarette. Sharon was watching it, waiting for it to fall when Nancy looked up and saw her standing there. "Oh, hi, I was just about to stuff the turkey."

Sharon was a little hurt that Nancy left her sitting alone, but she didn't think it was personal. Nancy just liked to be by herself. She preferred her conversations brief, then she withdrew like a visitor going home. Uneasily, Sharon reflected that this was the woman who taught her husband how a person should be.

How different these Salazars were from her family! In her family nobody ever did anything alone.

Many newly married partners go through a period of wishing to be adopted by their in-laws. Here, too, opposites attract. But often this attraction passes. Just as Stewart found Sharon's parents intrusive and chaotic, she gradually concluded that his parents were too reserved and cool for her. They, especially Nancy, didn't seem to want to get involved. Her parents wouldn't let go.

## Invisible Loyalties

Stewart could tell from Sharon's voice who she was talking to on the phone. There was that animated eagerness in her voice, a readiness to share some bit of news, or get annoyed. "*Mother,* he's already an assistant professor. Most people start out as an instructor." The nicest things he heard from her were often things he overheard.

Sharon didn't talk about him for long. She was already onto the subject that interested her most, the thing that kept her connected to her parents and separated from him: her family. Aunts and uncles and cousins and husbands and wives and children. Everything they did, everything they said, was still vitally important to her. Aunt Zelda was in the hospital and cousin Fredda didn't even visit! Cousin Ralph's wife, Suzi, was having her whole house painted. *Where* did she get the money?

Stewart was annoyed. If Sharon loved him, she would forget all that nonsense.

Stewart never put it (even to himself) in so many words, but he had expected to replace Sharon's parents. Two human beings, bound together in love and kindness—they shouldn't need anyone else. Like so many expectations, this one wasn't thought out or discussed, and so was never examined.

To Sharon, it seemed that he wanted to keep her hermetically sealed off from her family. But—and this is what made it so unfair—he didn't in return give himself to her. He wanted all of her but didn't give all of himself.

One of the great mistakes we make in love—in any relationship—is wanting to change the other person. When you choose someone, you choose the whole package, not just the parts you like. Part of that package is your partner's relationship with his or her parents.

Stewart saw Sharon as overly attached to her mother. Why all these calls? What he didn't see was that Sharon had wanted to leave her family, but finding Stewart less emotionally available than she'd expected, she turned back to her family to satisfy her need for intimate connection.

Sharon and Stewart and her parents formed a triangle, with sides of interchangeable length. The more distant he was from her, the closer she moved to them.

❖

The people who most jealously oppose their partner's bond to their parents are usually insecure—about themselves and about the relationship. They often don't have strong ties to their own families, or many friends. My advice to clients is to allow their partners as much freedom as possible to relate to their parents; otherwise, resentment, spoken or not, will create tension and become a source of irritation.

Sharon never imagined that the man she loved would turn out to be so stubborn and possessive. But she had seen only half of his nature then, as one sees the crescent moon when it's masked by the shadow of the earth. She saw the full man now.

The more hostile Stewart grew toward her family, the more Sharon felt like a victim of his jealousy. When Stewart criticized her mother, Sharon felt herself attacked. Not only did his criticisms set up a loyalty conflict within her, but she also realized that his attack on her mother was a displaced attack on herself. He felt free to call her mother shallow, dependent, and unimaginative. Weren't these the things he secretly thought about her?

❖

A therapist can help resolve in-law triangles by encouraging couples to clarify what is properly the province of their relationship to each other from what is the adult child's relationship to his or her parents. The can of worms that such discussions may open up occurs when the jealous partner complains and the mate then starts talking about *why* he or she feels the need to spend so much time with his or her family. Such discussions can be painful, but they can also be productive.

In the case of interfering in-laws, it's useful to invite them to a session with the couple. Start by giving the older generation a chance to talk about their point of view. Let them get their feelings off their chests. Acknowledge those feelings. This—the opportunity to have their feelings acknowledged—helps clear the air and makes them more likely to be receptive to their children's perspective. A rule of thumb in family therapy, or perhaps a gross oversimplification, is that the more people who are present, the simpler it is to get somewhere—just giving people a chance to air their point of view without attack is often very useful.

❖

Aside from whatever demands they actually make, in-laws are easy scapegoats for family tensions. Some mothers can't accept that their sons want to put distance between them. They prefer to hold their daughters-in-law responsible for alienation of affections.

Ultimately, what makes relationships with in-laws difficult is our ambivalence about our own parents. Sharon expected Stewart to pull her away from her family's suffocating clannishness, which to some extent he did. And Stewart handed the phone to Sharon when his mother called. He wanted the connection but didn't know how to make it.

In-laws are notoriously difficult, but they aren't the most feared species in the family jungle. Sharon may have mixed feelings about Stewart's parents, but she had less at stake than he did. After all, in-laws are only in-laws. Her in-laws were his parents.

## Past Tense and Imperfect Future

By the time we grow up, each of us has two relationships with our parents. One is based on the past. It consists of the memories we have of growing up, of how our parents treated us, and of how we felt about them. This is the repository of fond memories and frustrated longings. The second relationship is the real, ongoing relationship we have (or don't have) with the flesh-and-blood parents who exist in the present.

Ironically, the first relationship, the one in our minds, is more alive for many people than the second one. The real relationship is often frozen in place by the one in memory.

The family is made of strange glue—it stretches but doesn't let go. Even in families like Stewart's where contact is cordial but distant, the family adheres to the next generation in the form of unfinished emotional business.

This unfinished business is known as *fusion*—the blurring of psychological boundaries between the self and others that is so ubiquitous in families. The opposite of fusion is emotional maturity and independence, or *differentiation*. An easy mistake is to confuse the pseudo independence of the person who avoids his or her family with genuine differentiation. Differentiation is achieving an autonomous identity, not putting distance between yourself and your family. When it comes to family, you can run but you can't hide.

Sharon and Stewart were both still emotionally fused with their families, though they demonstrated it in opposite ways. Lack of differentiation may take the form of continued intense involvement, as in Sharon's case, or as in Stewart's case, emotional cutoff. In the process of differentiation, "I" becomes increasingly differentiated from "we." But Sharon was leaving one "we" (her family) for another (she and Stewart as a tightly bonded unit). Her plan had been to create a new family, an improved version of the old one, in which she would take care of Stewart and he would reciprocate. But the old family didn't disappear, nor did its claim on her, and she faced a struggle to balance the old relationship with the new.

Unfortunately for Sharon, the man she was trying to bond with was allergic to intimacy. Stewart was leaving a family that denied and avoided connection to form a marriage where he instinctively tried to do the same. For a poorly differentiated man like Stewart, sustained intimacy is threatening, as though it might negate his separateness entirely. Getting too close feels like losing control. Stewart wanted love but was afraid of being absorbed. In the face of his anxiety, his natural reaction was to keep his distance.

❖

Although the past is gone, we can't seem to let go of it. When we think about our parents and when we visit them, there's that tension. Slow to accept that they are who they are, and that whatever happened happened, we go on wanting something from them. We long for that someday when they will make up for what we missed; when they will change; when they will apologize; when they will finally treat us the way we want them to. We want everything from them—everything but the real love that's available.

Some people, like Sharon, long for their parents to start respecting them; others, like Stewart, long for missing shows of love and attention. Somewhere, lost in the heart, is a part of us that never really grows up until we stop needing our parents to make things right.

Some people invest their whole lives in a struggle with their parents. I've met men and women of fifty who are still furious with their parents' lack of attention or because their mothers don't visit them as often as they visit other members of the family. Such bondage!

In his stinging satire, *Portnoy's Complaint*, Philip Roth has Portnoy confess to his analyst his lifelong ambition to liberate his father from ignorance:

> *To this day our destinies remain scrambled together in my imagination, and there are still too many times when, upon reading in some book a passage that impresses me with its logic or its wisdom, instantly, involuntarily, I think, "If only he could read* this. *Yes! Read and understand—!" Still hoping, you see, still if-onlying, at the age of thirty-three. . . .*[2]

In reality, of course, the only thing that can be changed in the present is the future. Once you quit struggling to make your parents into the people you wish they'd been, you can begin to form a relationship with them as they are.

And what about the past? Your mother's harsh treatment, your father's neglect, all the ways they let you down? Does all that go away or cease to matter? No, but it's over. The best thing you can do about the past is to remember it and try to understand what happened, what effect it had on you, and how you can avoid acting out the same scenarios with your own children. As for the parents you remember,

---

[2]Philip Roth, *Portnoy's Complaint*. New York: Random House, 1969, p. 9.

forgive them. Perhaps you can understand why they did what they did. Perhaps not. But believe this: The did the best they could. We all do.

❖

One of my patients, a man of thirty-five, had the kind of childhood people like to forget. His mother alternated between angry tirades and periods of depression. When she was depressed, she neglected her six children; when she was angry, she beat them. His father was a heavy drinker and rarely at home. Growing up in this atmosphere, my patient learned to be self-reliant, to keep his feelings to himself, and not to trust anybody. This may have helped him in business; it did not help him as a husband and father. Exploring this past and its impact helped my patient understand himself better, and once he could see how he'd become so closed off, he was able to start opening up more with his wife and children. But when it came to reestablishing a relationship with his parents, he balked.

"Okay, so the past is over," he said. "But they still haven't changed. They still ignore me. Last week was my birthday and they didn't even send me a birthday card."

Like a lot of us, this man was still collecting grievances. Maybe that isn't quite fair. Perhaps I should say that his parents were still disappointing him. What he complained about was absolutely true. He was perfectly justified in complaining. What he missed, though, was understanding that relationships are circular. What they do is a function of what we do, and what we do is a function of what they do, et cetera. True, my patient's parents didn't send him a birthday card. But that isn't too surprising since he hadn't called, written, or visited in years. Am I saying it's his fault? No. It doesn't matter whose fault it is. The point is this: Relationship problems are kept going by both parties, and either one can break the cycle. This truth is easier for most people to accept with regard to relationships where they feel more powerful—with their children, or young friends, or junior colleagues. With big people we often feel one-down and don't see as easily our ability to turn things around. Nowhere is this truer than with our parents.

❖

Why bother? A lot of people ask that when therapists start suggesting that it might be a good idea to work on their relationships with their parents. Why bother? Because there are two benefits of almost incalculable worth. The first is mastering unresolved emotional sensitivity to the things our parents do that drive us crazy. The second is increasing the active network of our relationships. (The same two benefits accrue to developing better relationships with one's in-laws. Getting to know and accept their in-laws helps people understand and come to terms with their partners, as well as adding to the size of their families.)

The best clue to the nature of unfinished business with parents may be the triggers that set off emotional reactivity. Those who are cut off from their families, like Stewart, may be a little unclear about what their parents do that stirs up adolescent overreaction in them. Stewart thought that the link of dependency that united him and his parents had been completely severed, but little by little he was reminded that it still had a palpable existence. It was as thin as a hair, but there were moments when he seemed to hear it vibrate.

❖

Stewart still called his mother when he achieved some professional success, and she still responded with that cool lack of enthusiasm that punctured his pride like a needle in a balloon. His mother was the one audience who would never give Stewart a standing ovation.

Stewart wanted to be admired but was afraid he wouldn't be. That's what made him rein in his excitement over his accomplishments. "Don't play games," Sharon would say when he'd be coy about some accomplishment. His game was to minimize his success in hopes that it would provoke her to praise him lavishly. But how could she praise him when he was so indirect?

The emotion we're talking about is shame—that gnawing feeling of being unworthy that lurks in dark places of the heart, poisoning confidence and self-respect. Stewart held so much back because he was afraid of not being responded to or, worse, shot down for thinking he was special. Fearing that his craving for approval might lead to rejection, Stewart kept a lot inside. Sharon chided him for being a pessimist. The reason for Stewart's pessimism was that he didn't allow himself to get his hopes up; he was that afraid of disappointment.

Stewart carried a different legacy from his father. Earl Salazar exercised iron control with a velvet glove. As a boy, Stewart was allowed so much freedom that he never learned to rebel. At eight he was permitted to go anywhere he wanted on the bus, and by the time he was ten he often took long train trips to visit his relatives. It wasn't until he was seventeen that Stewart's idea of what he should be allowed to do exceeded his father's tolerance.

One Friday night as Stewart was about to go off to the movies with his friends, his father asked what picture they were going to see. It was a Brigitte Bardot movie. "Absolutely not!" his father said. Stewart was stunned. His father had never told him what movies he could or couldn't see. How could he start now? But Stewart didn't argue. You don't argue with your father.

That's when he started doing things on the sly. Previously, he'd never felt the need. But he was too old to start taking orders, and it didn't make sense to get into a hassle. Why bother?

Stewart brought this sneaky streak into his marriage. It wasn't that he did anything wrong; his own conscience was too strong for that. But sometimes, in little matters (like spending extra money or staying after work to have a drink with somebody), he found it easier not to say anything than to risk an argument.

❖

Those still actively embroiled in their families, like Sharon, usually know exactly what their parents do that drives them crazy. They loved her but treated her as an extension of themselves. This meant that, on the one hand, they placed a lot of expectations on her; on the other hand, they didn't take her seriously.

Sharon's family needed someone to play the part of "the good daughter," and she was it. Roles, like this one, may not describe the reality of the person so much as that person's place in the family system. In Sharon's family, where the collective sense of "family" was more important than the individuality of its members, such roles were extremely powerful.

When she got married, Sharon imagined that her parents would take her more seriously. They would see her grown up, happily and comfortably married. At last, they'd give her what she wanted: attention *and* respect.

Stewart did not look forward to his in-laws' visits. He didn't like seeing Sharon so frantic about how the house looked, what she would cook to please her father, and where they could go to entertain her mother. Worse, he felt smothered when they showed up.

Stewart didn't like it when Sharon got so frustrated with her parents (Why did she let them bother her so much?), but he didn't mind when she turned to him for support. He could sympathize with her when she said how awful they were, and he didn't have to risk saying the same thing himself. This was, however, only the immediate result of Sharon's stormy relationship with her parents. In the long run, she transferred her thwarted needs onto Stewart.

The idealized in-love phase of intimate partnership renews the hope for the perfect parent who will make up for old disappointments. The more impossible the expectations and longings, the more certain it is that the partner will become a source of disappointment and frustration. No wonder Stewart couldn't understand Sharon's anger with him; it carried so much weight.

❖

The degree to which the personhood of either partner remains tied up in unresolved conflict with his or her family shapes how flexible and accommodating the pair will be. This is really just another way of saying that unfinished business gets in the way of working on new relationships. Once people begin to resolve how they feel about their parents—the minute that happens—they can get on to the business of relating to their partners as real people, not as shadows of the past.

The best way to improve relationships with parents is to build a personal connection with each of them, and then to discover—and change—one's part in destructive patterns of interaction.

Sharon, for example, might have tried to spend some time alone with each of her parents. This wouldn't have been easy; her parents came as a matched pair. A surprising number of people who think they have a decent relationship with their parents never spend time alone with either one of them (especially the parent of the opposite sex). Sharon was occasionally alone with her mother, but the intimacy of this contact was limited because they always talked about other people. Sharon's mother was fond of complaining about various relatives; their crime was usually paying insufficient attention to her. Sharon, interested and sympathetic, listened, but she would have done better to try to make the conversation more personal by talking about her mother and herself.

To spend time alone with her father, Sharon might have offered to take him out to lunch. With her mother, the goal would have been to make the conversation more intimate, more personal. With her father, her goal would be to notice what he did that got her so upset and learn to control her reactivity—not necessarily to suppress her feelings, but to respond in a less volatile way. Her old pattern with her father was to initiate conversations, telling him what Stewart was doing at the university, or about someone interesting she had met, or some plans she had. He listened, but not for long. When he changed the subject, she felt totally discounted. If tensions were low enough, she'd just shut down; if anxiety was running high, she'd explode.

To break this cycle Sharon could have done a number of things. She might have begun by asking her father about himself. Perhaps by showing some interest in him she could have relieved him of the urge to interrupt when it was her turn. Or she could have told him directly that she felt bad when he cut her off.

Once you see what the old unsatisfactory pattern is, you can make improvements with almost any change. The trick is to remain calm and not respond reflexively. By the way, this is easier to do on a planned outing than in the heat of the moment during hectic family get-togethers.

❖

For Stewart to improve relations with his parents, he'd have had to find a way to get a little closer to his mother and to be more honest with his father. Getting closer to his mother wouldn't have been easy. Pressing shy persons for intimacy only scares them away. Telling her directly that he wanted to be closer, asking her personal questions, or even fishing for her approval could have had the opposite effect from the one he intended.

It helps to remember that there are degrees of intimacy, from friendly, superficial conversation, to expressing personal but not revealing information, to sharing more intimate thoughts and feelings, and finally to talking about the relationship itself. To become more intimate with someone, take one step at a time.

Stewart was closer to his father. In fact, they got along pretty well. The one thing Stewart might have done differently was to disagree more openly and let his father know when he was annoyed with him. Stewart was already an expert at ignoring what offended him and going along when he didn't feel like it. He needed to practice speaking up. In fact, he and Sharon would have been good coaches for each other.

❖

Sharon and Stewart might have made these changes but they didn't. The pressing demands of young adulthood—forming families and building careers—make most people defer working things out with their parents. If contact is painful, we protect ourselves with distance the way Stewart did or, like Sharon, endure it as inevitable. Most people know what their parents do that they don't like, but make the mistake of thinking that nothing will change unless they can get through to their parents, or maybe lightning will strike and transform them into the people we think they should be.

❖

Many married couples have a relatively short interval between marriage and the birth of their first child. (This is changing but not as much as people think.) Therefore, most young people have only a short time to adjust to this phase of life before moving on. It's hard to take on new tasks while still carrying the burden of what's left unfinished.

Loyalty commitments to parents are especially pertinent to the raising and training of children. So even though Sharon only shrugged when her parents asked their favorite rhetorical question, "So, when are we going to be grandparents?" she felt some responsibility not to disappoint them. Consciously, she was a long way from being ready to become a mother; unconsciously, she felt an undischarged obligation to give her parents what they wanted.

# 6

# THE DEPRESSED YOUNG MOTHER

One soft summer night when they were driving home from a party, Stewart said, "Let's have a baby. I want a little Sharon." They'd been married four years. Stewart was teaching at the state university in Albany, and Sharon was working in the department of admissions. She didn't know what to say. She assumed they would have a baby someday. . . . Was this "someday" already? All she said was, "Okay."

Sharon's doctor said it might take six months to conceive, something about the pill causing a hormone imbalance. But seven weeks after she said okay the gynecologist confirmed that she was pregnant. Sharon was just about to call Stewart when the phone rang. It was Stewart. "Well, what did the doctor say?"

"We're going to have a baby," she answered.

Stewart shouted something into the phone; it sounded like "Yahoo!" For once, there was no mistaking his feelings.

That night he came home with flowers and took her out to the little French restaurant she liked so much. He really made a fuss over her. It felt good.

The first three months of the pregnancy Sharon was sick to her stomach every afternoon. The first few days of nausea were bad enough. What made it hard to bear was the way it continued, day after day. Finally, she went to the doctor, who gave her some antinausea medicine. She wasn't crazy about taking medication while she was pregnant, but on the other hand, she wasn't crazy about spending every afternoon throwing up.

As her body swelled to adapt to the growing fetus, Sharon's mind slowly adapted to the idea of becoming a mother. Nature, she guessed, was resolving her ambivalence. When she first felt the baby turning inside her, it became a reality. Stewart got excited when he felt the baby move, but after that he wasn't particularly curious about what was going on inside Sharon's belly. He was a bystander. He was concerned when she said the baby was kicking ("Does it hurt?"), but his concern was limited to her. The new life growing inside her seemed beyond the reach of his imagination.

As slowly as the first weeks of pregnancy dragged on, the last few raced by. Labor began three weeks early. Sharon woke Stewart and said she was having contractions.

"You couldn't be," he said. "It must be a false alarm." After that the contractions stopped, and Stewart went off to work. "Call me if anything develops."

At two that afternoon Sharon called to say that the contractions were coming regularly and the doctor said it was time to go to the hospital.

Labor was hard and long. Lamaze helped. At least Sharon knew what to expect. Stewart was good, too. He was always calm in emergencies. When the pain made her lose concentration, Stewart was right there. He helped her get control of her breathing. Still, the night dragged on. It was well after midnight when they finally wheeled her into the delivery room. Sharon was groggy now, but she knew it was almost over. For the rest of her life, she would remember lying there in that theater of lights, with the doctor and nurse urging her, "Push—push—push!" God, it hurt.

Sharon saw the baby when his head and shoulders were out. *"There's a baby coming out of me!"* She had known it all along, but suddenly there he was. The next thing she saw was Stewart holding the baby, crying and smiling at the same time. *Maybe there will be a rainbow*, Sharon thought dreamily. Then they handed the tiny bundle to her. Her heart was bursting with love. She had loved him in her belly, but this was different.

When Stewart returned the next morning, Sharon was sleeping. The baby was in the nursery. Stewart stood in front of the glass watching all the little babies, full of feeling. But he didn't stay long, he wanted to see Sharon. He sat down next to her bed as quietly as he could. Sharon looked exhausted, and frail, and very beautiful.

Sharon opened her eyes and smiled when she saw Stewart. "Did you see him?" she asked.

"Yes, he looks just like you."

Just then the nurse knocked softly. "Anybody in here want to see a baby?" She wheeled Jason in on a little cart and handed him to Sharon. Sharon couldn't stop looking at him: his fat cheeks, his curly dark hair, his perfect little body. She was taken by surprise by the wave of love she felt for her baby. *Her baby!*

While Sharon looked at the baby, Stewart looked at Sharon. She had never looked so angelic as she did then, lying propped up on her pillows, with her hair cascading over her shoulders and the tiny infant in her arms.

For the rest of her days, there were many moments from that day Sharon would always remember. Most of all she loved looking at Jason. *God*, she thought, *made babies that helpless and adorable so everyone would want one, and want to take care of it*. In sleep, Jason looked like a little doll or an angel, defraying the suggestion of all the effort to come.

❖

Riding home with a new baby was one of those emotionally charged experiences that takes only a few minutes and lasts forever. Sharon's heart was full and everything was vivid. The sunshine was bright on the lawns and flowers, and the air was warm but not hot—perfect.

Sharon kept looking down at the baby. It was like coming home from a shopping trip with some wonderful new purchase. She remembered how she felt when they brought home the big air conditioner for their bedroom. Once they wrestled the heavy box up the stairs and finally got it installed, it was great: instant relief. But a baby—what were they going to do with a baby?

The house was more or less ready. Stewart had talked her into putting the baby in a separate bedroom ("You want to get some sleep, don't you?"). Friends had lent them a cradle, and they'd bought a changing table from Babyland with a padded top and lots of little compartments to put things in. What else did they need, really, except a few little sleeper suits and diapers?

Since it was Stewart's idea to use disposable diapers instead of cloth, he'd gone to the store to buy a supply. He showed Sharon the four boxes of infant-size Pampers and said, "This ought to last us a while."

❖

Sharon worried about the baby. He looked so tiny and helpless. How would she know if he needed something? She found out.

Nature, it seemed, had designed things so that parents *had to* take care of their infants. At least that's the way it was with Jason. He hollered to be fed and wailed when he was wet—he seemed so sensitive to a wet diaper—and sometimes he cried just to be held. Jason's demands were so intense and unrelenting that the first month was a blur of fatigue and frustration. Nothing had prepared them for this.

It was quite late that first day home from the hospital when Sharon finally fell into a deadening sleep. She was still exhausted when she woke, thick and groggy with dreams. She'd been on a train, speeding through the night, its whistle shrieking. When she tried to focus on where the train was going, she became aware that the whistle was really a baby's cry. A baby? Then she remembered. She glanced at the clock. It was 2:00 A.M.—oh, she was tired! She kept her eyes shut, hoping Stewart would get the baby so she could drift off again. She waited. Nothing broke the sound of the baby's persistent cry. After another minute she said, "Stewart, do you want to bring me the baby?"

"Aw, come on, Sharon! I have to be up early for work; why don't you get him? You're the one who's going to have to feed him anyway."

Sharon didn't say anything. As she went to get the baby she thought, *So this is how it's going to be.*

Over the next few weeks the weight of the baby's demands sapped Sharon's strength to the point where she felt she was in a fog. In those unbroken days and nights, it was like having the flu, but one that doesn't go away—and nobody sends you to bed and brings you ice cream. You're the mother now.

Sharon hadn't fully recuperated from childbirth. She still had pain and soreness from the episiotomy, and engorged breasts. Her back ached, and she could feel it getting worse every time she bent over to pick up the baby. And she still had vaginal bleeding with clots and cramps. Add to this her anxiety about the baby and her disappointment in Stewart for leaving everything to her and you have a recipe for postpartum depression.

According to a recent study by Eugene Paykel and his associates, 20 percent of new mothers experience mild to moderate depression during the postpartum period.[1] Among the contributing factors are worry, fatigue, and lack of personal time. Sharon didn't actually become clinically depressed, but she was among the two-thirds of new mothers who, according to Ramona Mercer, are blue and cry easily.[2] Sadly, many of these women are ashamed of themselves for being unhappy. It isn't supposed to be this way, is it?

## The Impossible Job

Being a parent is the ultimate training in humility. Nobody expects having an infant to be as stressful as it turns out to be, and few remember afterward how hard it was. The mind blurs the memory of all the effort and anxiety. Besides, there are plenty of incentives. When the children are babies, we can—and do—provide almost everything they need. And we exert such a profound control over them. They're ours. It's a good feeling.

❖

While she was still in the maternity ward, Sharon was surprised to learn that it would be a couple of days before real milk began to flow through her breasts. (Before that, a small amount of fluid known as colostrum is all that comes out.) It took a little while to get the hang of nursing, but when she did, it was an indescribable source of satisfaction. She held the baby in her arms, and when he felt the nipple near his mouth, he rooted around trying to get hold of it. He'd make a little *O* with his tiny mouth—Sharon called this his "foody face"—and search eagerly until he found what he wanted. He looked so blissful when he suckled. When Sharon's milk began to flow, she had the sensation of letting go and feeding the baby as though straight from her heart.

Sharon wanted Jason to have a pleasant, stimulating environment, and so she bought a collection of artistic greeting cards, sealed them in plastic, and hung them around the inside of his cradle. She chose ones with bright, pleasing colors. Mondrian, Klee, and Rousseau were her favorites. When she made mobiles to hang over the cradle, she took pains to turn the shapes—little boats and animals—sideways, so that Jason could see them when he looked up. She even read to him in French, so that he would get used to the sounds. But it was two or three months before the baby noticed much of what was going on around him.

---

[1] Eugene Paykel et al., "Life Events and Social Support in Puerperal Depression," in *British Journal of Psychiatry*, 1980, *136*, 339–346.

[2] Ramona Mercer, *First Time Motherhood: Experiences from Teens to Forties*. New York: Springer, 1986.

Jason proved to be a demanding baby. Not until he was eight months did he start sleeping through the night. He was a greedy eater, but it was hard to tell when he was going to want a big feeding or a small one. And Sharon never knew what to expect when she put him down for a nap or to sleep for the night. Sometimes he would lie quietly and give himself up to sleep. At other times, outrage twisted his face into an angry red mask, and then the wailing started.

When Jason cried, Sharon felt sad and helpless. Should she pick him up, like she wanted to, or let him cry himself out, as Stewart and the pediatrician suggested? She was never sure. Meanwhile, she felt guilty and frightened.

Sometimes after a late-night feeding, Jason would shriek on and on, while Sharon lay there, hoping he would drop off to sleep. The wailing would stop the way it started—all of a sudden there was silence, and Sharon felt like a hostage released.

At two months Jason began to suck on his fingers and smile. At four months he enjoyed being pulled up to a standing position. He was so full of life! His favorite thing was splashing in his bath, but there never seemed to be a time when he was content to be alone, amusing himself. Someone always had to be there. And so the responsiveness that was Sharon's major reward carried with it additional burdens. If she played with him, she was rewarded with loud, explosive laughter, but it took a lot of work to keep him entertained.

When Jason was six months old Sharon returned to work, as she had planned. It felt strange getting up at 7:30, dressing for work, and leaving Jason with a sitter. He cried and clutched at her arm when she tried to leave. Even after she got into the car, she could still hear him crying. All day long, that was the image that stuck in her mind: Jason crying and reaching for her. She quit at the end of the week.

Sharon told Stewart that she was too worn-out to return to work. Maybe it would be better if she stayed home with Jason. He said, "Fine, do what you want," but he thought she would feel better if she could get away from the baby for a while. Sharon stayed home but felt guilty because she saw so many other women who managed to work and raise babies, and because she never really believed that Stewart supported her decision.

Sharon wondered how Jason could have been so good in the hospital and so fussy at home. Maybe she was doing something wrong.

❖

Why is it that parents with easy babies think they're lucky, while those with difficult infants worry that they're doing something wrong? Perhaps it's a testament to the average person's enormous capacity for self-criticism.

One of the things that makes parents unnecessarily susceptible to self-blame is the lack of awareness that babies are born with wide variations in temperament. Some parents say that their babies were always fussy, or always easy. But they can't quite believe it. When things don't go well, they can't let go of the idea that they must be doing something wrong.

It's now clear that part of a child's personality is a matter of inborn temperament. Alexander Thomas and Stella Chess, who are among the most respected researchers to look at infant temperament, concluded that babies are born with one of three dispositions: "easy to handle," "difficult to manage," and "slow to warm up to other people."[3]

Jerome Kagan, summarizing the available evidence, concluded that two qualities persist from the first birthday onward. Some children are *inhibited* (restrained, watchful, gentle), while others are *uninhibited* (free, energetic, spontaneous). As infants, inhibited children are more irritable during the early months. Moreover, this irritability seems to be related to higher levels of physiological arousal (which also leads to more stomachaches, allergic reactions, and other physical discomforts).[4]

Parents can, of course, influence the direction that a child's predisposition will take. But this influence works both ways. An infant who is easy to care for and predictable makes life much easier for parents. On the other hand, a difficult baby like Jason greatly increases the stress of parenthood. Innately irritable infants tend to cry for long periods of time and aren't easily comforted. So, in addition to the stress of the crying, parents are discouraged by their inability to relieve their babies' distress.

All of this makes caring for a fretful infant extremely stressful. Studies by Carolyn Cutrona and Beth Troutman demonstrate that bringing home a difficult infant frequently leads to maternal depression.[5] The link between infant temperament and maternal depression may arise from the mother's feelings about herself, Cutrona says. When a woman has trouble comforting her child, like Sharon did, she feels less competent as a mother. She may develop ambivalent feelings toward her child, causing guilt and further lowering of her self-esteem.

Although there isn't much parents can do to alter their baby's basic temperament, they can lower the level of stress by working together to develop a network of support. Women who received high levels of support from their partners, parents, or friends before their babies were born had more confidence as parents and felt less depressed three months after delivery, according to Cutrona and Troutman. A woman can help fend off the postpartum blues by cultivating supportive relationships and by realizing that she isn't to blame for feeling stressed by a demanding baby.

"Support" is one of those blessings that conjures up envy on the part of those who feel the lack of it, especially when they see others lucky enough to have plenty. I've known many young mothers lucky enough to have lots of support, and the harder they worked at it, the luckier they got. I don't deny that some women are fortunate in having partners, friends, or family members who freely and willingly help out. But for the most part, support, like love and friendship, isn't something you "have"; it's something you create.

❖

The job of bringing up baby is so consuming and the tasks so many and so demanding that it's easy to lose sight of the context. We think of ourselves as

---

[3]Alexander Thomas and Stella Chess, *Temperament and Development*, New York: Brunner/Mazel, 1977.

[4]Jerome Kagan, *The Nature of the Child*. New York: Basic Books, 1984.

[5]Carolyn Cutrona and Beth Troutman, "Social Support, Infant Temperament, and Parenting Self-Efficacy: A Mediational Model of Postpartum Depression, in *Child Development* 1986, *57*, 1507–1518.

individuals—mommy, daddy, and baby—rather than as a family unit. So, it's natural that when we think of change, we think of individuals changing. Because the baby changes so fast, we concentrate on that. At one month, the baby does this; at four months, the baby does that. There's no danger of parents failing to notice the baby's development (ask parents how old their baby is, and they'll tell you in weeks.) What we do lose sight of, however, is that the family has developmental needs of its own.

## The Family Life Cycle

When we think of the life cycle, we think of individuals moving through time, growing and changing, mastering the challenges of one period and then moving on to the next. The cycle of human life may be orderly, but it's not a steady, continuous process. We progress in stages with plateaus and developmental crises that demand change. Periods of growth and change are followed by periods of relative stability during which changes are consolidated.

Families, too, have cycles. By this I mean more than the parallel progress of parents and children. A consistent theme in the life cycle is the interconnectedness that reverberates between generations. Even when these connections aren't apparent, they still exert a powerful, if unseen, influence. As parents move through young adulthood into middle age, their children metamorphose into teenagers, growing more willful and independent, until sooner or later they're ready to leave home. (Sometimes sooner, sometimes later.)

Changes in one generation complicate the adjustments in another. A middle-aged father may become disenchanted with his career and decide to become more involved with his family just as his children are growing up and pulling away. His need to hang on to them may frustrate their need to be on their own, and may lead to war between the generations. Or, to cite another example becoming more and more familiar in the nineties, just as a man and woman begin to do more for themselves after launching their children, they may find their children back in the house (after dropping out of school, being unable to afford housing, or recovering from an early divorce) and are therefore faced with an awkward, hybrid version of second parenthood.

Cultural groups vary in the emphasis they place on various life transitions. For example, while death is a fact of life for everyone, Irish families tend to hold elaborate wakes, whereas families of African descent spare no expense for funerals. Jewish families devote seven days after a death to intense mourning in a period called *shivah*. Unlike other groups who attempt to put death behind them once the funeral is over, Jews encourage prolonged and communal mourning. *Kaddish*, a prayer for the dead, is recited by the bereaved as often as once a day for a year and thereafter on the anniversary of the death.

Mexican Americans see early and middle childhood as extending longer than the dominant American pattern, while Jews mark the end of childhood at age thirteen with a bar or bat mitzvah, a transition that other groups don't celebrate at all.

Anglo-Saxon parents are likely to feel that they have failed if their children don't move away from home and become independent, while Latin parents may feel like failures if their children *do* move away.

One property that families share with other complex systems is that they don't change in a smooth, gradual process of evolution, but rather in discontinuous leaps. Falling in love and revolutions are examples of such leaps. Having a baby is like falling in love and undergoing a revolution at the same time.

❖

Now that Sharon and Stewart had a child, they were more than a couple, they were a family. Because Jason was such a demanding infant, Sharon needed more support from Stewart. She hated seeing him go off to work. Here she was stuck at home with the baby—she was a mother—but he could be a father or not. He could stay home or go to work. She had no choice. To Stewart, Sharon seemed to demand constant attention. He felt her demands on him; she felt his neglect. What they couldn't see was that every single thing that happened between them was now part of a triangle.

The more Jason wore her out, the more Sharon needed from Stewart. The more stressed Stewart felt from work, the less available he was to Sharon. Nothing any one of them did would ever again be independent of the other two.

Jason's birth destabilized Sharon and Stewart's uneasy harmony. The addition of a new element is a *perturbation* to the system, which is destabilized and must be reorganized into a new arrangement. In mechanical systems these changes are automatic. When the "new element" is a living child and the "system" consists of two very human people, destabilization goes right to the heart of things and shatters the peace. Because stress is highest at transition points, it's at these junctures that we tend to get stuck. The unhappy irony is that at precisely those periods when we most need to be flexible, we're least likely to be. This isn't only because as individuals we tend to fall back on familiar coping strategies (strategies that have worked in the past), but also because one family member's rigidity provokes equally rigid reactions in others.

In response to the burden of caring for Jason, Sharon became more dependent; Stewart became more isolated. The more Sharon complained, the more distant Stewart became; and the more distant Stewart was, the more Sharon complained— et cetera, et cetera.

❖

One of the things that makes conflict inevitable is that parents come in pairs. Every parent is different. One will have a shorter fuse than the other, and each of them will respond to different triggers. He may get angry when the kids make noise; she may not get angry until they start shrieking. She may be more annoyed by the children fighting with each other than by their arguing with her; he may not care about fighting but may be unwilling to tolerate disrespect.

What makes parenting so difficult is that these contrasting styles aren't static. Parents polarize each other.

Imagine a little boy who scrapes his knee and runs to his daddy. The father wipes the scrape and tells the boy he's okay and can go back outside and play. His wife, watching on, may feel that the father was insufficiently sympathetic. She calls the boy over and gives him a little extra attention—bathing the scrape, applying first-aid cream, and inviting him to sit on her lap while she reads him a story. Seeing this, the father may feel undermined and that the boy is being spoiled. In response he may try harder to toughen the boy up, or he may pull away (*If she doesn't like the way I do things, let her do it herself*). Thus conflict is inherent. It's neither good nor bad, it just is.

The hardest thing about family life isn't that we're different; it's that we don't accept these differences. Some differences are hard to live with—how much time to spend together, how often to have sex, what temperature to set the thermostat at—but what makes them infinitely harder is thinking that one way is right and the other is wrong. Even before people find a way to compromise their differences, it helps to accept them: *Okay, so she thinks the children should take music lessons, and I don't. Fine. What are we going to do about it?* This makes it so much easier than *This is awful!* or *What's wrong with her?*

So, the new organism starts in conflict. Then what? The first thing to keep in mind is the nature of the life cycle. The family goes through phases of stability, interrupted by transitional points at which the family's structure is destabilized and then reorganized. It's at these points that family members must make active efforts to readjust, changing the way they interact; otherwise the family will get stuck.

Some people fail to appreciate transitions and the need for reorganization. In-laws may interfere with a new couple's adjustment by intruding into their relationship so much that the couple doesn't work out mechanisms for solving their own problems. A new husband may fail to recognize the need to spend less time doing things alone so that he and his wife can learn to do things together. Even though he's married, he still acts like a bachelor.

Transitions, though disruptive and stressful, don't last long. If the appropriate adjustments are made, the family moves on to a new plateau in the life cycle. *But the clock doesn't start until they begin to make the adjustments.*

❖

One of my patients had a stormy relationship with her emotionally disturbed daughter. The daughter was given to impulsive outbursts of rage and violence. Despite her impossible behavior, the parents did everything they could to keep the girl in school, until at age seventeen she ran away to Miami, where she got involved in the drug culture and became a prostitute. When she was arrested and released to her parents' custody, they agreed to support her in an apartment near—but not too near—the town where they lived, until she could learn to be independent. When the daughter got to be twenty-one and showed no signs of supporting herself, the parents realized that they should "be firm" and stop paying her expenses so that she would be forced to get a job. However, because they feared the girl's volcanic temper and worried about her inadequacy, they kept prolonging their support.

These parents knew what they should do. They just couldn't face their daughter's anger or the chance that she would fail. I told them that I understood their fears, but when they said they knew they "had to change," I gently but firmly told them no, they didn't have to change. They could go on as they had been, until their daughter was twenty-eight, thirty, forty-five. If they did decide to stop supporting their daughter, I said, there probably would be a period of protest in which she would test their resolve. Moreover, I said that period could last for several weeks, even a few months—but the clock wouldn't start until they made the change.

❖

The birth of a child requires a radical shift in the family organization—a shift for which one or both parents may be unprepared. The partners' functions must differentiate to meet the infant's demands for feeding and changing and bathing, and to adjust to the constraints imposed on the parents' time.

❖

For a helpless baby, Jason was pretty powerful. He was utterly and completely dependent on his parents' care. As far as he was concerned, there was being alone—which meant sleep—or there was being nursed and changed and petted and played with. Sleep, which he resisted, did not come upon him gently but overtook him as if by surprise. He woke demanding to be fed. He wanted Sharon. If she didn't come right away, he was subject to flash rages.

Sharon tried to keep up with her son's fierce progress, but she also needed time alone. She tried to get him to nap, but never was there a baby who slept so little. She tried to find things for him to do while she read or just sat and rested. She put him in his playpen outside in the sunshine, gave him armloads of soft toys—but he didn't want to *do* anything; he wanted Mommy.

While parents are busy trying to keep up with the demands of an infant, one thing that invariably gives way is the couple's time alone together. With so much to do, so much anxiety and tension, and so little sleep, it's natural for parents to long for time to themselves—time to rest, time to relax. One thing Stewart made a point of doing for Sharon was taking the baby out for little trips on Sunday mornings, so that Sharon could sleep late and maybe read the paper.

Caring for an infant is so consuming that if parents think about themselves at all, they mostly think about getting a break. In the process, they lose sight of their couplehood, which slowly deteriorates.

## 2 + 1 = 2

According to a familiar lyric from the song *My Blue Heaven*, two plus one equals three. How does it go? Just so-and-so and me, and baby makes three, we're happy in—etcetera. But the addition of a new baby can be calculated differently if you consider that the family now consists of two subsystems: the parent-child unit and the couple unit.

The new addition is also a subtraction. No matter how much a couple cherishes their baby, his or her arrival also threatens the fantasy of exclusive ownership and love. Not all young parents are consciously jealous of the attention their partners devote to the baby, yet inevitably these feelings are stirred beneath the surface of awareness. New fathers are especially prone to feeling displaced. Suppressed rivalrous and rejected feelings at this time propel many young fathers to overwork, overeat, or drink too much.

For Sharon, breast-feeding rekindled archaic memories of the blissful time when as infants we're merged with our mother's tender love. Sharon was everything to Jason. These were moments of happy fusion. Moments Stewart couldn't share.

The father's exclusion from the magic circle of mother love, and the heavy burden on the mother of caring for the baby, may lead to an erosion of the couple's relationship. Too bad, because that relationship can be—should be—a haven that provides the partners a refuge from the stresses of life.

Revitalizing their couplehood is the greatest support parents can give each other. This may seem obvious, but the demands of caring for an infant distract many couples from the need to work at preserving what brought them together in the first place—their love for each other.

That's how it was with Sharon and Stewart. The infatuation of their courtship was more like a tropical fever than a relationship. Their love affair was filled with rich mysteries of emotion that simply descended on them—as the song says, "It's Magic." It never entered their calculations that they might have to work to re-create this mystic sentiment.

Here's what I tell young parents who've gotten out of the habit of enjoying each other: You can't breathe life back into a relationship by wishing or waiting for your partner to initiate something, or even necessarily by taking advantage of existing possibilities. You may have to create the possibilities.

Try this exercise. Close your eyes and think back to your courtship. What are your happiest memories? Chances are you may remember going for long walks, opening your hearts to each other, conversations that lasted long into the night, dancing slow and close, kissing for hours, watching the seasons change—just being together. You may even remember Johnny Mathis singing "Chances Are."

These memories make the heart ache. What happened to that magic? "Where Did Our Love Go?" Chances are the magic is still there, submerged beneath all the dirty dishes, wet diapers, late nights, and early awakenings that never figured in the romantic songs you used to listen to.

Even when things have cooled off or gone stale, both partners know what the *other* one could do to bring the couple closer. The trick is to figure out what your mate would like from you, and start to re-create a warmer, more romantic relationship by paying a little more attention to him or her. Think of it as getting the ball rolling.

Paying attention means noticing the other person—how does your partner look? feel? what has he or she been doing?—and acknowledging what you notice. Understanding can be as simple as recognizing that your partner looks tired, or asking about how the day went, and actually *listening* to the response.

For a couple with a new baby to enjoy doing things together, it's probably a good idea to get out of the house—away from guess who and the atmosphere of responsibility and tension. A couple can hire a babysitter or find friends with whom they can trade baby watching, and get out. They can go for a walk, go shopping for some new clothes, go out to dinner, go to the movies—get away, be together; enjoy themselves. One of the nicest things young parents can do for themselves is to have a relative spend the night with the baby, so they can have a whole evening of peace and relaxation.

It's more difficult to create an affectionate mood when you're around the house, but it can be done. Try holding hands, having wine and cheese by candlelight, giving your partner a backrub, taking a shower together (remember, it saves water), have dinner in a different part of the house, play Scrabble. Young parents won't feel like doing these things all the time, but breaking the usual routine and closing some of the distance between them can be the beginning of a positive spiral that will regenerate tender feeling in the relationship.

Some unhappy couples are so bitter and resentful that they give up on each other and settle for a pale version of domestic peace. At least they can be decent parents, they think. Actually, when two people drift away from each other, to the extent that all they share is their children, they're unlikely to be good parents. The inevitable conflicts about raising children are heightened to a constant state of tension if the parents can't escape from parenting long enough to enjoy each other's company without the presence of the children.

## Heather's Birth

By the time Jason was one-and-a-half, things settled down a bit. Neither Sharon nor Stewart forgot the sleepless nights, but as with other normal awful things, time softened memory's edges. Besides, Jason was so cute now: a chubby, waddling, smiling miracle of their own creation. Every day there was a new astonishment of the heart.

Sharon didn't let herself think about having another baby and she was surprised when Stewart brought it up. "I don't know," she said slowly. She didn't want to go through all that again, but she didn't want Jason to be an only child. What could she say?

Two weeks later she was pregnant, and six weeks after that she knew it.

Sharon was astonished, numb. It was all starting again, without her ever really having made up her mind. Stewart was elated. "Great!" he said. "Now Jason will have someone to play with." Sharon didn't dare tell him what she was feeling. Mothers weren't supposed to feel that way.

❖

The second baby was as late as Jason had been early. Sharon just kept getting bigger and bigger. Her due date came and went. Ten days later she went into labor. This time she was sure, and this time she waited as long as she could before calling Stewart. When she finally dialed his office at two in the afternoon, her contractions were coming every four minutes. He came home immediately.

Stewart was more considerate this time. He seemed genuinely concerned about her. At least that's what Sharon thought. Maybe she'd finally gotten through to him. He thought the change was in her—she wasn't as bewildered this time, or as demanding, or as critical.

Labor was easier this time. Jason hadn't wanted to leave her; this one couldn't wait to get out. It was only 6:00 P.M. when she finally finished panting and pushing.

"It's a girl!" Stewart shouted, tears streaming down his face. *That's nice,* Sharon thought. She couldn't see.

Heather was an easy baby, as good-natured as Jason had been demanding. They didn't even look like brother and sister. Jason was a chubby baby, with a thick mat of dark curls. Heather was smaller, almost slender, and her wispy hair was reddish-blond. By some miracle, Heather slept through the night from her second day home from the hospital. Sharon's gratitude for this blessing transformed her whole outlook.

Another thing that won Sharon over was that Heather was so pliable; she liked to be hugged, and she was as flexible as a kitten mauled by a house full of kids. Jason had always been stiff when Sharon held him. He arched his back, grew rigid, and wriggled to get down as soon as he was able to crawl.

Unlike Jason, who had always demanded attention, Heather seemed content to amuse herself. She'd lie in her cradle, her eyes wandering around the room, fascinated with her little corner of the world. She liked to play with crib toys and would do so until her eyes drooped and she slipped off to sleep. Sharon marveled at how much this baby slept. It was almost as if having paid her dues the first time, she'd earned a respite.

Jason was delighted with the new baby. Only once did he show his jealousy directly. When Sharon hung the mobile that had been his over the cradle, Jason climbed up on his little wooden chair and snatched it down. "What's that?" Sharon asked when she saw him take it into his room. "MINE!" he said. Sharon made another mobile for the baby.

After that, Jason was very nice to his sister. He tried to help Sharon as much as he could with changing diapers. Even though he always fastened the adhesive tabs so loosely that they popped open, Sharon let him do it anyway. What he loved most was to hold the baby. At first Sharon was afraid Jason would drop her, but he was so happy with Little Sister in his arms that Sharon helped him sit down on the rug and then handed Heather over. At least the baby wouldn't have far to fall if Jason dropped her. When they went for walks, Jason pushed the stroller, and if Heather started to cry, he handed her a toy and said, "Don't cry, baby Heather. Look at this."

Mommy's little helper was a good big brother but more clingy. In one month he went from two-and-a-half to one-and-a-half. Now instead of walking he wanted to be carried when they went to the store. "You have to walk, Jason. Mommy has to carry the baby. You're a big boy now." Jason wasn't so sure he wanted to be.

On the whole, though, life was more peaceful. There was no repeat of the endless days and nights when Jason had been so irritable and Sharon felt so alone. As Heather got bigger, the two children kept Sharon busy, just by being children. She never had any time to herself. Even when she went to the bathroom, she'd hear a knock at the door and a little voice calling, "Mommy . . . ."

## The Young and the Restless

Stewart liked to watch the children sleep. In sleep, their faces looked so heart-stoppingly tender. Jason's mouth made a little "o", and his breath came gently. It was as still as he got. Heather, curled up in a fetal position, clutched Blankie in her hand and sucked her thumb. Stewart loved them. In those soft, warm faces was a quality of trust so absolute and pure it made him feel selfless. But he only watched for a minute or two.

There was no doubt in Sharon's mind that Stewart loved the babies, but he was so intolerant of what to her were normal, expectable changes in their moods. He always thought there was something wrong, something she should fix. When Heather got a little whiny, Stewart would say, "She's tired." He was always finding something. Either they were teething, or hungry, or tired. He could never just let them be little children with feelings, little children who needed a certain amount of tending and a certain amount of tolerance.

If he wasn't fussing at them, he was jostling them, taking them for walks, trying to distract them from their own games, their own moods. When they went out to supper, Stewart was in a constant state of anxiety. He was acutely sensitive to the reactions of other diners. Maybe they were only projected images of his own discomfort.

One night Stewart took the whole family out to dinner at Sharon's favorite restaurant, and the evening unrolled in its usual tense fashion. Stewart viewed the children as little bombs who might go off at any minute. To diffuse them, he fed them rolls and let them drink from the little coffee-cream containers that restaurants so thoughtfully provided. He used all his ingenuity to find things for them to play with—quietly—at the table. He dangled his keys in front of the baby until she squealed and grabbed them. He gave Jason the spoons and taught him how to build things with them. He made puppets with the napkins and drew faces on them. Stewart was trying to be a good daddy, but he wore himself out.

When the food came, he expected the children to eat quietly. It was his turn. Between mouthfuls, he told Sharon what was going on in the English Department. She listened, even though, when she was tired, the doings of Stewart's department were about as interesting as the marshmallow music piped in from the ceiling. Jason felt free to break in. "Mommy, you have the same soup as Jason." "That's right," she said and then turned back to Stewart. Too late. He was sulking. He ordered a third Michelob and withdrew into himself.

Conversation grew tense, polite, strained. Sharon could tell that Stewart was mad, although he wouldn't admit it. "Would you please pass the salt?" Then silence.

Jason didn't let the silence last long. Did he feel the tension, or just see an opportunity to seize Sharon's attention? In either case, Sharon seemed happy for the distraction.

"Can I get down now?" Jason asked.

"Wait a minute, honey, don't you want to finish your supper?"

"*No*, want to *get down*!"

"What do you like best about coming here," Sharon asked, "the pretty decorations, or the soup, or the crackers, or the nice desserts?"

"You know what?" Jason said brightly, "I don't like anything!"

"Oh, honey . . . but what's the best part?"

Jason giggled. "No, nothing was the best part," he said happily.

This was a wonderful game. But Sharon took it seriously. She wanted somebody to be having a good time.

Stewart continued to sit in stony silence, staring out the window. Heather just watched, her eyes round and clear.

When they got home, the tension of the evening hadn't dissipated. Sharon decided that she was overdue for calling her parents. "Jason do you want Mommy to call Grandma and Grandpa?"

"No! *Jason* do it," he said, and with Sharon's help he placed the call.

## Renegotiating Boundaries with Grandparents

Sharon's parents were, as always, delighted to hear from their grandson. The conversation went on for several minutes. Sharon listened as Jason babbled on, and wondered what her parents were saying.

Now that she had babies, her parents seemed more eager than ever to visit. It was nice. They fussed over Jason and Heather, who of course thrived on the attention.

Two things young parents don't like about grandparents is that they spoil the children and don't always take them seriously. Actually, these two problems are related, and they both strike a nerve.

Sharon's mother loved to give the children candy and take them shopping. The second of these Sharon didn't mind.

On one visit, Sharon's mother took Sharon and Jason shopping for clothes. They bought two cute little shirts and a pair of shorts. Then they went to the Junior Bootery for shoes. Sharon picked out three pairs of shoes she thought suitable, and asked Jason to pick the ones he liked best. Her mother didn't approve of the ones he chose.

"Sharon, you shouldn't let him pick out his own shoes, he's only a baby."

"He has very definite ideas, Mother," Sharon said archly. "He is a person, you know."

Sharon was mad. So, *this is how they treat children*, she thought. *Act all nicey-nice, but don't really respect them. They're too wrapped up in themselves to recognize the children's real feelings. If they treat Jason like this, imagine how they must have treated me.*

❖

Grandparents dote on their grandchildren but sometimes treat them more like domestic pets—to be cuddled and fed and spoiled—than like little people with minds of their own. Jason's grandparents spoiled him, and he ate it up. His love for his grandmother was absolute. Nothing was held back. She was mindless of discipline, so there were none of the hard feelings that complicated his love for his mother. Sharon, of course, resented this. Her son, the child she did everything for, could be bought for the price of a candy bar.

❖

The underlying issue here is a boundary dispute. Will the grandparents recognize their children's authority as parents? And will the new parents recognize the grandparents' right to be grandparents? Young parents bristle when their folks don't respect their new role as parents. They have certain rules they consider important—such as how much television to watch or what to eat—and they don't want anybody (not even, or especially, their own parents) to violate these rules. Parents must speak up about the rules they consider important and ask the grandparents to respect their way of doing things.

On the other hand, parents can learn their first lesson in letting go by allowing the grandparents a certain amount of discretion in how they treat the grandchildren. Up to a point, let them do what they want. Some parents worry that their children will get confused if the grandparents let them stay up late and watch television when they aren't usually allowed to do so. Stop worrying. Children learn, very quickly, to discriminate. Parents should be clear about what they consider essential rules for their children. When they're at home, the parents are in charge. But when they're with their grandparents, the parents should let go—as much as they can.

## Reciprocity

Asked what's wrong with their relationships, most people are pretty generous in giving credit to their partners. Oh, first you may hear something like "We don't communicate," or "We don't have many interests in common." But when you get down to why, it's likely to be: "He doesn't share his feelings with me," or "She's always nagging me about something," or "He never wants to do anything with the family."

What these complaints have in common isn't just blaming, but also a one-person psychology. What happens is a function of what someone else does. Family therapists don't think this way. We see relationships as circular, such that what one person does is a function of what the other does, and so on. Their behavior is reciprocal.

*Reciprocity* is the governing principle of every relationship. I don't simply mean the obligation to return one kindness for another. This, by the way, is a happy view of human nature, based on the hope that doing nice things for others will make them feel grateful and reciprocate. By reciprocity I mean the descriptive principle that, in a relationship, one person's behavior is functionally related to the other's.

A popular expression of this principle is "What goes around, comes around." Once you realize that behavior is linked in an ongoing circular pattern, you can stop worrying about who started what, and start thinking about what to do about it.

As a family therapist I frequently turn the burden of complaints back on the complainer

*Husband:* My wife's boring.

*Therapist:* How do you approach her that she responds that way?

*Mother:* It's our son, he's so immature. He doesn't even tie his own shoes.

*Therapist (to the boy):* How does your mother keep you so young?

Less often, but occasionally, family members blame themselves. This is just another way to deny connections and avoid conflict. A lot of women come to therapy because they're "depressed." It's them. Something inside them. This is easier for some people than facing up to the fact that family life is disappointing, or that their partners are depressing them.

*Therapist:* What's the problem?

*Wife:* It's me. I'm depressed.

*Therapist:* Who depresses you?

*Wife:* No one; it's just me.

*Therapist:* No one in the family contributes to your depression? I don't believe it.

The aim of these questions is to bring out the interrelatedness of behavior, to shift problems from something *inside* one person to something *between* two (or more) persons, and to provide alternatives to solutions that have been tried and failed.

A gentler way to confront linearity is to simply follow up one person's complaint by saying, calmly, "That's his (or her) contribution. . . ." Leaving the rest unsaid minimizes the likelihood of an argument.

❖

Neither Sharon nor Stewart recognized the reciprocity in their relationship. The stress of caring for two small children heightened the emotional vulnerability that already existed between them.

How might a therapist have helped Sharon and Stewart recognize the reciprocity in their relationship? One possibility would be to talk with them about the painful scene in the restaurant. You could ask each of them to talk about what effect Jason's fussiness had on them. When Stewart got quiet, did Sharon notice? She knew what she was feeling; did she think about what he might be feeling? Did he consider what she might be experiencing? Did each of them feel supported by the other? What might have happened differently that would have felt more supportive? If they had teamed up and supported each other in dealing with Jason, would Jason have noticed? In other words, what might each person have done that would have been more in line with his or her wishes?

People have learned to be skeptical about the old bromide that having a baby brings a couple closer together. Actually, it does; but closer may be too close—closer than the partners have learned to accommodate to each other. Jason's constant demands triggered anxiety in both Sharon and Stewart, making them emotionally reactive, each in their own characteristic ways. Stewart needed more time to himself; Sharon needed him to be more involved and concerned.

## Bitter Fruit

When you have small children, colds sweep through the family like a plague, from child to parent and parent to child. If the spacing is right, the last person to succumb will give the cold back to the person who brought it into the house in the first place.

Heather and Jason both had colds. Heather was such a good baby, but when she was stuffy she couldn't sleep, and so she woke up several times in the night, scared and crying. The vaporizer helped some, but not enough. Jason was well enough to sleep through the night, but he complained constantly during the morning. "My throat hurts!" "Give me 'lozenger.'" "Give me aspirin." "I want juice."

Stewart stayed as far away as possible. If he could only avoid getting close to them for a couple of days, he thought, he could avoid getting sick and missing work. So it was Sharon who carried Heather around when she woke in the night, put drops in her nose, gave both of them Tylenol, and tried to get as much ginger ale as possible down their throats. In the middle of the afternoon, both children fell into fitful sleep, and Sharon plopped down on the sofa, exhausted.

Looking out the window into the backyard, she made an interesting discovery. Stewart had given her two dwarf apple trees for their first anniversary, and each spring since then one of them flowered and then in the fall had apples. For some reason, the other one never bloomed or bore fruit. Looking at them now, Sharon could see that the tree that bore apples was much shorter than the other one. Apparently its strength had gone into producing fruit, for it was gnarled and twisted; the other one was taller and straighter, and much healthier looking. All of a sudden, she started to cry.

Sharon cried a lot these days. She felt so vulnerable and isolated. Being a mother was sapping her strength, just like that poor little tree. She thought of how little Stewart did for her. As the days went by, she sank increasingly into bitterness and self-pity.

❖

When we speak of self-pity, it's usually with disdain. Feeling sorry for yourself is a sin in our culture. It's okay to feel sorry for someone else; when it comes to ourselves, we're expected to be selfless and strong.

What's wrong with self-pity? *Pity* refers to the sympathetic suffering of one person, excited by the distress of another. *Self* is the core of the person, the heart of the personality. Self-pity, therefore, is the suffering of a person excited by distress in his or her own inner being. It's a natural response to a bruising of the self. Its purpose is to fill in the soothing and consolation that isn't forthcoming from someone else.

Sharon moved from hope to despair. She expected marriage to bring emotional closeness and sharing. When it didn't, she felt, first, disappointment; then hurt; then anger. Having the babies—and most of the burden of caring for them—only made things worse. Eventually, she could no longer stand the vulnerability. It hurt too much. So, she moved to what family therapist Philip Guerin calls an "island of invulnerability."[6] She built a wall around her feelings, so that she could no longer be hurt or even reached emotionally.

When hope is abandoned, alienation sets in.

Once in a while Stewart surprised her by doing something nice. He liked to feed the children supper, and sometimes he took them for long walks, giving Sharon a chance to rest. But the good feeling from these small kindnesses didn't make the bitterness go away. She couldn't get her mind off all those times when he could have helped but didn't.

Stewart felt sorry for Sharon. He looked at the girl he used to be in love with. She looked old, with permanently tired eyes. He felt sorry for her, but why did she have to blame him? Women had been raising babies for thousands of years, and with a lot less help from their husbands than she got from him.

It was as though each of them had an emotional vault in which they collected grievances. With every aggravation, they put in a deposit. Interest was collected in the form of resentment.

Sharon *or* Stewart could have put the concept of reciprocity to good use by forgetting about who started their problems and shifting their attention to what they, themselves, were doing to prolong them. Instead of thinking of their problems in linear fashion (Stewart's neglect *made* Sharon bitter; Sharon's nagging *caused* Stewart to withdraw) they could begin to think of a mutual exchange, a circular chain of behavior *that could be changed at any point in the chain.* Circular thinking helps combat the unfortunate assumption that the other person must act first.

If he started thinking, not about what he wanted from Sharon, but about what *he* was doing to provoke the anger he was getting, Stewart might have realized that he never took time to ask about how she was feeling. He behaved as though her anxiety and depression infected him, and he couldn't listen without offering suggestions for things *she* should do to get over what she was feeling. He could have started listening. Simply listening.

As for Sharon, she was in a vicious cycle: She was too tired to go out and too bitter to think about Stewart's needs—*and* the less she went out, the more tired she got; the less she considered Stewart's feelings, the less he considered hers. She

[6]Philip Guerin et al., *The Evaluation and Treatment of Marital Conflict: A Four-Stage Approach.* New York: Basic Books, 1987.

knew what she wanted, what Stewart didn't give her, and that knowledge filled her heart with such bitterness that there was little room for anything else.

❖

What is it possible to give? How is it possible to divine what is helpful? It's not so hard. But first a person may have to clear away the belief that thinking about how he or she can change the relationship isn't fair. *Why must it all be up to me?*

Fairness isn't the point, effectiveness is. Both parties contribute to the problems in a relationship. Looking at one's own contribution, ironically, gives a person power, power to change the relationship. I'm not advocating one-sided or unconditional generosity. I'm talking about how changes in one person's behavior toward others lead to reciprocal changes in their behavior toward him or her. We continuously influence the "situations" of our lives, as well as being influenced by them, in mutual, organic, two-way interactions. Too bad more people don't see it.

# 7

## WHY CAN'T JASON BEHAVE?

From the day they brought him home from the hospital Jason was a handful. At most he slept two or three hours at a time, then he was up, screaming, demanding to be changed and fed; then cuddled, carried, tickled, and played with. He was adorable but consuming.

Sharon was exhausted. The only peace she knew was sleep. Yet even when she finally got to bed at 11:30 or midnight it was with the knowledge that Jason's cries would jolt her awake in a couple of hours. She hardly had time to dream.

When you're a new parent these things seem unforgettable and at the heart of everything. But they slide away and are gone sooner than you think.

After about eight months things settled down a bit, at least enough for Sharon to start catching up on her sleep. Jason now slept through the night, and he could sit up and amuse himself briefly while Sharon read the newspaper, one paragraph at a time.

At about this time Stewart started taking an interest in his little son. Previously helpless as a newborn father, Stewart now took Jason for outings every Sunday morning. It was a chance for Sharon to rest and for him to be alone with his little boy.

It wasn't long before Jason could pull himself up to a standing position. Once he discovered this trick he loved to do it over and over again. When Sharon and Stewart watched their pudgy little baby haul himself up to vertical, they knew he would soon start walking. Stewart tried to speed things up by putting his finger in Jason's tiny hand and helping him take a few halting steps. But practice or no, it was weeks and weeks between almost walking and the first solo steps.

Six months later it was hard for Sharon to believe she'd been in such a hurry for Jason to start walking and talking. Now he was a little talking machine, and all over the house, into everything. He was cute but impossible to keep up with. If she tried to hold him back, he struggled free like a little animal. When she went shopping in the mall, he always wanted to get out and push his stroller. "Jason push!" If she tried to strap him in the seat, he cried and cried until she let him up.

As Jason got to be two and then three, Sharon discovered so many things to do for him. By this time Heather was born, but she demanded so little attention that Sharon still spent most of her time trying to please Jason. He loved to play dress-up, and she was happy to provide him with a series of capes and hats and parts of Daddy's old Army uniform from the attic.

And there were so many things to buy. Cuddly blanket-sleeper suits, bright colored overalls, books, and toys—and toys, and toys. Hasbro, Playskool, Milton Bradley, Ideal, Child Guidance—they all made so many clever and charming things to play with. Every time Sharon went into the store, she saw something new Jason would like. Jason's favorites were the bad-guy toys: King Kong, Darth Vader and, later, when he got a little older, innocent-looking cars and trucks that transformed into killer robots. There didn't seem to be any bad-guy toys aimed at little girls. That didn't stop Sharon. When Heather was old enough, she bought duplicate versions of the toys Jason liked. But despite Sharon's effort, Heather's favorites were Barbie and Ken.

With every new purchase Jason was briefly delighted. Once Sharon bought him a pair of gerbils and a cage with a series of clear plastic tubes for them to explore. Jason was enchanted. For two days. Then he wanted rabbits. Guess who got stuck feeding the gerbils and cleaning their cage?

As the first grandchild, Jason's birth was a magnet for admiring relatives. It was visible proof that Sharon had fulfilled her maternal role. He was so adorable, she loved to show him off. But he was cute only as long as things were going his way. When anything frustrated his whim, he turned nasty. Nasty? Sharon was ashamed for even thinking it.

The defenses that supported Sharon's wish for the family to be whole and happy had also supported a grand illusion: that motherhood was good and she was content. Emotions growing secretly in her heart since the baby was born now worked themselves to the level of conscious awareness.

Things that were supposed to be fun weren't. Going to the park was a good example. If anyone had asked, Sharon would have said she loved taking Jason to the park. But he always spoiled these trips. As long as she gave him her undivided attention he was happy, but if she wanted to sit on the bench and watch or read the paper, he'd yell, "Swing me! Swing me!" And when it was time to leave he shrieked and clung to the swings. When she finally yanked him away he bawled until she promised him a treat when they got home.

Life with Jason was a constant struggle. Guilty and uncertain, Sharon thought maybe something was wrong. But how do you know? It was against her nature to go outside the family, but she had to do something, so she talked to a friend whose children were already teenagers.

Emily was somewhat sympathetic. "Yes, little ones are a trial." But when she heard that Jason had kicked Sharon in the shins and bit her, she agreed that things had gotten out of hand. "Maybe you should talk to your pediatrician. Jason might be hyperactive."

Hyperactive? That would explain a lot.

At first Dr. Magruder was dismissive—"All kids are a handful." But Sharon wasn't about to be put off. (Hadn't this same doctor said the spitting up that turned out to be an allergy to milk was nothing?)

"Last Friday I was playing with him on the floor and I had to stop to cook dinner. So I bent down to kiss him, and he punched me in the mouth. I screamed at him—real bad—and said 'Go to your room!' Then he came over and hugged me and said, 'Mommy, I'm sorry. I love you.' So I felt bad and I had to hug him."

"Maybe you do have a problem. I'll give you the number of the child guidance clinic."

When Sharon finally got up enough nerve to call for an appointment, she was surprised that they wanted to see the whole family.

## Fix My Child without Disturbing Me

The Salazars went to the child guidance clinic anxious and uncertain. Each of them had private reasons for being apprehensive. Jason worried that his parents were bringing him to another grownup to crack down on him. Even when you're sick, doctors hurt you. Imagine what they do when you're bad!

Sharon was eager for help but felt that seeking professional assistance was an acknowledgment of failure. Still, if the price for gaining control was accepting blame, she'd pay.

Stewart, quietest of the three, was also the most worried. His best hope was that this so-called expert would see that Sharon was too easy on the boy. He was spoiled. His worst fear was that more would be asked of him.

The young doctor assigned to them was an Indian, Dr. Singh, who was completing a dual residency in psychiatry and pediatrics. Sharon thought Dr. Singh seemed nice—but he was *so* young. Stewart couldn't help thinking of the Sherlock Holmes movie in which Basil Rathbone disguised himself as an Indian named Rajni Singh. This guy didn't look a thing like Basil Rathbone.

Speaking in a low voice, as though she didn't want Jason to hear, Sharon began, "Doctor, what we want to know is, why can't Jason behave?" When Dr. Singh asked her to elaborate, she burst out like a dam giving way to a springtime flood: "He never sits still. He always has to be doing something, running around, getting into things; you just can't tell him no." Her voice rose and her eyes watered, but she held her emotions in check enough to continue.

As Sharon put the problem into words, Jason put it into action. When they come to therapy, family members vie to say what's wrong and who's at fault. The real story is how they interact. Are the parents in accord or in conflict? Do they speak plainly to their children, or do they give vague orders? When the children speak, do the parents listen, really listen, or only go through the motions?

Sharon and Stewart and Jason demonstrated what their lives were all about. It took only a minute to see. Sharon complained endlessly about Jason's behavior, meanwhile doing nothing about it. Jason jumped from one activity to the next. He didn't appear to be having much fun, but rather seemed too anxious to settle down. Meanwhile, Stewart sat silently, studying the linoleum while Sharon complained.

Left to their own devices, Sharon and Stewart were passive and ineffectual. To test their flexibility, Dr. Singh asked Sharon to quiet Jason down. Half turning to him, she said, "Jason, honey, be quiet so the grownups can talk, okay?" Then she turned back and resumed her chronicle of complaints. Dr. Singh pushed: "He's ignoring you." Once more Sharon said, "Jason, please go over there and play so we can talk, okay?" Two minutes later Jason was back again. This time Stewart said, "Jason!" But Dr. Singh put his hand on Stewart's arm and said, "Let her do it. She's the one at home with him all day."

Jason continued to interrupt and show off, determined to hold the center of attention. Meanwhile, Sharon continued to reason with him. It's tempting to think of the problem as her problem—she wasn't strict enough. We could even give reasons for Sharon's laxity: for example, that the bond with Jason was so important to her that she couldn't jeopardize it by forcing him to do anything against his will. But shifting the problem from one person to another, from Jason's "hyperactivity" to Sharon's "leniency," doesn't add much. The whole story involves the whole family.

Watching while Sharon tried unsuccessfully to control Jason, Stewart kept his mouth shut but his feet busy, fidgeting around, crossing and recrossing his legs. Finally he couldn't stand it any longer. "Jason! Get in the goddamn chair and don't make another sound!" Here was the mirror image of Sharon's forbearance: Stewart's impatience. First to respond was Sharon—"Honey, don't be so harsh"—then Jason, who came over to sit in his mother's lap with a pitiful look on his face. Now the circle was complete.

Dr. Singh saw the Salazars only twice. In the second meeting Sharon and Stewart touched on the conflict they'd been avoiding. Stewart thought Sharon was overinvolved with Jason and too easy on him. Sharon felt neglected by her husband; that's why she spent so much time with her son. She was afraid to be too strict, afraid to be like Stewart, because she was afraid of his anger.

Sharon and Stewart were using Jason to avoid each other. His misbehavior was a product of their conflict over what to do about it. No four-year-old can stand up to the united front of two parents in agreement over how to control him. The child who misbehaves stands on one parent's shoulders.

Dr. Singh assumed a didactic role. Sharon's mistakes were so obvious that it was compelling to step in and offer suggestions—as though being a good parent were merely a matter of having good information. But even though Dr. Singh wasn't a family therapist, the conflict between Sharon and Stewart was too apparent for him not to comment on. So, Dr. Singh talked briefly about how Jason seemed to be pulling his parents apart. "If you two don't start harmonizing—working as a team, yes?—it's going to be difficult to get Jason to behave." They listened, knowing what the doctor said was true but hoping he wouldn't press them to open up the painful feelings that had built up between them. To their relief, he didn't.

As far as Dr. Singh was concerned, the problems in the Salazar family were too minor to warrant further treatment. Besides, the parents seemed to understand what he had told them.

## Family Rules

Family life is governed by a set of invisible laws that are never ratified and rarely conscious. As a result, trying to solve family problems can be like trying to win at a game when you don't know the rules.

If you asked Sharon what the family rules were, she would have recited a set of *do's* and *don'ts* she expected from Jason. *Do* brush your teeth at night, *do* turn the lights out at eight; *don't* leave the yard without asking permission.

When family therapists speak of *family rules* they mean something quite different—not what's supposed to be, but what is. The *rules hypothesis* is a descriptive term for recurrent patterns that characterize any social system, of which the family is a prime example. People in any continuing relationship develop modes of interaction that become regular and predictable. *Rules* describe regularity, rather than regulation.

The rules hypothesis was originally formulated by Don Jackson, who observed that families function as cybernetic systems.[1] Their organization is governed by feedback. A familiar example of a cybernetic system is the whistling tea kettle. You put it on to boil, and then its little steam siren goes off just when you get busy reading the paper or watching the news.

Similarly, Jason could get away with murder until his misbehavior reached Sharon's rather high boiling point. Although the regulation in families isn't mechanical, it almost seems to be. This is because family rules—what is, not what's supposed to be—are established through trial and error and are generally not carefully thought out. The rules may be products of our own creation, but because they are complex and unspoken, we often become trapped in patterns not of our choosing. Moreover, because no one ratifies the rules, they're hard to examine.

❖

The rules describing how things worked in the Salazar family were not at all the same as Sharon's official version. Take bedtime, for example. If we were to observe what actually happened, we would see that after she put the baby to sleep, Sharon usually told Jason when there were fifteen minutes until bedtime. Like most children, he struggled to prolong the inevitable. Either he'd find something pleasant to do with his mother—"Mommy read to me"—which postponed bedtime for at least twenty minutes, or he'd whine and fuss, which mobilized Stewart to take over. When Sharon told Jason to go to bed and he defied her until Stewart yelled at him, an interactional pattern was initiated. If it's repeated, it may be perpetuated

[1]Don Jackson, "Family rules: Marital quid pro quo," *Archives of General Psychiatry*, 1965, *12*, 589–594.

as a family rule: Sharon isn't good at setting limits, so Stewart becomes the heavy. The corollary is that Sharon becomes closer and more affectionate with Jason, while Stewart, the disciplinarian, moves further outside.

❖

In the early days of family therapy, the rules families lived by were thought to be primarily of their own making. Recently, however, we've come to appreciate the ways in which culture and ethnicity shape the rules by which families operate.

Consider, for example, a daughter living with her family in Brooklyn who decides to go to a small college in Oregon. If her parents were Puerto Rican, they might have a very different reaction than if they were white Anglo-Saxon Protestants. Puerto Ricans share with other Latinos a deep sense of family commitment, obligation, and responsibility. The family provides a high level of support but in return expects a high level of loyalty. Leaving home isn't a rite of passage; it's a defection.

Because of relative differences in the value they put on professional achievement versus starting a family, these same two families might reverse their differences if their daughter decided to get married and have a baby. The point isn't that going away to college or starting a family at eighteen is a good idea or a bad idea, but that a family's response to such decisions is shaped by their heritage.

When we think of culture as helping to define a family's rules, it's easiest to think about someone else's culture. The more foreign the culture, the more striking its ways. Our own culture works more like a stealth indoctrination program, teaching us what to expect of men and women, but doing so largely out of our awareness.

❖

In some ways Sharon was the archetypal parent of our time. Family life has become democratic. We believe so strongly in individual freedom that lines of authority are blurred, even, or perhaps especially, within the family. We believe in treating children with respect, and it's fashionable to be aggressively child-centered ("Have you hugged your child today?"). Sharon accepted without question the rights of children. She was committed to togetherness. She believed that understanding and persuasion should replace coercion. In earlier, less democratic times, things were harsher but simpler. Children did things because "Mommy (or Daddy) said so." Today more improvisation is necessary. As a result many parents get confused.

Modern parents, conditioned by a fear of being accused of child abuse, are even more afraid of their own anger. They try harder "to communicate." In principle, increased communication should make for a more nurturing family. In practice, it means that the method of authority shifts from physical to verbal control. Instead of spanking children or sending them to their rooms, we argue with them.

Sharon played the role of a controlling but ineffectual parent who could be manipulated and pressured and who didn't feel able to enforce limits or openly express anger. Any good child-rearing manual would spell out her mistakes. She gave too many orders ("Jason do this, Jason do that"), put them tentatively ("—, okay ?"), and failed to back them up. One could say a great number of cogent things to this mother about setting and enforcing clear guidelines. But she might not listen. If she did, she might find herself somehow unable to take charge. And like most mothers, she would blame herself. Until she sees it, the family triangle imposes invisible limits on her actions.

## Family Structure

Family rules are tenacious and resistant to change because they are embedded in a powerful but unseen structure. Rules describe the process of interaction; structure defines the shape of relationships within which that process takes place. Initially, interactions shape structure; but once established, structure shapes interactions.

Once a social system such as a family becomes structured, attempts to change the rules constitute what systems theorists call *first-order change*. The enmeshed mother is caught in an illusion of alternatives. She can try to be strict or lenient; the result is the same because she remains part of a triangle. As with all relationship triangles, two people are close and one is distant. As long as Sharon remained close to Jason and distant from Stewart, she was unable to transform the nature of her interactions with Jason.

Stewart now had competition for Sharon's attention. Like any rival male, he responded by trying to pull Sharon away from the baby. But the new structure had already begun to coalesce, and the three of them were held harshly by a network of nebulous rules, constrained by the structure of a fixed triangle.

Sharon and Jason were so much together that they developed their own mutually defined relationship, in which the child conditioned the parent to accept limited control. (Army officers are forbidden from fraternizing with enlisted personnel precisely to prevent this erosion of authority that comes from blurring hierarchial distinctions.)

What's needed is *second-order change* —a change in the system itself. Without some change in the overall pattern of their relationships, Sharon and Stewart and Jason would continue to be caught in an invisible network. First-order change usually appears commonsensical but often turns out to be more of the same. Suppose Sharon tried to be stricter with Jason. Instead of arguing with him, she tells him once what she wants and if he disobeys she makes him sit on a chair in the corner. Fine. But unless their overinvolvement with each other is changed, Sharon would find it difficult to enforce these rules. Moreover, as long as parents aren't united they'll tend to undercut each other's authority. Second-order change involves a shift that transforms the structure of a relationship, and it is sometimes counterintuitive, as in the following example.

❖

The Jacksons were a family not unlike the Salazars. Corrie left most of the discipline to Rodney; she was enmeshed with the two girls, Lateesha and Cecily. Rodney was disengaged. This pattern, so common in middle-class America, is stable but unsatisfying. The mother's closeness to the children stabilizes the distance between husband and wife but does little to assuage the bitterness of love gone sour. If you want to find fertile soil for an extramarital affair, this is it. In the most common instance, the man has the affair. Eventually he confesses. She's hurt and angry (in varying proportions, depending on her style) but forgives him, or at least takes him back. Chastened, like a naughty child, he keeps his eye from roving. She keeps her eye on him to make sure. They resume their former pattern, only now prepared to avoid future shocks.

There are, of course, at least as many alternatives as there are verbs in the above description—confess, forgive, resume. Now that most mothers also work outside the home, there is equally likely to be a change in the subject of who has the affair. That was the case with the Jacksons. It was Corrie who had the affair, and Rodney was about as able to forgive as most men. After the divorce, Corrie wanted more time for herself and with her friends. She discovered how indulgent she had been with Lateesha and Cecily. They expected her to do so much around the house, and they did so little. They loved her all right, but they didn't mind her. Unfortunately, unlike many African American families, the Jackson's were isolated from their extended families, who might have helped lessen the load.

Now, absent the family disciplinarian, Corrie was it. She didn't have to think or plan or read a book about how to discipline the children. The change in the family structure led to a changed relationship between her and the children.

❖

Divorce is one form of second-order change, a revolutionary form. The trouble with revolutions is that you never know what will follow.

Realizing that we're all embedded in family structures reestablishes the limits of "parenting" as a skill susceptible to endless criticism and improvement. Family structure isn't easily discerned. Family members see what others in the family do, but not how what the others do as a function of what they themselves do. You can't change individual family members' lives without affecting the larger system. The first step in mastering the power of the family is to discover how families are structured.

## The Structural Model

Families, like other groups, have many options for relating. Very quickly, however, interactions that were initially free to vary become regular and predictable. As they are repeated, family transactions establish enduring patterns. Once these patterns are established, family members use only a small fraction of the full range of behavior available to them.

Family structure is built up from the covert rules that govern transactions in the family. For example, a rule such as "family members should always protect one another" will be manifest in various ways depending on the context and who is involved. If a boy gets in a fight with another boy in the neighborhood, his mother will go to the neighbors to complain. If a teenager has to wake up early for school, mother wakes her. If a husband is too hung over to get to work in the morning, his wife calls to say he has the flu. If their parents have an argument, the kids interrupt. The parents are so preoccupied with the doings of their children that it keeps them from spending time alone together. All these sequences are *isomorphic:* They're structured. Changing any one of them may not affect the basic structure, but altering the underlying structure will have ripple effects on all family transactions.

❖

Families are differentiated into *subsystems*—determined by generation, gender, common interests, and functions—which are demarcated by interpersonal *boundaries*, invisible barriers that regulate the amount of contact with others. Boundaries safeguard the separateness and autonomy of the family and its subsystems.

A rule forbidding phone calls at dinnertime establishes a boundary that shields the family from intrusion. Subsystems that aren't adequately protected by boundaries limit the development of relationship skills. If children are permitted to interrupt their parents' conversations at dinner, the boundary separating the generations is eroded, and the couple's relationship is subverted to parenting. If parents always step in to settle arguments between their children, the children won't learn to fight their own battles.

Rigid boundaries are overly restrictive and permit limited contact, resulting in *disengagement*. Disengaged subsystems are independent but isolated. On the plus side, this fosters autonomy. On the other hand, disengagement limits warmth and affection. Disengaged families must come under extreme stress before they mobilize mutual assistance. If parents keep their children at a distance, affection is minimized and the parents will be slow to notice when the children need support and guidance.

*Enmeshed* subsystems offer a heightened sense of mutual support but at the expense of independence and competence. Enmeshed parents offer their kids closeness, but too much closeness that cripples their initiative.

❖

Several years ago I received two phone calls on the same day, both requesting therapy for sixteen-year-old boys. Both mothers complained with equal concern about their sons. In the first family the boy was, according to his mother, a behavior problem: He rode his bicycle around the neighborhood sometimes for fifteen minutes past his 6:30 curfew; he often forgot to take out the garbage; and when he got mad at her, he slammed the door to his room. The other boy, whose mother was about equally concerned, was profoundly, suicidally depressed. He had been slipping into a deep depression for several weeks before his parents finally noticed. The enmeshed mother was so exquisitely attuned to her son's behavior that she was upset by the slightest hint of adolescent rebellion. The disengaged mother, while no less loving, was so distant from her child that she didn't realize a problem existed until it became profound.

❖

Like most enmeshed parents, Sharon was unaware of the amount of interference and coercion that characterized her relationship with Jason. They were preoccupied with each other, and their intense mutual focus limited each one's participation in other relationships. The more involved Sharon was with Jason, the less time and energy she had for Stewart and the less freedom Jason had to be with his friends.

Enmeshed parents usually produce children who are well behaved outside the home, in large measure because they are adult-oriented. By the same token, these children are somewhat more likely to have trouble making friends. Children who become behavior problems at school often have a distant or unstable relationship with their parents. Disengaged parents are more likely than enmeshed parents to be indifferent or preoccupied than permissive. So, the children of disengaged families probably don't cause trouble (at least not that anyone notices) at home, while children from enmeshed families don't cause trouble outside the home.

❖

A common misconception about boundaries is that whole families are enmeshed or disengaged. This is only loosely accurate. Some families, especially from northern cultures, are generally more private and independent of one another, whereas in other families the members are about as independent as peas in a pod. But enmeshment and disengagement are more accurately applied to specific boundaries around discrete family subsystems.

Was the Salazar family enmeshed or disengaged? Even if it were one or the other, so what? The fact that Sharon and Jason were enmeshed while Stewart was disengaged is not only more accurate but also more useful.

If Stewart became aware of the pattern, he could change it by ceasing his interference with Sharon's discipline, move closer to her by suggesting activities they both enjoy (instead of making excuses for why he can't do all the boring things she suggests), and spend more time alone with his son.

If Sharon became aware of this pattern she could pull back from Jason as a way of getting Stewart more involved as a parent. Giving up control, asking for help, or simply being "unable" to do everything are more effective methods than nagging Stewart to do more or criticizing his lack of involvement.

❖

It should not go unnoticed that these arrangements are gendered. That they are doesn't make them any more right or wrong. But it should make us careful not to blame mothers for cultural expectations and arrangements that perpetuate their role as primary caretakers of children. A therapist who recognizes the normative nature of the enmeshed-mother/disengaged-father syndrome but puts the burden on the mother to let go should consider why it doesn't occur to him or her to challenge the father to take hold.

❖

Although it isn't possible to understand people without taking into account their social context, notably the family, it's misleading to limit the focus to the surface of interactions—to social behavior divorced from inner experience.

Psychoanalytic theory emphasizes the development of interpersonal boundaries, while describing how individuals emerge from the context of their families. Beginning with the separation and individuation from symbiosis with the mother that characterizes "the psychological birth of the human infant,"[2] psychoanalytic clinicians describe repeated and progressive separations that culminate first in the resolution of oedipal attachments and eventually in leaving home.

This is a one-sided emphasis on poorly defined boundaries between self and other. Psychoanalysts pay insufficient attention to the problems of emotional isolation stemming from rigid boundaries. They describe this preference for aloneness as an artifact, a defense against a basic lack of psychological separateness. This belief in separation as the model and measure of growth is an example of overgeneralized and unquestioned male psychology. The danger that people will lose themselves in relationships is no more real than the danger that they will isolate themselves from intimacy, which is part of the full expression of human nature.

To avoid the pain of conflict, Sharon and Stewart built up an invisible wall between them. The rigid boundary separating Sharon and Stewart kept them from talking over their opinions about how to discipline Jason.

Another important point about boundaries is that they are reciprocal. Sharon's enmeshment with Jason was related to the emotional distance between her and Stewart—related as cause and effect. The less she got from Stewart, the more she needed from Jason; and the more involved she was with Jason, the less room in her life for Stewart.

## Blueprint for a Healthy Family

What is the ideal structure for a family? There isn't one. Families come in a variety of functional forms, reflecting cultural preferences (for example, child-centered versus adult-oriented) and unique demands (for instance, in single-parent families it may be necessary to invest considerable parental responsibility in the oldest child). Or, to cite another example, many couples function quite happily even though they see very little of each other. Some commuter marriages only seem to be compromises with necessity, when in fact the practical "necessity" of working in different cities actually suits one or both partners' need for a high degree of independence. The stability of these relationships depends less on some abstract norm ("families should be together") than on whether or not the disengagement suits both partners. However, although I have seen happy, successful commuter marriages and "companionate marriages" (where the spouses are like friendly roommates), the only place I have seen successful "open marriages" is in European films.

Although there is no single standard for optimal structure, healthy families do share three structural characteristics: clear boundaries, a hierarchal organization, and flexibility.

---

[2]Margaret Mahler et al., *The Psychological Birth of the Human Infant*, New York: Basic Books, 1975.

## Clear Boundaries

Strong families manage to balance closeness and separateness, to satisfy individual and group needs, resulting in personal freedom as well as belonging and togetherness. This is a lesson Stewart had yet to learn. Like other disengaged fathers, he sought satisfaction outside the family. As a result, he got less out of family life and the family got less out of him.

Stewart had to learn that being more involved doesn't necessitate giving up your identity or autonomy. What makes it feel like that is going along without standing up for your preferences and opinions. Being a self *and* a member of the family means taking other people's points of view into account—and speaking up for your own. When you negotiate in good faith with your partner, you win by winning *and* you win by losing. Both cohesiveness and honesty are essential for a healthy family life.

Strong families have *clear boundaries*. Like the membranes of living cells, their boundaries have enough integrity to permit a highly involved interaction within, yet are permeable enough to permit an exchange of energy and information with the outside world. Sharon's enmeshment in the family limited her involvement in the adult world and deprived her of emotional energy and enrichment, as well as limiting her own and Jason's autonomy.

Recently, I spoke to a man whose wife was thinking about going back to work after six months of maternity leave. Naturally he was concerned about the balancing of household responsibilities that her return to work would necessitate. Still, he had no doubt that her going back to work would be best for all of them. "Sure, we can use the money," he told me, "but—more important—I just don't think she would be as happy or as interesting a person if she gave up her career."

Healthy families also have clear boundaries between members. They understand and respect that each of them is somewhat different. Dad likes Chinese food, Mom likes salads and seafood. Johnny likes swimming and ice skating, Suzi likes ice skating but prefers hiking. They don't attempt to establish a façade of pseudomutuality that says they must all like the same things. Yet they manage to work things out. Negotiation consists of accepting differences and working toward shared goals. In such a differentiated family group, individual choice is expected, family members speak up, and even the youngest are respected as autonomous individuals with sovereign rights and responsibilities.

## Hierarchal Organization

In healthy families there is an unambiguous hierarchy of power, with leadership in the hands of the parents, who form a united coalition. There are clear generational divisions: Parents have more power than children, and older children have more responsibilities and privileges than younger ones.

A clear boundary between parents and children makes room for a private relationship between the spouses, excluding the children from certain adult activities—

making important family decisions, lovemaking, adult conversation. But what really separates the generations isn't distance but modes of relatedness. Effective parents relate to their children from an unquestioned (and unself-doubting) position of authority. They rule with good-humored effectiveness. They don't overcontrol their children, but neither do they feel obligated to disclaim their adult power.

When parents say in despair, "I can't control anything!" I usually ask them if their children run in front of cars. The point of course, is, that all parents teach their children to obey those rules they're serious about.

Most parents could profit from making fewer—far fewer—rules. But there should be one superordinate rule: *The parents are in charge.* Too much discipline, control really, is as bad as too little. An excellent guideline is to let children learn for themselves the consequences of their own behavior. Overuse dilutes authority.

## Flexibility

In healthy families, roles are clear yet flexible. Boundaries and alignments are adjusted to accommodate to changes in the life cycle. As we've seen with the Salazars, a new couple must strengthen the boundary separating them from their parents in order to protect the autonomy of the new union. With the advent of children, a boundary must be drawn that allows the children access to both parents while excluding them from spousal functions. Some couples who do well as a twosome are never able to make a satisfactory adjustment to a group of three or four. And the familiar example of two people who live happily together for years but suddenly break up after they marry can be understood as a failure to tolerate the stronger boundary that marriage vows imply.

What makes being a parent so damned difficult is that just when you start to get the hang of it, the children get a little older and throw you a whole new set of curves. When they're little, children need little more than unconditional and extravagant love.[3] Later, control and guidance also become important. The growing child's developmental needs tax the parents' capacity for flexibility. As children mature, their developmental needs for both autonomy and guidance put pressures on the parental subsystem, which must be modified to meet them.

❖

When Jason was a baby, Sharon was the perfect mother, tending to his needs with love and devotion. When he got a little older, however, she had trouble shifting from a purely nurturing role to one of nurture plus control. To think of this simply as Sharon's failure to exercise discipline would be to ignore the context. Responding to the shifting demands of children requires a periodic transformation of the positions of all family members in relation to one another. A parent's relationship to the children always reflects his or her relationship to the other parent or, in the case of single parents, the relationship to other significant adults.

[3]Some people lecture their little ones, but it's only practice—for further sermonizing and future deafness.

If we understand the family as a social system in transformation, we get away from blaming everything on the mother, and we get away from labeling the family as pathological. Instead, we see the Salazars as a family stuck in transition.

Problems of transition may be produced by developmental changes, as in the Salazar family, or by a member's increased involvement beyond the family, as when a wife and mother begins to work outside the home. When this happens, family members have to realign roles and boundaries to accommodate to changing circumstances. Another classic dislocation occurs when children enter adolescence. Teenagers become more involved in the wide world and less willing to submit to parental authority. If adolescents are to move a little away from the sibling subsystem and receive increased autonomy and responsibility appropriate to their age, boundaries must shift and parents must change. But in order to change their relationship to their children, parents must change their relationship to each other.

Sharon viewed the problems in her family from a subjective point of view, which didn't include her own role. She saw that Stewart was distant from her and distant from Jason, but she tried to change him, not her part in these relationships. Trying to change other people is an exercise in self-defeat.

Sharon told Stewart she wanted to spend more time together, but she didn't appreciate that her tight bond with Jason made this difficult. When Stewart did try to talk with her, Jason was always around. By the same token, Sharon's enmeshment with Jason made it difficult for Stewart to spend time with the boy. When Sharon objected to the two of them going off to see an adventure movie ("He sees plenty of that stuff on TV") or gave detailed instructions for dressing Jason, Stewart got mad and decided, *To hell with it; let her do everything if that's what she wants.*

Had she gone to individual therapy as a result of her unhappiness, Sharon might have discovered connections between these events and her feelings and her own family history. She might, for example, have learned that her efforts to be the perfect mother to Jason were founded on her own insecurity, which in turn stemmed from her parents' failure to take her seriously. But being insecure is a little like having a big nose or fat hips: How you got that way is somewhat irrelevant.

In family therapy, Sharon would have learned a different lesson. She would have learned to see connections between Jason's actions and Stewart's actions and her actions. What would have been most useful was thinking of the three of them as a triangle, so that if she wanted to get Stewart more involved she would realize that what she said was less important than that she make room for him. Specifically, when Stewart and Jason were together she might leave them alone. Once in a while she might even find reasons to be out of the house. In short, she could have started building a clear boundary between herself and Jason, which would have made room for Stewart to become more involved. Could have, should have. . . .

## Uncovering the Structure in a Family

If a parent is enmeshed, most of his or her conversations are about the children, their problems, and their accomplishments. Disengaged parents, on the other hand, spend relatively little time with the kids and get a glazed look in their eyes if you talk for long about children. You can diagram this as follows. Use a dotted line to represent a diffuse boundary, dashes for a clear boundary, and a solid line for a rigid boundary.

| Enmeshment | Functional | Disengagement |
|:---:|:---:|:---:|
| · · · · · · · · · · · · · · · | – – – – – – – – – | ━━━━━━ |
| Diffuse Boundary | Clear Boundary | Rigid Boundary |

If you think a man is disengaged from his children, draw it as below. Remember, if you're thinking of his relationship with his children, he's a father, not a husband.

Dad
———————
Kids

The trouble with this diagram is that it leaves out the other relationships, and it leaves out the leverage for change.

Put the rest of the family in the diagram.

Mom          Dad
· · · · · · ·
  Kids

When you think of things this way, you can see that there are three ways things can change: by strengthening the boundary between Mom and the kids, by Mom and Dad moving closer together, or by Dad moving closer to the kids. *Any one of these changes will help bring about the others.*

A clear boundary between parents and children exists when the parents allow the children a fair amount of control over their own lives. It's easier to be flexible and tolerant if you realize that they are them and you are you. Once parents accept a diminished need to manage their children's lives, most of their interactions take one of two forms: nurture or control. Disciplinary issues, however, will be short and sweet. When the parents are clearly in charge, battles are few and quickly settled.

Remember that breaking down a rigid boundary means moving closer emotionally. It means spending time together and opening up whatever is being held back in the relationship. If two people are disengaged, it may be best to begin to break down the distance by spending time together in as pleasant a way as possible. Real closeness may, however, require airing dormant complaints and working through conflicts.

❖

The first thing a therapist should seek to improve in families with misbehaving children is helping the parents to become consistent and united in their response.

This should not, however, be the only thing. Effective therapy means not only establishing control but also strengthening relationships, improving communication, and making sure that the parents are serving as guides and supports for their children. It's also important to highlight what the family is doing right. Parents who are firmly in charge can listen and be understanding, rather than alternate between the kind of controlling and ignoring of children that plays such havoc with their self-esteem.

## Building Children's Self-Esteem

Parents who don't control their children's actions often try to control their feelings. When they express feelings, children are asking both to be understood and to be allowed to do something. A common example is bedtime.

*Daddy:* It's time for bed.

*Child:* I don't wanna ago to bed! I'm not sleepy.

A father who never doubts that he's in charge can sympathize with the child's feelings. "I know, honey, you hate to go to bed. You wish you could stay up as late as you want, don't you?" Little more need be said.

Parents who doubt their control confuse the instrumental and expressive functions of feelings, and they fight back. By the way, unless their three-year-old has very big muscles from lifting blocks all day, her parents can make her go to bed, if they have to. And they may have to. But only once or twice, *if* they start early. It shouldn't be necessary to argue that a small child feels something she doesn't (tired) to get her to do something that her parents want her to do (go to bed). In my practice I've seen dozens of young couples who have no peace or privacy in the evening because their toddlers "don't get tired" until ten or eleven o'clock.

Unhappily, children who are punished or ignored when they express how they feel learn to conceal and submerge their emotions. Eventually they no longer recognize their own feelings. Instead, they feel only the residues of suppression: boredom, anxiety, and apathy.

❖

Jason's mother was always there, but not always there for him. In her way, she loved him completely. But her response to him was often a projection of her own moods and tensions. Sharon could be counted on to soothe and bandage hurts, to hold him when the shadows of night took on scary shapes, and to protect him from his father's anger. But—and this bewildered Jason—she scolded him for fighting, wouldn't tolerate his anger, and occasionally yelled at him just for being muddy. Her tenderness made him run to her with blind confidence, but sometimes he ran blindly into a wall of criticism.

As he got older Jason turned more to his father, but here too he was unlucky. He saw his father defer to his mother, steer clear of her, avoiding at all costs the fights in which, when they did occur, he quickly caved in before her shrill attacks. Jason never put it to himself in so many words, but he became aware that the father he loved and admired was a coward. Maybe that's the way men are with women.

Mommy's love was like a warm sweater on a winter night. But sometimes it chafed. He'd want to go play outside, and she'd tell him it was too cold and why didn't he stay inside and listen to a story. Since she was always trying to control what he did, he didn't always have a clear idea of the difference between her preferences and her rules. Sometimes when he was naughty she didn't notice; sometimes she yelled at him. This kind of high-volume denunciation had little measurable effect on his behavior but a far greater effect on his self-image. Later he would react with unforgiving rage; now all he felt was hurt and diminished.

❖

Suppose things have gotten out of hand; how does a parent regain control over a young child who has become impossible? By doing two things. First, by balancing discipline with affection. If rewards can be used to shape good behavior, so much the better. But even just starting to be nicer to a child for no special reason will help cement a positive relationship and make it easier to start setting limits.

The second thing to remember is that parents must work together as a team. The essential point isn't that they share equally in parenting—though that certainly is a fine thing—but that they agree to support the same set of rules.

Some experts say that parents shouldn't tell a child "You're a good girl (or boy)," but should instead praise only specific behavior—the things they want them to do more of. That's good advice for training behavior, not so good for building self-esteem.

It's impossible to overestimate the importance of a child's self-esteem. Being appreciated is what builds self-respect. When they're little, children need lavish praise. They need to feel special. When they get older, it isn't fawning that they need but to have their ideas listened to and acknowledged. Efforts to control and discipline young children should be specific and forceful. It's a shame to let the relatively few things parents need their children to do become battlegrounds. The best way to avoid that is to fight few battles but get them over quickly. Teaching children to treat their parents—and all adults—with respect is an investment in their own future. If they learn to walk all over adults, what do they have to look forward to when they become adults themselves?

# 8

# THE TWO-PAYCHECK FAMILY

It was raining the morning Heather was due to start first grade. Only September and already there was a chill in the air. From the kitchen window Sharon looked out at the rain coming down hard, swept sideways by intermittent gusts of a strong, early autumn wind. There was no light on the horizon of the gray, leaden sky. It would rain all day.

In the kitchen it was warm and bright. Jason was playing on the floor with his Legos while Heather finished eating her cinnamon toast. Because it was raining so hard, Sharon offered to drive Heather to school, but Heather wanted to ride the bus, just like all the other kids.

Sharon watched from the doorway as Jason dashed through the rain and onto the bus. Heather walked slowly, deliberately. In her slick, yellow plastic raincoat, she was a big girl. Big girls aren't afraid of the rain. Sharon's heart opened and she started to cry, but only for a minute. She put on a big smile and waved as the bus pulled away. Watching as the bus disappeared into the rain, Sharon became aware of a strange sound in the house. Silence.

Now that the children were gone all day, Sharon felt like she had her life back again. The last few years now seemed a blur, from round-the-clock feedings and diaper changes to lugging the children everywhere, the cleaning up of a thousand messes. So much to do and never enough time to do it. Now it was different. No longer were the children in charge of her days. She supposed she should feel liberated. In fact, she felt adrift.

Having small children is like being in the Army. Every aspect of life is regimented, but there is one great freedom: the freedom from deciding what to do. Sharon's little commanders didn't exactly give orders, still they just as effectively set the agenda for her days. Together with Heather, Sharon had looked forward to this day. It meant that Heather would ride the bus with her brother and go to school all day with the big kids. Sharon wasn't so sure what it would mean for her. Would she feel lonely or just relieved? As it turned out, she didn't feel much of anything.

There was lots to do around the house. When the children were around it never seemed possible to catch up.

After a second cup of coffee, Sharon stripped and waxed the kitchen floor. Then, after weeks of not getting around to it, she finally took the cracked basement window to the glazier for a new pane of glass. On the way back she stopped at the library. It seemed strange not to go right to the children's section. She picked up three novels and leafed through some recent copies of *The New Yorker*. *My god*, she thought, *it's been years since I read one of these.*

Sharon knew how she felt about going back to work—she didn't want to. She would have been perfectly content to stay home. There were plenty of things to do. Besides, she didn't want to be away when the children came home. And what about summers? What would happen to them in the summer if she were working? She could argue the case for staying home quite effectively with anyone who claimed that women *should* work. Still, in her own mind, she didn't feel quite right about it. Once again, though, Sharon didn't really have to sort out her ambivalence. She agreed with Stewart that they needed the money. They were just getting by. There was no way they'd be able to save anything for the kids' college expenses unless she took a job.

Stewart thought maybe she should go back to school, get a master's degree so that she'd have some real earning power. But Sharon didn't want to go back to school. She wanted a job, not a career, and she didn't want to work summers. That pretty well limited her to something at the college, and a friend of Stewart's in personnel found her an opening in the psychology department. It was a large department, with six secretaries, or "support staff" as they were now called. Sharon wouldn't exactly be a secretary—more like an assistant to the departmental administrative assistant, in charge of coordinating some of the professors' research projects. The salary wasn't much, but the job sounded interesting, and most important, the hours were flexible.

Stewart was pleased. It was more than the money. He thought—though he would never say it out loud—that Sharon had regressed in the past few years. Taking care of the children, she had become one. Working would be good for her. Get her out of the house, meet interesting people; let the children look after themselves for once. He knew there would be some changes around the house, but he could handle it.

The night before Sharon's first day at work, Stewart had a little talk with the kids. He told them that they'd all have to help out more now that Mommy was starting a new job. They'd have to keep their rooms clean and take their dirty clothes down to the laundry. Jason would have to start putting the dishes in the dishwasher and Heather would have to help set the table for supper. He, Stewart, would start planning the menus and helping out with the shopping and cooking. The kids nodded.

In the morning, Stewart and the children made a special breakfast for Sharon: eggs and yogurt and cinnamon toast. They were so sweet.

Sharon's first day was a mess. Everyone was nice but nobody seemed to know what Sharon was supposed to do. So she hung around a lot. Her hours were 8:00

to 2:30, so she got home just about the same time as the kids. Jason was very solic-itous, very grown up. "How did it go, Mommy?" Heather wanted to know if she'd done any "speriments" yet. "Not yet, honey." When Stewart came home he was very mysterious. "Why don't you go upstairs and read for a while? We'll call you."

Forty-five minutes later Jason bounded up the stairs, calling out, "You can come down now!" Excited, impatient, he burst into the bedroom and took Sharon's hand. "Close your eyes," he said full of mischief. He led her out to the back porch, where Stewart was grilling lamb chops. On the table were flowers and a card. "Sit down and have a glass of wine while I finish these," Stewart said. She could see that he had his hands full trying to manage everything. Sharon opened the card. On the front was a child's drawing of a woman with black hair driving a little red car to a large gray building. Inside it said, *Happy New Job!* And it was signed "Jason and Heather and Daddy."

❖

The first several days at work were hard for Sharon. Everyone seemed to know what they were doing, except her. Not only was she new, but her job was ill-defined and she was supposed to find things to do. When she told Carmen, one of the secretaries, that she was confused, Carmen said, "Don't worry, you'll get the hang of it." Carmen was maybe twenty. It was disconcerting. Sharon had grown used to being a mother, in charge and in control. When it came to her house and her children, she was the expert. Now she was a beginner, starting over—and ask-ing a twenty-year-old for advice.

By the third week, Sharon was beginning to feel better. She knew her way around the department and pretty much what was expected of her. The thing she liked most about the job was working with Alice, the departmental administrative assistant. Alice was so organized. It was a pleasure to see how efficiently she planned teaching schedules, arranged meetings, and handled the prima donnas.

The hardest thing for Sharon was getting out of the house in the morning. She was used to coming downstairs in her bathrobe and helping the children fix break-fast. After they left, she would sit down with a cup of coffee and read the paper. In the warm weather she sat out on the back porch where she could listen to the birds. In the winter she sat by the window and looked out at the cold, happy to be inside. This brief period of unhurried solitude helped her ease into the day. With-out it she felt rushed and tense.

Stewart and the children tried hard to make accommodations. Stewart worked out a schedule for suppers, two weeks at a time, which included what they would eat and who would cook. He cooked as often as he could. Heather and Jason fixed their own breakfasts, and Jason helped Heather put together her lunch. These lunches consisted of more Fruit Loops and granola bars than Sharon liked, but she figured they would survive. All four of them were anxious about the change, and all were on their best behavior. Sharon had planned to be home in the afternoon before the school bus, but once or twice a week she didn't quite make it. At the end of the second week, Jason, now eight, told her, "Mommy, I don't mind that you're not here anymore when I come home. I can take care of myself."

The easiest adjustments were the things Stewart and the children volunteered to do. It was nice to have their help with meals, but nobody volunteered to help with the laundry or the cleaning. Sharon hesitated to ask, but after a while she just couldn't keep up. Why couldn't Stewart see that she needed more help?

Stewart thought everything was fine. He liked seeing Sharon dressed up for work in the mornings—she looked more like the woman he married than the house-wife she'd become—and he was proud of himself for doing the shopping and cook-ing. The first he knew anything was wrong was on a night when he was particularly tired. He'd just finished grading the last of twenty-six papers on Fitzgerald's por-trait of Jay Gatsby and was lying on the couch watching a Humphrey Bogart movie on TV. Sharon came up from the basement and dropped a laundry basket stuffed to overflowing on the floor in front of him, then stomped off upstairs.

Stewart's stomach started churning. He could tell she was mad, but why did she have to slam things down without saying anything? He went back to his movie, trying his best to ignore her. He'd be damned if he was going to give in every time she had a tantrum. But after a few minutes he could hear her sobbing in the bed-room, and he decided to go up and make peace. Unfortunately Sharon was ready for war. She screamed at him: "You said you were going to help out; you don't do anything except sit there in front of the *goddamned television*, while I do six loads of your dirty laundry. You're a fine one when it comes to making speeches, but you don't *really* help out. Once in a while you cook supper—when it's convenient—but what about everything else around here? Who does the laundry? Who takes the kids everywhere? Even when you do condescend to clean up, I have to go around and clean up after you. You put dirty dishes in the dishwasher and I have to scrape them off after the crud is all baked on. You don't have an ounce of compassion in you! *You don't give a damn about anyone but yourself!*"

Stewart tried to listen, but he couldn't stand it—her yelling and exaggerating everything all out of proportion was more than he could take. When he said, "I'm sorry," and reached out to put his arm around her, she slapped him. "Don't touch me, you bastard!"

He was stung, livid. He got up and walked out of the bedroom in a cold fury, down the stairs, out the front door, and into his car. But then he wasn't sure what to do next. He was scared of leaving but too angry to go back into the house. So he drove to the bar across the street from the university. This wasn't him. He'd never walked out before, and he never went into bars. But he didn't know what else to do. He sat there nursing a beer and thinking about all the awful, unfair things Sharon had said. Sure it was hard with both of them working, but why did she have to blame everything on him?

For the next two days they avoided each other. Stewart was angry and hurt, too upset by Sharon's yelling to take in what she'd said, and definitely too mad to dis-cuss it. Sharon was hurt and angry, and determined to wait for Stewart to come to her. After all, he was the one who walked out. After a couple of days of nursing his resentment, Stewart calmed down and thought about what Sharon had said. She was exaggerating, of course, but maybe he *could* do a little more. Half out of a sense of fairness, and half just to appease her, he decided to try to make peace. He began as he usually did, with an apology. "I'm sorry, honey." Sharon didn't say anything. She just waited to see what he would say next. "I know you have a lot to do, and I'm sorry if I'm not doing my share. What else would you like me to do to help you out?"

For a while things were better. Stewart did help out more, though Sharon couldn't help noticing that he asked a lot of questions about things he could have figured out himself. She'd be trying to read to the children and he'd interrupt. "Honey, where does this go?" She wanted to scream.

Another source of resentment was looking after the children. When they fussed about doing their homework, he might ask them what was wrong or just tell them to quiet down; it never seemed to occur to him to help them. The same thing with cleaning their rooms. If they cried and started banging things around, he yelled at them to cut that out and get busy. He didn't seem to understand that little people need help. They have feelings too.

One rainy morning when everybody was running late and the kids were cranky and whining, Sharon asked Stewart if he would mind driving them. "No, I can't," he said. He had an article to edit before he went in. Besides, it was their job to catch the bus. Another time he promised he would be home in time to drive Jason to a skating party, but he called at the last minute to say he couldn't make it. By then it was too late.

Sharon was incredulous at Stewart's letting them down. She thought he was acting out of a selfish, stubborn unwillingness to be a fully sharing member of the family. Stewart wanted to do more. But in his life the payoff was for succeeding at work. No one cheered when he helped out at home. In fact, it infuriated Sharon that he expected to be praised just for doing his share. They rarely argued about the children, though. By some kind of mutual agreement, differences about the children were consigned to the realm of Things Not Safe To Discuss. That left housework as the primary subject of contention.

They seemed to fall into a pattern. For a while after a blow-up, Stewart would do more. Then he'd start slipping. Forgetting to do certain things, lapsing into the old habit of expecting Sharon to take care of everything. She tried not to say anything. She didn't like their fights any more than he did. But after a while she'd get to the point where she couldn't stand it any longer. There'd be another fight, and another cooling off. Promises made, and promise broken. They seemed to go in cycles. And they both thought these arguments were unique to them. The truth is that Sharon and Stewart were struggling to adjust to the new form of the American family.

## The Two-Paycheck Family

In the early 1970s, the women's movement put the nuclear family on trial and found it guilty of oppression. Housekeeping and child care were drudgery, and home-makers were little more than domestic slaves. Even moderates like Betty Friedan claimed that the average middle-class household was a "comfortable concentration camp."[1] At the same time, a corrosive cycle of inflation and recession made it increasingly difficult for most American families to subsist on one income. The rising divorce rate and the fact that women are still overwhelmingly awarded custody created a legion of single mothers who suddenly found themselves dropping out of the middle class into poverty. As a result, more and more mothers are now working outside the home to support themselves and their families.

It's important to note that most of the increase in women working for pay has occurred among married women with husbands and children present in the home. Victor Fuchs, an economist at the National Bureau of Economic Research, notes that four of every five single women ages twenty-five to forty-four work for pay, and this proportion hasn't changed since 1950. Divorced and separated women have also traditionally worked, and their participation rates (about 75 percent) have grown only slightly. The really revolutionary change has taken place in the behavior of married women with children.[2] The two-paycheck family has become the new American norm.

Despite the hopes of feminists that entry into the sphere of production would be the ultimate road to women's liberation, so far it has proved to be just the reverse. The problem is, of course, that most married women who work carry a double load.

Between work and chores and the kids, most working parents are worn out. There's much to do but little to enjoy; overwork chokes their zest for life. If they lived alone, they'd have only their own particular brand of neurosis to keep them from taking a hard look at what they're doing with their lives. Working couples are not alone. Sadly, though, instead of providing support and enrichment for each other, many couples find the stresses of two careers driving a wedge between them.

When both parents are busy working, leisure is often the first thing to go. Here, too, the burden falls disproportionately on women. A UNESCO study showed that working mothers around the world have less than two-thirds of the free time enjoyed by their husbands.[3] Working mothers have little time for reading or sewing or letter writing or exercise. This is unfortunate because one of the most important ways to keep stress from leading to exhaustion is taking time to relax. Sitting down in the morning with a cup of coffee for a few minutes makes a big difference in your frame of mind. Few working parents have, or take, this time.

Tired and busy, many working couples get into a rut and stop having fun. Their inertia is doubled because if either one is tired, neither of them goes out. Because one or the other is usually tired, they fall into a pattern of staying home, or going out only when they feel they have to—to after-school activities or shopping with the children.

A further cause—and effect—of resentment in many two-career couples is the deterioration of their sex life. They're too tired. They're too tense. Their schedules

[1]Betty Friedman, *The Feminine Mystique*. New York: Norton, 1963.

[2]Victor Fuchs, *How We Live*. Cambridge, Mass.: Harvard University Press, 1983.

[3]UNESCO study cited in Caroline Bird, *The Two-Paycheck Marriage*. New York: Rawson Wade, 1979.

conflict. It's wives who are most often "too tired" for sex, and what usually makes them "too tired" is housework. It isn't so much the physical effort of having to do it all as the enormous resentment that builds up.

Sex is one of the things couples are reluctant to discuss. At the end of a long day, who wants to argue?

The problem of avoiding hard discussions doesn't arise only in the lives of our clients. We hesitate to bring up tough issues when we anticipate an angry response. If you think your partner will become defensive or critical if you voice your complaints about sex or housework, you're probably right. The mistake people make, though, is thinking only about the other person's response, rather than their own reactions.

Conversations go downhill, not because of what the other person does—acts hurt or angry or whatever—but because of how we (1) approach and (2) react to them. Think of the difficult conversations as a pattern of what-you-say and what-he (or she)-says, and so on. You probably know how it goes (if you don't, it's easy to find out—just pay attention). Try anticipating what usually happens and control your side of the discussion. If one person changes, the system changes.

## The Need to Restructure the Family

The family isn't a static entity; it must change to accommodate to the growth and development of its members. A long-range view of any family would show great flexibility and many stages of reorganization. Yet between these periods of reorganization are steady states during which family members are beguiled into thinking that the current structure of the family is the permanent structure of the family. Alternative patterns are available within the system, but any deviation that goes beyond the system's threshold of tolerance elicits mechanisms that reestablish the accustomed patterns.

❖

Before Sharon went back to work, the Salazars had evolved a style of living together that worked. Stewart's disengagement and Sharon's enmeshment, though not ideal, made up a functional parental unit. Likewise, Stewart's being the sole breadwinner allowed Sharon time (and made her feel it was her responsibility) to do the vast majority of household chores. Sharon's return to work destabilized the system. Stewart was dismayed to discover how many things he now had to do for himself. Going to the dry cleaner, taking his car in for repairs, buying birthday presents for his mother—these were just a few of the services Sharon had provided, services he had taken for granted. Sharon had one foot in the fifties, one foot in the nineties.

Trying to be a wife and mother as well as a working woman, Sharon kept having the feeling she was supposed to be in two places at once. Trying to do both jobs, she was afraid she'd succeed at neither.

When Sharon demanded a transformation in the family rules, the remaining family members resisted. Fluctuation, either internal or external, is normally followed by a response that returns the system to its steady state—people always resist change. Stewart tried to help out more but forgot some things and refused to do others. Jason and Heather knew Mommy was working and knew they weren't supposed to rely on her as much as before, but old habits die hard. When Mommy is around, children just naturally go to her when they want something. And Sharon, though she wanted things to be different, tended to pick up the ball when Stewart dropped it. She didn't know how to say no to the children. The family organism, proceeding according to its own rules, was stable enough to persist with a structure that no longer fit the circumstances.

❖

We've all seen the difficulties people go through in adapting their structure to changing developmental needs. In a similar way, the American family itself is in transition from the stable (though limiting) complementary marriage—with a division of labor based on gender stereotypes—to a new form, the symmetrical marriage.

The traditional division of labor allowed each partner to concentrate on his or her own specialties. Conflict was minimized because interaction between roles was minimal. The spouses divided roles—men were aggressive and career-centered (and, incidentally, a little selfish); women were soft and sensitive (and perhaps a little too selfless for their own good). Complementary relationships tend to be stable, like interlocking pieces of a puzzle that hold each other in place. The trouble was, the division was unequal. We had stability without fairness.

When a wife and mother returns to work, complementarity unravels and a new balance must be created. The division of labor needs to be more equal, but "equal" doesn't necessarily mean "the same." What's needed is a rebalanced interdependency, with the couple operating as a team.

The most successful two-paycheck couples divide and distribute functions. They achieve a more symmetrical, more equal relationship, not by sharing the same chores but by dividing them up. They don't try to do everything together. They may alternate, or one may do most of the shopping and cooking while the other does most of the washing and folding of clothes. This sharing is sometimes confused with equality. Don't kid yourself. Equality? Most working wives would settle for 70-30.

*Equity*—a sense of fairness—is achievable; equality is rare and elusive. Moving toward equality may lead to a better balance, but insisting on complete equality may produce frustration and bitterness.

Therapists differ in how they go about addressing gendered inequity in couples. Some, like Betty Carter and Monica McGoldrick, favor advocacy over neutrality. Even if couples don't bring up issues of fairness, they will. Once these issues are on the table, Carter and McGoldrick take a strong stand in favor of equality, to the point of telling women that if they aren't making substantial incomes they aren't going to have substantial bargaining power in their relationships. A less direct (and directive) approach is to ask questions about the partners' intentions and preferences. These discussions serve two purposes: helping couples talk about the division of labor in their relationships in nonblaming ways may promote more equitable solutions and such discussions *will* promote greater empathy.

# Empathy

At the end of a long day, most working parents come home to a household in disarray and a host of noisy claims on what little energy they have left. There isn't a whole lot you can do about that. Unfortunately, many people also come home to partners equally worn out by a grinding routine that strains their capacity for sympathy.

In unhappy families people are cut off from kindness and compassion. Some of them develop whole reservoirs of feeling they believe their partners don't know or care about. The persistent pressure of these private concerns works a strong claim on the mind. As long as feelings and desires go unshared, they separate the individual from the group.

The uninvolved partner or cold mate isn't just "not participating"; he or she is actively engaged in feeling something. When a partner continues stewing in unspoken resentment or anxious worry, there is little room in his or her heart for anything else.

Shared experience is the first step toward mutual understanding. Sharing emotional experience helps us regulate our feelings. Unhappy feelings don't just go away if we talk about them, but it's impossible to overestimate the soothing effect of talking over the upsets of the day with someone who cares enough to listen. The sharing of emotional experience is the most meaningful and pervasive feature of true relatedness.

Empathy starts with listening but doesn't end there. Listening is a strenuous but silent activity, rare in busy families. Most of the time we're too eager to get a word in edgewise, or to get off by ourselves, to really hear what anyone else is saying. Foremost among the obstacles to listening are those that stem from our need to "do something" about what's being said: defend ourselves, disagree, or solve whatever problems are described.

One popular technique for fostering empathy is to have couples take turns talking and listening. This is useful but doesn't, of itself, teach empathy. It teaches taking turns. Taking turns is fine, but it isn't empathy.

Empathy has as much to do with understanding as with dialogue. Open conversation and empathy are related in circular fashion; one begets the other. Ordinarily we achieve empathy for other people when we think about them, not just when we talk with them. Ironically, sometimes it is while watching strangers that we begin to develop empathy for those closest to us. A woman sees male emotional reticence portrayed in a television drama and begins to understand that her husband may be more shy than cold. A man sees a child in a playground, anxiously looking for someone to play with, and realizes—perhaps for the first time—how much his children need him.

Empathy is often confused with sympathy, but there's a crucial difference. Sympathy is more limited and limiting; it means to feel the same as rather than to be understanding of. It is an emotion that makes us suffer *with* unhappy people, and that feeling motivates us to avoid them or try to do *for* them.

Here is a small example that caused my wife and me needless friction for years. She loves to talk about fixing up the house. For years she would describe her plans for knocking out this wall or that, putting in cabinets here, and buying new furniture there. These conversations made me very uncomfortable. *Why do we need to do that?* I'd think, and *Where's the money going to come from?* I had no patience for these discussions and she knew it. But like a lot of people we refused to discuss what seemed obvious: She wanted to remake our house from top to bottom, and I didn't want to hear about it. In fact, my wife just likes to imagine most of these projects. Oh, maybe someday in the next century, when we can afford it, she might actually remodel the place, but for now she just likes to daydream. It hurt her that I wouldn't listen. After all, doesn't she listen to my hopes and dreams? My unwillingness to listen stemmed from an unfortunate but common confusion about where her dreams ended and my responsibility for fulfilling them began.

Over years of living together partners learn to hide away their feelings. Not all of them, of course, but enough. These silent areas fester and assume more than their share of importance, eventually perhaps becoming preoccupations. We retreat into our own personal and subjective worlds, hiding away our real feelings, sometimes even from ourselves. As a result, everyday family life is taken over by obligation and habit; real feeling is controlled and limited, and the people we say we love are kept at a distance and seen through a curtain. We get by, but intimacy slowly dies. To meet, truly meet, means that we must open up part of ourselves, feel our feelings and share them.

Will empathy solve a family's problems? No, that only happens when Walt Disney writes the script. Empathy doesn't extinguish conflict, but being understood makes conflict bearable.

❖

Communication doesn't solve very many practical family problems. Action, not talk, is what counts. However, talking things over is usually a good place to start; it is, for example, when you are trying to rebalance the housekeeping and parenting after a mother returns to work. What's needed is a revisiting and renegotiating of previous issues of power and sharing. It's time to update the marital *quid pro quos*, the (largely implicit) patterns of exchange in every marriage. These discussions work best if the partners can be helped to avoid the following expressions: *You should, It's not fair, I always, You never*—; you get the idea. Have them start with their feelings: "I'm too busy and tired to do all the shopping," or "I can't keep up with everything." Then encourage them to make specific requests—*requests,* not accusations or guilt trips. (Save those for emergencies.)

Therapists should remember that change can occur in small steps. If she's doing most of the housework and he starts doing a little but she acts like there's been no change, he may feel unappreciated and decide that there's no use in trying. Is it fair to have to praise someone for doing his share? No, but it may work. If you can teach a squirrel to ride a bicycle by rewarding successive approximation to the goal, you should be able to teach a husband how to fold the laundry.

When it comes to family life, men have trouble taking hold and women have trouble letting go. If a woman wants her spouse to take more responsibility around the house she has to give it to him. Wives can be encouraged to try a little "strategic helplessness." It's harder to argue with *I can't* than *I won't*. Most husbands, incidentally, are experts at strategic helplessness—they must give classes in the subject to bridegrooms.

❖

So far I've been talking primarily about couples and their need to shift from the traditional complementarity to a new, more symmetrical balance. The limits of this analysis stem from taking the couple out of context. This is a mistake many therapists make when thinking about families—looking at one part of the family, while ignoring the whole system. The husband and wife are the architects of the family, and they are the ones with the greatest capacity to change the system. Remember, though, that husbands and wives are also often parents, and unless they change in relation to their children, as well as to each other, change may not last.

The major transformation required when a mother returns to work is from a diffuse (. . . . .) to a clear (- - - -) boundary between mother and children. This, in turn, permits and encourages the father to move closer to the children. Families, like all of nature, abhor a vacuum.

A family realigning its boundaries to accommodate to a mother returning to work looks like this:

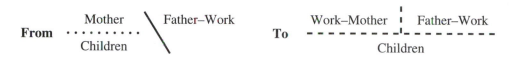

As you see, changes must be made in the boundaries between both parents and their careers. He needs to be a little less involved, she more involved. Both of these modifications require complementary shifts in the relationship of each parent with the children. He needs to be more involved, she a little less.

In many families, the subsystem of the children should be subdivided; children of different ages should be differentiated, given different rights and responsibilities. This can be diagrammed as follows:

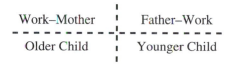

The point to keep in mind is that all these changes are interrelated. A concerted effort to change only one boundary—say, that between husband and wife—may create a ripple effect and alter the whole system. A more likely possibility, however, is that change begun in one part of the family will not take hold if other subsystems resist and block the new patterns. The most effective way to restructure a family is to keep the whole system in mind and coordinate efforts to change on several fronts.

## Shared Parenting

Too many men continue to think of caring for the children as their wife's problem. Many find it hard to back off from work and get more involved at home. This is due not only to male reticence, but also to the way our society is structured. Greedy occupations may resist a working father's efforts to spend more time with his family. But fathers are as responsible as their wives for finding a way to reconcile their professional ambitions with the interests of their children.

If both parents work, then both should share the burden of looking after their children. The solution to the instability created in a family after the mother goes back to work is to move from the traditional family setup, in which the mother is the primary parent, toward shared parenting.

Among the many advantages of shared parenting are: (1) relieving women of the dual oppression of being a paid worker and the sole parent; (2) liberating women from full-time mothering to pursue other interests; (3) affording the opportunity for more equal relationships between men and women; (4) allowing men more access to their children, and vice versa; (5) enabling children to be parented by two nurturing figures, and thus freeing them from enmeshment with one over-involved parent and possible alienation from an underinvolved one; (6) breaking down gender stereotypes as role models; and (7) putting pressure on political, economic, and social structures for changes, such as paternity and maternity leaves, job sharing, more equal pay, and freely available child care.

The advantages of shared parenting range from the purely practical—having two people working together to do a job that is virtually impossible for one to do alone—to changing the way children are brought up, and even to leading the way toward social change.

The crisis of the two-paycheck family is a result of trying to adjust to new demands with an outmoded and unchanged family structure. Like individuals, families cling to the familiar and resist solutions that require breaking old habits.

Mothers may have trouble backing off from their kids. (This is a secret known only to mothers, their children, their husbands—and their employers.) Even couples who try to move toward sharing the physical tasks of parenting have trouble reversing the rule that says "Mother's in charge." The system—embodied in the expectations of both parents and their children—will resist significant change. No matter how much Dad does, in the final analysis it's up to Mom to make sure that someone takes the kids to the dentist, that they have clean clothes, and that they get to their after-school activities.

This perception is also shared outside the family. One morning when I was home writing, the elementary school nurse called and asked to speak to Mrs.

Nichols. I said she was at work; I was Dr. Nichols, could I help her? She then asked if she could reach my wife at work. I asked again if I could help. She said that our son, Paul, had gotten sick and threw up in the boy's bathroom. Could she have Mrs. Nichols's phone number at work, so she could call her to come and take Paul home? I said I'd come. Oh, she said.

The sexual division of labor remains intact, embedded in the American way of life and in the hearts and minds of most mothers and fathers. Years spent in female-dominated households have led many to believe it cannot be otherwise. Motherhood is a woman's "natural" calling, and it is her sphere of influence and power. Recently, women have challenged the belief that the home is their rightful place, and they have sought power and influence in the workplace. Most of these women did not, however, abandon their aspirations to have families; they thought they could have everything if they worked at it.

❖

Unlike their more traditional sisters, who are rebalancing their lives by going back to work, many younger and more career-oriented women have already had a bellyful of the professional world. After successfully climbing the corporate ladder, they're discovering that the bottom-line mentality of modern business, coupled with the crass materialism of American consumer culture, can crush your spirit and devour your family life. Perhaps it's time for someone to write "Death of a Saleswoman" or "The Woman in the Gray Flannel Suit."

Career women are learning what men have been saying for decades: climbing the ladder of success can be a soul-deadening experience. The difference is that women are less willing to take this state of affairs for granted. After achieving success as a powerful editor at major publishing houses, Elizabeth Perle McKenna writes:

> *Most of us love what we do and none of us would trade our right to do it. But we don't like the way business works. We are increasingly sick of the petty politics, the unmanageable workloads. We are tired of working harder and harder with less satisfaction. We want to work more humanely, with more respect, recognition and flexibility.*[4]

Perhaps if enough men and women begin to feel trapped and miserable at work and long to change how work relates to family life, we will begin to create alternatives to committing oneself either to a career *or* to the family.

Privileged young people in the seventies thought they could lead the way to more egalitarian marriages and families. Young women graduated from college not wanting to be trapped in the narrow domesticity of their mothers. Encouraged by the rhetoric of the women's movement, many of them put careers first; families would come "later." They wanted challenge; they wanted to "have it all." They were pursuing an attractive but untested image, that of the Superwoman. Theirs

---

[4]Elizabeth Perle McKenna, *When Work Doesn't Work Anymore: Women, Work, and Identity*. New York: Delacorte Press, 1997.

was an individualism that underestimated the conservative forces in society and ignored the conservative structure of family systems.

## The Best of Intentions

Sharon and Stewart tried to become more equal parents, but despite the best of intentions, they gradually slipped back into familiar roles. Their relative failure is instructive because it illustrates the trouble men and women have in changing their approach to parenting.

Stewart tried to become more involved with Jason and Heather because he felt he could do some things—like enforce discipline and teach the children to be adventurous—better than Sharon. He also thought that freeing Sharon from some of her burden would make her a happier and more agreeable person.

Stewart started coming home early on Friday afternoons and taking Jason and Heather on outings. One week it was hiking in the woods, the next week it was teaching them how to throw a football. On school nights he made more of an effort to get after them to put away the dishes and do their homework—things Sharon usually spoke to them about.

One evening after supper, Stewart told Jason to pick up his dirty socks from the living room floor and put them in his room. Jason snapped at him, "You're getting to be just like Mom!"

Stewart was furious. How dare Jason speak to him this way! "Pick up those goddamned socks and get up to your room. Don't you ever take that tone of voice with me, young man!"

Stewart wondered what happened to make Jason react like that. Was he losing his authority?

In contrast to the children's overtly conflict-laden relationship with their mother, their relationship with their father is usually smoother because it's diluted. He's a once-in-a-while, feared and idealized figure. That's why fathers are often better disciplinarians. They aren't around enough to get housebroken. Stewart was around more now, and the kids tried to mold him to their way of doing things. It didn't work. He wouldn't bend.

Daddy's Friday afternoon outings with the kids started getting canceled. Usually it was something at work that got in the way. It's hard to be really involved with your career and your children. Few men manage it.

Most successful careers require some backup at home—a supportive person who frees the career striver to concentrate on the demands of work. Traditional men had this support from their wives. When a man came home at the end of a long, hard day, his wife was waiting for him with a drink and a sympathetic ear. By the time he had a chance to relax, dinner was ready. If he had to stay late for a meeting, all he had to do was call and dinner would be delayed or waiting to be warmed up in the oven. Sharon could no longer play that part, even if she wanted to. Stewart couldn't get this vision of marriage out of his mind.

So, they muddled along. Stewart continued to help out in some ways—washing dishes, mowing the lawn, and, when he remembered, planning the menus. He wasn't really satisfied with these contributions, but he felt he couldn't do any more. With the children, he did what he felt like doing. Sharon did what had to be done. (Visit the waiting room of a pediatrician or an orthodontist and count the number of fathers sitting there waiting for their children.)

❖

Shared parenting seemed to elude Sharon and Stewart, not because their intentions were ignoble but because old habits are hard to break. They were often at odds about the children and had difficulty understanding each other's position. Stewart often put his own needs ahead of the children's, and he couldn't understand why Sharon didn't do the same. "Parents have to take care of themselves," he told her. "Satisfied adults make good parents." To Sharon, it sounded like just another excuse.

# 9

## THE OVERINVOLVED MOTHER AND PERIPHERAL FATHER

When did it happen? Sharon's life was consumed by two small children, and though she was married she might as well be a single parent. She did so much, and Stewart did so little. Was this the way it's supposed to be?

Some days all she seemed to do was chauffeur the kids around—soccer practice, swimming, Sunday school, piano lessons, skating parties. Why was everything so far apart?

On the rare occasions when Stewart drove, he expected to be thanked profusely. Husbands sometimes "help out," but that's a lot different from sharing. He seemed to resent the children's needs. It scared her. If he could not love them, he could leave. But this thought, only vaguely apprehended, just made her mad.

Sharon hadn't wanted kids. Never really saw the need for them. She wanted Stewart. He wanted kids, seemed to think they were essential, and his certainty overruled her doubt. Besides, she thought he would make a fine father. He was so boyish and playful. When they visited friends with kids, he loved to play with them. But things didn't turn out the way she expected.

The day they brought Heather home from the hospital Stewart was at work before lunchtime. She did not, as he accused her, resent his work. What she did resent was the way he used work to rationalize his lack of involvement with the children. He usually managed to show up for the really important events, like birthdays, but even then he was likely to come late or leave early. He was not a loiterer. His entrances and exits were justified in the name of work. "I'll be a little late, honey. I have to tie up some loose ends before I can leave the office." He never let go and gave himself to them.

By the time she was thirty-five, Sharon was used to doing everything for the children. They trained her well—Jason and Heather, and Stewart. She might get annoyed at having to drive Heather to play at Tammy's and then take Jason to the other side of town for Cub Scouts, but she rarely bothered asking Stewart and never really questioned the need for all this driving.

When she did say no, she felt guilty. Once, when she didn't feel up to driving Jason to the Great Escape amusement park, she got into a big argument with him. Afterward, Jason went off to play and forgot completely about the Great Escape; still, Sharon couldn't stop hearing his accusation, "But all the other kids are going."

Most of the time she enjoyed doing things with the children: reading to them, going to museums and concerts, taking them on picnics and field trips, helping out with special events at school. In the winter they went ice skating and sledding; in the summer, there were outdoor concerts and rock collecting expeditions. Stewart was usually busy working.

When she did succeed in dragging him away from his separate existence, the results were mixed. Sometimes he was agreeable, even fun, but you couldn't count on it. When the kids were exceptionally good, or if they played while she listened to him talk about his job, they could have a nice time. But even when she planned things he liked, time together could turn sour.

One Friday she took the kids to meet him after work at T.G.I. Friday's. It was the kind of thing he liked to do—a drink after work. Jason was a little cranky and couldn't decide what he wanted to eat, so Sharon gave him a little of the attention Stewart couldn't seem to share. That was it! "These kids are so spoiled, why don't you leave them at home? We can't even finish a conversation with them around." And that was that. They sat languishing in a nice restaurant over a speechless meal. She sometimes thought he saved his sourest moods for their most expensive outings.

Lately she was tired all the time. Thirty-five years old and only now did she finally feel grown-up. Grown-up and tired. Too much work, too much stress, and not enough sleep. Once she daydreamed about men; now her fantasies involved taking a vacation in the sun. She would love to go to one of those resorts they showed on "Lifestyles of the Rich and Famous." Maybe Club Med. Seven days of sleep would set things right.

❖

Sharon's counterpart, the peripheral father, is a familiar role. So familiar in fact that it evokes a stereotype: the unfeeling male, obsessed with achievement, not caring about intimacy or his family, except as an obligation. Like many stereotypes, this one is simpler and thus more commonplace than the truth. It reduces an unhappy interaction to the problem of one person, and suggests that person is willful and selfish.

The truth is somewhat more complicated. Like most problems that occur in families, a father's remoteness can be understood on three levels: *monadic* —his personality; *dyadic* —the couple's interaction; and *triadic* —her bond with the children and his with work that stabilizes the distance between them.

❖

Stewart's life was about self-reliance and privacy. As a young man he had his privacy, and with it loneliness. He didn't choose solitude. Who would? He learned it from his mother, who taught it by example and by leaving him to his own devices much of the time.

In college he shunned dormitory small talk and noisy fraternity parties. Why did everything have to be so loud? Besides, he didn't have time. His program of serious purpose kept him busy working and studying, while at the same time masking his anxiety and covering his insecurity. He felt himself too sophisticated to join in, so he stayed outside.

With Sharon it was different. She cared about important things, like music and art, and she seemed genuinely interested in him. He married for many reasons but perhaps none so compelling as to escape from loneliness. He thought Sharon would always be there when he needed her.

As it turned out, she was always there, but not always in the way he needed her. The painful discovery that she was a being in her own right, separate from him, with a different and often conflicting agenda, made him depressed and resigned. At times Stewart felt Sharon had no life of her own and tried to live off his, which didn't give him any room to breathe. Once again the thing he sought was privacy.

Now Stewart thought that Sharon spent too much time with the kids. He had some intuition that she turned to them because he was too independent to suit her. A few years ago he'd welcomed that, felt that because of the kids she left him alone more. But now he and Sharon were older, calmer, more flexible. Maybe they could be closer—except that the kids were always in the way. She let them interrupt whenever they wanted, she hardly ever wanted to go out without them, and they couldn't do anything together on weekends because there was always some children's activity going on. There were soccer games and Little League baseball and swimming lessons and puppet shows and children's theater and birthday parties and school outings, and on and on. Work often kept him from going, but he didn't always regret missing these outings.

Stewart didn't exactly plan to be so busy, he just was. When he did have some free time, he wanted to relax. He loved Heather and Jason, but he had little left to give at the end of the day. Sharon didn't seem to understand that. Without trying, she was more open to the children and more sensitive to their needs. She was more ready to connect with them, even when she was tired, and so she had little patience with Stewart's unwillingness to do the same. She thought he was acting out of malice—a stubborn refusal to be a fully involved member of the family, a kind of selfishness she couldn't understand. Take, for instance, the night she asked him to go to one of Jason's Cub Scout meetings.

Stewart was riding home in heavy traffic, hurrying to Jason's school for the Cub Scout meeting. He hadn't questioned his need to be there. But now he was resentful. It had been a long day. He wanted nothing more than to have a drink or two, tell Sharon about his day, eat some supper, then maybe watch a movie or a ball game. He loved his son and enjoyed their time together, but Cub Scouts was different—an organized activity, "for boys" maybe, but conceived and run by adults. Hell, adults ran these kids' lives! But Stewart didn't feel that he could tell Sharon he didn't want to go to this stupid pack meeting. So he went, and left early with a reluctant Jason.

And what was it that Stewart worked so hard to insulate himself from? Certainly not physical effort. No, he even sought that out, like when he ran hard on a hot day. Something about unstructured, unplanned, everyday family life just made him uneasy. He'd always been like that, although when he was single he hadn't really noticed. His habits were carefully constructed to isolate him from casual social contacts. People who didn't know him confused his cultivated reserve for aloof uncaring. It wasn't that, really; more that he liked to pick and choose when to socialize. This pattern of privacy may work for a single man; it does not work for a married one. To be this isolated from everyday intrusions, small talk, and children who want attention, it's necessary to keep busy. Stewart kept busy at work.

Like many workaholics, Stewart was too preoccupied to drift along with the currents of everyday family life. His schedule absorbed his time and energy, so that daily family events, moods, and irritations were not inflicted on him. He depended on hard work in pursuit of achievement for rejuvenation and maintenance of his morale.

He knew how *he* felt, but what about Sharon? There was a part of her he could not fathom. At times a terrific feeling of love for her washed over him, especially when she wasn't around to mess it up. Most of the time, though, he thought she was too demanding, too dependent, and *way* too committed to togetherness. Why did she always want to do everything together? The truth was that outings with all four of them usually ended up in quarreling and bickering. Why couldn't she understand?

❖

It's good to understand Stewart's and Sharon's separate psychologies—her need for togetherness and his craving for privacy. If only Stewart and Sharon could understand each other, they might begin to get over their resentment and learn to relax the drive to change each other.

Remember that human problems are created and maintained on three levels: monadic, dyadic, and triadic. Stewart's emotional distance from Sharon reflected his personality, the couple's pattern of interaction, and their other involvements—hers with the kids, his with work. If Sharon wanted to get closer to Stewart—if she wanted results—she'd have to act counterintuitively. She'd have to stop trying to pull him toward her. First she'd need to see the pattern of their relationship. Understand first, change second. As we shall see, Sharon's understanding of the dynamics of the relationship led to the painful but liberating discovery that she could change him by changing herself.

## Pursuers and Distancers

Pursuers feel neglected; distancers feel crowded. The more neglected they feel, the more pursuers pressure their partners to come closer. When that doesn't work, they criticize them for being selfish. The more demands distancers feel are placed on them, the more they withdraw. From a distance these pairs resemble two ponies on a merry-go-round—one chases the other but never catches up. Up close it hurts too much to be objective, so both continue to play out their parts.

❖

For years Sharon tried to get Stewart to spend more time with her and the children. At first she just assumed he would help out with the responsibilities of parenting and share in the fun. The only trouble was, Stewart didn't agree with her about what the responsibilities of parenting were or about what constitutes fun. He didn't think they should enroll the kids in so many activities and then have to drive them here, there, and everywhere. And Sharon's outings to museums and concerts and art galleries weren't always his idea of fun.

Sharon tried so hard. She tried asking him nicely to come along. She tried having the kids ask him. When nothing else seemed to work, she screamed at him in frustration. These unhappy outbursts usually got his attention. For a few days he would make an effort to spend more time with her and the kids. But then he would revert to his usual disengaged self. From her point of view, Sharon tried nearly everything. But notice how her various strategies all revolved around a common theme: her attempt to pressure Stewart to change his lack of involvement.

Stewart played out the other half of this complementary pattern. When they were first married he felt a tremendous pressure coming from Sharon. It was as though she wanted to take him over, subjugating him to make up for some emptiness in herself. Helplessly he felt the pressure of her need for constant companionship weighing him down, the weight of domestic quietude.

She seemed to have no life of her own. "Why should I go by myself. We're married, aren't we?" She objected to his playing volleyball—"How come you have time for that when you never have any time for me?" She criticized his friends, and she always wanted to know what he was doing—"You never tell me anything!" Usually he caved in. He felt humiliated, hurt, attacked; all of these were safer than experiencing his underlying fury. So he stopped playing volleyball and gave up most of his friends, except one or two whose wives Sharon happened to like; in short, he stopped having fun. It had nothing to do with his own conflicts about enjoying himself; oh, no, it was her fault. Neurosis recruits accomplices.

Stewart promoted Sharon's complaints about things he liked to do into an ironclad, blanket prohibition. It was a negative, grudging compliance. Since he felt criticized and controlled, he made little attempt to enjoy being with her. He felt trapped. The one place he could escape was work.

Things changed after the kids were born. As she became more involved with them, she demanded less of him. Over the years they evolved into a stable pattern: Sharon and Jason and Heather did all the everyday things together, while Stewart was busy working. Once in a while the four of them went to a movie, or more often, Sharon insisted that they all go to a show at the museum or a concert. Her insistence that Stewart join them on these occasions which he so disliked only served to reinforce his wish not to. No more, though, than his own failure to suggest that they do things he liked. Sometimes he felt guilty about not being more involved.

Occasionally he planned little trips for the whole family. What seemed to put him in the mood were periods during which he didn't see them at all for a couple of days—while he was on business trips or when Sharon took the kids to visit her parents. Most of the time, however, he felt like a prisoner, too busy longing for escape to consider letting go and getting involved.

❖

Sharon's relationship with Stewart fits such a familiar pattern that we may be tempted to take it as natural. Stewart was independent, concerned more with professional accomplishment than with everyday family life. Sharon was the opposite. For her, family life was the number one priority; she respected hard work and achievement but thought that doing things together as a family was equally important. Are we really talking about masculine autonomy and feminine relatedness? No. Stewart's separateness wasn't autonomy, it was isolation. He wasn't so much self-sufficient as reclusive. Unlike Stewart, the truly autonomous man can be himself, as well as flexible and self-possessed, in relationships. Stewart wasn't independent of others; in fact he was quite dependent on Sharon to look after the house, the kids, and him. What he was, was allergic to intimacy. He disengaged himself to create a protective wall of distance. Failing to acknowledge his reliance on Sharon, he lived under the illusion of independence.

In pursuer-distancer relationships, the pursuer is often, though not always, a woman. Perhaps "often" because of culturally induced values. However, autonomy and relatedness aren't essential aspects of male and female nature, but depend on the pattern of relationship as much as personal history. True, most women are more relationship-oriented than most men. But couples tend to polarize each other. Even small differences tend to become exaggerated and stabilized.

The pursuer-distancer pattern may reverse at different times in a relationship. Many husbands, for example, ignore and take their wives for granted until they become jealous of their own children. It's not at all uncommon to see a father competing with his children for his wife's attention. Often this happens while she's too busy cooking dinner to pay much attention to any of these supplicants.

The pursuer-distancer pattern may also vary in different aspects of a couple's relationship. Stewart, for example, was the pursuer when it came to sex. When he and Sharon were first married, sex was pretty good. The only thing was, he seemed to be in the mood more often that she was. He got the feeling that she made up excuses. She felt like he was always after her. So, he "courted her" and she "avoided him"—or she "wanted a more balanced relationship" but he "had a one-track mind," depending on which one you listened to.

❖

Sharon made discoveries that many of us make when we calm down, though maybe we have to get to a certain age before we relinquish the habit of waiting for others to change to make us happy. Our relatives don't have any tricks up their sleeves. Their actions only surprise us because we keep looking for them to do what we wish they would do or what *we* would do. They do what *they* do. Once we learn this we can stop being so surprised and upset. We can let them be who they are. We might as well—they will anyway.

Sharon discovered the pattern of pursuit and withdrawal that she and Stewart were locked into, but the discovery came about in stages. The first real change occurred when she gave up on him. She stopped trying to figure him out, stopped underlining passages in self-help books for him to read, and started looking after herself. Focusing on herself rather than on the man in her life helped Sharon develop a healthy self-interest, and as she took more responsibility for her own life, she felt a diminished need to control him. Instead of trying to make him into the man she needed, she let him go to discover the man he was. She gave up on changing him and contented herself with the kids and her friends.

❖

With no one chasing him, Stewart stopped running. He had always been interested in self-improvement—as though his self was always in need of improvement. So, he decided to go to "est," a popular encounter-group program that promised to help participants get more out of life. Sharon didn't want to go, but she hoped it would do him some good.

The friends who encouraged him to attend wouldn't tell him exactly what went on at est—part of the effect depended on surprise and spontaneity—but they did prepare him for the austere restrictions. Two long weekends, with no trips to the bathroom or meals except those few scheduled by the staff. When the appointed weekend came, Stewart took the train to New York on Friday afternoon and checked into the cheapest hotel he could find. Why pay for a fancy room that he would only be using for a few hours? He went to Chinatown for supper with friends, but he was too apprehensive about the next day to enjoy himself very much.

The first thing that struck him when he arrived at the training site was the incredible regimentation. Everything was organized. Everything. He found his name tag, deposited his watch with one of the assistants—participants weren't supposed to keep track of the time—and took a seat in the auditorium. For the first time he felt really anxious. Two hundred wooden chairs were packed closely together in a relatively small room, and Stewart suddenly realized that he was going to be trapped in close quarters with a large group of strangers for two whole weekends. He liked people, but he also liked to keep his distance, and he liked to get up an leave when he wanted to. And that was fairly often.

Just about then, one of the assistants strode up to the front of the room and read off the rules. It sounded like the Army: Don't do this, don't do that. Stewart was bored and annoyed. He knew this stuff already. But some people apparently didn't; dozens of them stood up to question, protest, and challenge the rules.

"But what if I *have* to go to the bathroom?" someone asked. *That's asinine*, Stewart thought; *if you have to go, you have to go*.

Someone across the room rose to say, "This is bullshit! Nobody's going to tell me when to sit and when to stand; these rules are stupid and unnecessary!"

After each question or argument, the leader simply repeated the relevant rule, as if to say, "This is the way it is, take it or leave it." But the haggling went on and on. It seemed as though everyone in the auditorium had to stand up to declare that he or she was special, and to try to find some way around the rules.

Stewart was getting more and more irritated. *Why don't these people sit down and shut up so we can get on with it?* But they didn't. More and more people got up to say that they didn't like this or they didn't like that, and why do we have to do these things, and you can't make us. Then it hit him: *These people are me! The only difference between them and me is that they're willing to say what they feel.*

Then the trainer came in and helped spell out the significance of what was happening by connecting the rules of the training to the rules of life, which are often just as arbitrary, just as unfair. As he listened, it struck Stewart how much of his life was devoted to struggling against the rules—from running yellow lights to wanting Sharon to be a more independent person. How much easier it would be to accept things the way they are and deal with the world as it is, rather than piss and moan because life isn't the way it should be.

Not all of what followed was equally powerful. Some of it was interesting, some was annoying, and some was just plain boring. But there were moments. One of the most powerful came late on the second Saturday night. The trainer introduced an exercise wherein the participants were supposed to confront their inner fears. Normally, people don't even have access to their inner fears, much less are they willing to confront them. But the long hours and lack of familiar routine had worn away several layers of defenses.

When the exercise started, Stewart didn't expect much. He wasn't afraid of many things; besides it was only an exercise. Following an elaborate set of preliminaries, which acted as a form of hypnotic induction, the participants were guided into a vivid fantasy. They were to imagine walking into a dark city alleyway and then coming face-to-face with a desperately violent criminal. The effect was further enhanced because the room was absolutely dark and all around people were screaming. At first Stewart couldn't really get into it. Maybe if he lived in the city he would be scared of dark alleyways, but he didn't and he wasn't. Then something happened. *Holy shit!* Instead of some criminal, Stewart saw Sharon and the kids coming toward him. They were reaching out their arms to him—he could see that they loved him—but he was scared out of his mind. He screamed and tried to shut them out, but he could still see their faces. In that instant he knew that he was terrified. Stewart kept on screaming, but now tears gushed down his face and he was racked with aching sobs. He couldn't stop crying. *They love me . . . all they want is for me to love them back . . . and I keep running away.*

Tired as he was after the session ended that night, Stewart didn't go to sleep. He kept going over and over it in his mind. That was about all he could do—he kept seeing the sweet faces of Sharon and the kids, and the love in their eyes. And he thought about all the ways he contrived to keep his distance from them. Somehow Stewart had confused these people, who only wanted to love him, with something dark and sinister that lurked in an alleyway, something that wanted to suck him dry.

Love that blooms in the hothouse climate of an encounter weekend usually dries up on Monday. Stewart came back from that second weekend with the best of intentions to stop running away from Sharon and the kids. He started feeling that they loved him and that they didn't want anything from him but to be with him. He tried to let go and give himself to them. But, gradually, he lapsed back into his old self-sufficient, introverted self.

❖

So much of what we experience in relationships is clouded by our natural human inclination to be judgmental. Instead of observing carefully, we often note only enough to decide who's right (us) and who's wrong (them), and what's fair (very little) and what isn't (plenty). To learn about family dynamics, my advice is to take up the attitude of an anthropologist. Instead of ignoring the commonplace, these curious observers note everything. An excellent place to observe *Americanus middleclassus* is in the neighborhood shopping mall, America's living stage. Here adults come with their young to hunt for trinkets and clothing, or merely to escape the boredom of long afternoons in the nest. You'll see tired parents threatening their children—enough to hurt the children's feelings, but not enough to keep them in line—and you'll see mates tugging at each other and pulling away.

## Self-Defeating Cycles

Unhappy people are keenly aware of what others do to make them that way. "My boss takes me for granted." "My friend never calls me." "My husband always gives me a hard time when I ask him to do something with me and the children." Looking outward keeps them stuck. In psychotherapy, the therapist asks, "How do you *feel* about that?" This attempt to get at the personal equation emphasizes unresolved emotional reactivity. A family therapist would ask, "What do you *do* about it?" The first question—"How do you feel?"—may lead to new understanding; the second may lead to a new relationship.

The "What do you do about it?" question is designed to uncover the cycle of interaction that exists around all family problems. Who does what, when, where, and how? When I first ask my patients to look at what they've been doing in attempting to get what they want, many of them immediately reply, "I've tried!" The response is part defensive—it really *is* the other person's fault—part naïve. The naïveté comes from thinking that, like Gertrude Stein's rose, trying is trying is trying. In fact, the attempted solution often exacerbates the problem.

A woman once called me on a talk show to ask for advice about her husband, who, she said, at age forty-two was losing his sex drive. For years he used to want to make love more often that she did. Now the pattern was changing. He was less and less interested. I suggested that if she wanted more romance she try acting more romantic, but before I could explain what I meant, she interrupted to say, "Oh, I've tried that." What she'd tried was chasing him around the bedroom. Never pursue a distancer.

❖

We can break self-defeating cycles by subjecting them to a two-part analysis. The first reevaluation involves applying the principle of circular causality; the second is to consider the principles of reinforcement and shaping.

A distancing husband may be convinced that his wife's nagging (cause) makes him withdraw (effect). She is equally likely to believe that his withdrawal causes her to nag. From a family systems perspective we see their behavior as part of a circular pattern: the more she nags, the more he withdraws, *and* the more he withdraws, the more she nags. Yes, but who *really* started it? It doesn't matter. Once underway, the system—the circular interaction—is perpetuated by both of them, and *either one of them* can break the cycle.

The likelihood of a particular response being repeated depends on its consequences—what happens after the response. If the response is followed by positive reinforcement, it's more likely to be repeated. If the response is ignored or punished, it will gradually be extinguished. So? The principle of reinforcement—whether you call it that or not—is so obvious that it doesn't seem to add much. It does if you look at patterns of interaction.

Whatever a person's words might be intended to convey, interactions function either as positive or negative reinforcements. Yelling at a husband, "You never do anything around here!" is aversive. It doesn't work.

At first glance it would seem unlikely that family members reinforce undesirable behavior. Why, for example would parents reinforce temper tantrums in their children? Or why would a wife reinforce her husband's withdrawal, when it appears to cause her so much pain? The answer isn't to be found in some kind of convoluted motive for suffering, but in the simple fact that people often inadvertently reinforce precisely those responses that cause them the most distress.

As to the "convoluted motive for suffering," I believe that the concept of "female masochism" is a myth promulgated by men. On the surface it might appear that a woman's relationship with a distant man is a negative experience, something missing or absent. Actually it can be quite involving. All her time and energy is focused on him: wanting him, thinking about him, dwelling on how awful it is that he isn't around more. The relationship, bad as it is, absorbs her consciousness, and in this way it functions like an addiction. (Who says people only become addicted to things that make them feel good?) The relationship is addicting because it relieves pain—by detracting from the need to pay attention to and deal with other aspects of her life. She uses her obsession with him like a drug to avoid her own pain, emptiness, fear, and anger. The more painful it is, the more distracting it is. She may not know who she is or what she wants, but as long as she is embroiled with her unsatisfied longings for him—and it continues to be "his fault"—she can avoid holding still and finding out who she is and what she wants.

❖

Though she yearned for closeness with Stewart, Sharon didn't know much about real intimacy. She grew up in a family with plenty of closeness but little intimacy. What kept her parents together all the time were duties, obligations, social functions, family tradition, and habit. They did everything together, to be sure, but "everything" didn't include opening their hearts to each other. In fact, when she was a teenager Sharon felt all the pain and tension of this constant but shallow togetherness. All she wanted was to get away. What made Stewart so attractive was that he seemed quieter, more serious, and less demanding. But after they were married she automatically re-created the same environment she was accustomed to. We spend years fighting our heredity, but eventually it breaks through.

❖

Pursuers help create and maintain the very distancing that they complain about by resorting to *aversive control*. I've already explained how pursuing a distancer is only likely to make him or her feel pressured, which leads to anxiety, which leads to withdrawal. Never pursue a distancer. Some even more specific approaches make things worse. One is criticizing someone you want more from. Nagging someone to come closer works about as well as kicking your car when it won't start.

In unhappy relationships partners react to problems with attempts at aversive control—nagging, crying, withdrawing, or threatening. Rarely do these couples think to shape positive alternatives, and so the mates feel more and more negatively about each other. If someone yells at you to stop doing something, you will probably feel upset and anxious; you may understand what that person wants, but you certainly won't feel like going out of your way to please them. Of course, when I put it like that anyone can see the point. And probably you can readily identify all the aversive things your partner does. The aversive things you do are harder to see, because, naturally, no one means to be aversive and because what we do is often driven by feelings more than by rational consideration.

Ironically, pursuers get more of what they want when they stop trying so hard. Like a baseball player who learns to relax and swing the bat smooth and easy, you will get more closeness by relaxing your frantic pursuit. Letting go creates the space for other people to come closer *of their own accord*.

❖

Sharon got sick and tired of always having to be the one to buy clothes for the children, so she let Stewart know that Jason needed some socks. "No problem." The next day Stewart came home with two packages of socks. It was great for Sharon because the socks were her size, not Jason's. It wasn't hard for her to avoid making Stewart feel worse by criticizing him—especially since she thought it was funny. The hard part was not going out to get the socks herself. "Don't worry, I'll exchange them tomorrow," Stewart said. The next day he forgot, and the next. Sharon waited; she was not going to say anything. It was astounding to her how hard she had to try to ignore the holes in Jason's socks. When Jason finally came to her to complain, she just said, "Ask Daddy."

❖

If you're a distancer it may be even harder for you to bring about the changes you want. Maybe you've grown sour on the relationship and just want to be left alone. Okay, but you will find that you are freer to spend time alone if you begin to volunteer to spend a little time together. (A little giving makes a big difference.) One other thing, the feeling that it's awful when you are together—she (or he) nags, criticizes, complains, bosses, and bores—is partly a product of the process of getting together. She has to pressure you, feels you don't want to be there—and you don't. What I recommend is breaking the pattern. Switch from passive, grudging, defensive, reactive compliance and defiance to actively initiating contact. It goes a long way. You will reap two rewards: First, by initiating getting together you will lessen the pressure, demands, and criticisms you (both) have lived with. Second, if you initiate doing things you like, you may discover that being together isn't so bad after all.

There are, of course, those who question the idea that some people have an affinity for more closeness and that others prefer more distance. One woman might seem to be one way with her husband and children and another way with her parents. This is a valid and important observation. Although most people have a predominant style, a person's style can vary from relationship to relationship. That's what makes us able to change this dynamic—it's a product of the relationship, not fixed in our character.

Another often-asked question is, "Okay, but how can I change how I feel?" This is one of those "questions" that sounds more like a statement. If you really want an answer, I'd say first notice that your behavior is automatic in most relationships and that it is often part of a complementary pattern. Then all you have to do is experiment with changing the pattern. If you are pursuing a distancer, try backing off, spend more time with your friends. If you're a distancer, try initiating surprise contact with the other person. See what happens. You may begin to feel that you have an enormous ability to regulate the pattern.

Finally, some people complain, "It sounds good, but I've tried moving away and it doesn't work." There's a big difference between *planned* distance and *reactive* distance. If you move away when you're angry, your partner knows it and he (or she) feels a great deal of pressure. Planned distance is different. If you create more space when things are relatively calm, the other person won't feel obliged to come and make amends; he or she will just start to miss you.

Another thing: If you're a pursuer and you move back, then you must try to accept any movement toward you, even if it's done in anger. Some pursuers say they want the other person to express more feeling, but what they really mean is *positive* feelings. If you want the person to move toward you, to be more involved in the relationship, you may have to begin by putting up with some long-avoided complaints.

One final note about my suggestions. Try out one or two changes at a time, and stick with them. If you try a barrage of variations in rapid succession, they may cancel each other out.

# 10

## FAMILY FEUD

"Last one to the car is a rotten egg!" Stewart shouted, then raced off through the parking lot. Jason, now ten, wasn't far behind, running as fast as he could. Heather, panicky at being left behind, bolted in front of a car. The driver braked, but it was close enough to make Heather's heart race.

Stewart slowed his pace to let the kids catch up. Then, when they were almost to the car, he put on a spurt and got there first. He yanked open his door and jumped in. "Ha!" he said with a grin.

Two seconds later, Jason slapped the hood with his hand, just ahead of Heather. "I win!" he yelled triumphantly. "Guess who's a rotten egg?"

Heather looked miserable. "Yeah, but you had a head start."

"So what? You're a rotten egg, and you stink!"

"*Kids*, come on, it's only a game. Don't take everything so seriously."

When they got home, Sharon wanted to know, "How come you two look so grumpy?"

"It's Heather. She's such a big baby. We had a race and she lost. Now she's being a fuss-face."

"It's not fair," Heather said, close to tears. "Jason got a head start, and then he was teasing me."

"Is that right, Jason? Were you teasing your sister?"

"No! She's just a big baby."

At that, Heather broke into tears. "Leave me alone!"

"Jason, you apologize to your sister, right now."

"No, I won't. Why does she have to be such a baby? And you always take her side."

Sharon was furious. "I don't take *anybody's* side. *You* are constantly tormenting her. Why can't you be nice to each other? You're getting to be selfish and mean, and I won't have it!"

Stewart watched, full of anxiety, as Sharon yelled at Jason. He felt he should stop it, but he didn't know how. To Stewart's surprise, Jason yelled right back at her.

*"It's not fair!* You never listen to anything I say."

"That's it, young man. Go to your room."

Jason stomped up the stairs and slammed the door to his room.

"And don't come out until I tell you," Sharon shouted after him.

Stewart was upset. As far as he was concerned, Sharon only made things worse by trying to settle the kids' arguments. *Let them work it out by themselves,* he thought. But as usual, he didn't say anything. He didn't like to get yelled at any more than Jason. Maybe less.

If children learn to fight by watching their parents, then Jason and Heather had little to go by. When Sharon vented her frustration on Stewart, he rarely fought back, at least not openly.

A half hour later when Stewart went upstairs, he was surprised to see Heather in Jason's room. They were sitting on the floor playing Chinese checkers, as friendly as puppies.

*How could they do that?* Stewart wondered. One minute they were at each other's throats, the next thing they were playing together happily. Maybe that was part of the problem. They spent too much time together. That, Stewart was convinced, and Sharon's always trying to settle their disputes, instead of leaving them to fight their own battles, made a bad situation worse.

What he didn't realize was how he fostered competition by making invidious comparisons ("Why can't you be neat like your sister?"); playing one against the other ("I sure like it when you help me cook supper, Jason—you're a lot more helpful than some people I know"), and turning everything into a contest ("Last one up the hill's a stinkpot!").

Whatever the causes, Stewart and Sharon were suffering the effects. At least once a day, Jason and Heather got into a major fight. There didn't seem to be any way to predict or control them. The least little thing would set one of them off, and pretty soon there'd be name-calling and then tears. Going out for supper or to the movies used to be something to look forward to. But now, an escalating series of battles between the children took all the fun out of being together.

❖

Sibling rivalry. People joke about it. Parents are reluctant to complain—friends dismiss it as "normal." So it is, but so too are automobile accidents.

## Sibling Rivalry

*Sibling rivalry* is one of those facts of family life that familiarity has rendered a cliché, robbing the problem of emotional impact. "The kids are fighting? Don't worry, it's only sibling rivalry." Friends and grandparents smile when they say "sibling rivalry." Parents don't. The constant bickering, arguing over who's going to get what, and acute sensitivities that flare into tearful battles whenever the family is together can drive parents crazy.

Why do brothers and sisters fight so much? This familiar question, which has plagued legions of frustrated parents, has a familiar answer. Siblings fight because they're jealous. Every child wants the exclusive love of his or her parents, and with less and less parental time available in busy households, there's all the more reason for siblings to quarrel.

The seeds of sibling rivalry are sown when a new baby comes home from the hospital and gets so much attention. The regression we see in older children at that time is partly an involuntary reversion to more infantile modes of behavior, and partly a deliberate attempt to get more attention.

Most parents could tell at least one anecdote like the following, related to me by a friend.

"It's a story my mother loved to tell, about the afternoon my infant sister was sleeping and the house was suspiciously quiet. She checked the nursery at just the moment when my brother, a mere thirteen months older, had climbed up the side of the crib and was about to lower his rubber tomahawk on his baby sister's head. Mother swooped down, picked up her son and, cuddling him, explained that he couldn't hit Fran on the head with the tomahawk because she was just a little baby. My brother looked up at her and replied, 'But I just a widow baby, too.'"

No wonder the arrival of a new baby provokes intense jealousy: The older child's entire life is turned upside-down. Suddenly someone else has number one priority for mommy's attention. Despite this, we expect the displaced child to be pleased with the new arrival.

Even a child who was convinced to await a new brother or sister with happy anticipation may feel cheated after the baby's birth. The little sibling can't play, doesn't talk, and is little more than a nuisance. Children aren't kidding when they ask whether their parents can give the baby back.

Sibling rivalry is a theme that occurs several times in the Old Testament. The rivalry between brothers for their father's blessing—and, not incidentally, to inherit his estate—led Jacob to drive a hard bargain with the starving Esau and cheat him. Jacob later was deprived of his favorite son, Joseph, when his older brothers united to get rid of their rival. And most ominous of all, Cain's murder of his brother, Abel, stands out as a sinister warning of the consequences of fraternal jealousy. The message of these cautionary tales is clear: Rivalry between siblings is evil. Equally clear is the implication that such feelings should be repressed.

With such dire warnings, it's easy to forget that there is a value to all the fighting between brothers and sisters. Sibling rivalry is natural, and it takes place throughout the animal kingdom. Rough-housing and spirited play, whether between monkeys or kittens or puppies, or your own young monkeys, builds speed and agility. Tussling teaches youngsters how to fight for a place in the world. Incidentally, when animals play-fight they send signals that it isn't serious. So do children, though their parents often don't get the message.

Attempts to establish dominance, among friends and between siblings, makes kids tougher, more resilient. And if you'll notice, kids, like puppies and kittens, have their own ways of keeping their fights within safe limits—especially if they realize no one's around to step in and call foul if things get out of hand. Fighting teaches children how to assert themselves, defend their rights, and—if the scraps aren't interrupted—how, eventually, to compromise.

Much depends, however, on the parents' response. The way parents handle sibling rivalry determines not only how brothers and sisters get along, in childhood and beyond, but also how they feel about themselves and their parents.

❖

One patient of mine, a middle-aged woman, came to see me because she was depressed. Silvia White was the epitome of the self-sacrificing wife and mother, always ready to do something for anyone in need, rarely thinking of herself. Now she was fifty, her children were growing up, and she felt empty. She wondered why it was so hard for her to enjoy herself and why she was—in her words—"such a sucker for everyone else." Although her daughters, ages nineteen and twenty-one, were living in their own apartments, she continued to buy groceries for them and regularly did their laundry.

Like many patients, Mrs. White came to therapy with an idea of what she needed to do to improve her situation: learn to say no occasionally. She tried to use our sessions as morale boosters, telling me who was now demanding what and how she shouldn't give in. Only thing was, she couldn't seem to stop. She knew what she needed to do, but her habit had been programmed in childhood and was hard to change.

Silvia was the youngest of three daughters. When she was four, her father had three successive heart attacks and for the remaining ten years of his life was an invalid. The atmosphere in the house became that of a sick room. Silvia's mother, worried about the effect of any stress on her husband, cautioned the children not to make noise, not to argue, not to do anything that might upset their father. For a young child raised in such an atmosphere, the lesson was indelible: *Don't make trouble.* At least that was the effect on Silvia. Her older sisters weren't as affected by their mother's warnings; they continued to make noise, look after themselves, and quarrel with each other—in short, to act like children.

Silvia's mother, cut off emotionally from her chronically ill husband, turned to her "good girl" for solace and sympathy. She complained to Silvia about the thoughtlessness of her older sisters and came to rely on Silvia for help around the house. Silvia complied and became a little Cinderella—trapped every bit as effectively by love and duty as by threats and punishment.

❖

Another of my patients was a young man who became acutely anxious when he entered graduate school. Despite having achieved a fine record as an undergraduate, Hideki was afraid he had overreached himself. He was, he thought, an impostor who had gone too far and now would be found out. Whenever he was called on to speak in class, he suffered all the symptoms of a panic attack.

One of the things that struck me about Hideki's accounts of graduate school was how he constantly compared himself to his fellow students. He felt they knew more than he did and that he could neither compete with them nor be accepted socially. It wasn't hard to discover the roots of these feelings.

Hideki was a little brother. His big brothers, two and four years older, were intensely competitive. Instead of treating Hideki like a little guy who needed support, they treated him as a rival, one who, because of his age, was always easy to defeat. It seemed that Hideki's mother was always tired and preoccupied with various aches and pains, and therefore unable to fulfill the maternal function of supporting and protecting her youngest. He may not have needed her to interfere, but he did need her to sympathize. Hungry for attention, Hideki turned to his father. He wasn't lucky there either.

Hideki's father was a rough, aggressive battler, a successful businessman who believed that the world was a jungle and only the tough survive. He encouraged his boys in sports and taught them that winning was everything. Hideki couldn't win. Love was conditional, and the condition—defeating his two older brothers— was impossible. No wonder he grew up thinking that he was inadequate, and that when faced with any serious challenge, he was bound to lose.

❖

Most parents develop a repertoire of predictable responses to their children's quarrels, responses based on intolerance of fighting and an exaggerated sense of the parents' duty—and capacity—to control their children. These responses, which usually begin by reasoning with the little adversaries and end with threatening them, interrupt squabbles before the children have a chance to settle them.

Ironically, parents who try to muzzle their children's fighting contribute to their rivalry. Parents who foster competition, either deliberately or without thinking, lock their children into roles (such as calling one "smart" and the other "popula fan the flames of rivalry and resentment. Parents foster competition blatantly challenging one child to outdo the other, and subtly, by making comparison

Parents aren't stupid. Few of us ask younger children to perform as well a big brothers or sisters, and few of us goad older ones to defeat the little on child is different—in age, size, and capability—and therefore should be tre ferently. This makes sense, but feelings aren't always sensible.

Sometimes parents pit one child against another playfully. "Come or see you beat your sister out to the raft." "Who can build the biggest Men do this more than women. Many of us are highly competitive ours though common sense tells us not to encourage one child to succeed of another, in play we often drop our guard and turn a good time don't happen to agree that all children's games should be non point is simply to encourage parents, especially fathers, to be awa into a time where the only way for one child to win is for the ot

Parents also slip up and set their children in competition w they get upset (company's coming and they ask the children clean up the most) or when they're anxious about the outcome (getting good grades in school, behaving politely at important social events, making the "right" friends). Often, parents set up these competitions "in secret." "Don't tell your brother, but. . . . " (Don't tell one child anything "in secret" that you don't want repeated.) Parents wouldn't play these games if they thought about it. The problem is, sometimes they don't think.

Like competition, comparisons turn family life into a contest. Favorable comparisons ("I wish your brother was as helpful as you are") give one child vested interest in surpassing the other. Unfavorable comparison ("Why can't you be neat like your sister?") can prompt a child to decide that if he can't be the best, he can be the worst; to resent the "good" sibling; and to go through life measuring himself against others.

Whether they're praising or rebuking, parents should describe their children's behavior without reference to siblings:

> "Honey, it's so nice when you help me with the cooking. I really enjoyed working on the supper with you."

> "Your floor is covered with Legos; please clean them up, now. I'll be back in fifteen minutes to see if you did a good job."

❖

One of the more insidious ways parents foster rivalry among their children is by casting them into different roles. If one child is "the baby" and the other is "our big girl," the older child may be jealous of the attention lavished on the little one. Instead of feeling more grown-up, the older one may long to be babyish. By typecasting children parents thwart their development. For every positive image any role carries, there are, by implication, negative consequences—all the other roles that seem to be shut. When parents label their children ("my studious daughter," "the family the serious one") they're often projecting their own strengths and weaknesses their children. This not only limits the development of the child—either in the parents' directions—it also polarizes siblings. Putting one tends to cast the other into a complementary role. If one is "neat," if one is "bad" (wild), the other is "good" (tame).

and I were growing up, he was the "big boy" and I was "the gave me an unfair advantage. In any competition, he swim before me, so what? He was older. But if I did "the baby" beat him? He was also "the brain" and he was as athletic as I was (which he's demonstrated), and I was probably as smart as he was. But discovered, had powerful consequences. my best to be a star but never quite making for any teams. And in the brains department, I first-choice college (an Ivy League school) at the good grades and high SAT scores, my image of myself enough.

Perhaps you can recall what role or roles you played in your family, and how your parents fostered those roles. Try to remember; it's a good antidote to repeating the same stereotyping with your own children.

❖

One of the functions of a family therapist is to challenge definitions that limit possibilities. The narrowing of self into fixed roles is reinforced by highlighting behavior that fits the role and ignoring that which doesn't. If Jill comes to be seen as "willful," her parents will focus on the times she argues and overlook the many ways in which she cooperates. If Jack gets labeled as "a poor student," he, as well as his parents, may come not to expect much of himself.

When the construction of identities rests on comparisons among siblings, families pigeonhole their children. As a result, skills atrophy and the children's humanity shrinks. When families present themselves as defined and constrained in some ways, the therapist tells them they are wrong. "No," the therapist says, in effect, "You are more complex than you know."

When families describe themselves and each other, note what they emphasize to the exclusion of other things. It's not enough to appreciate the strengths that families demonstrate. It's also important to probe for untapped potential.

## Enmeshment

The biggest mistake parents make in dealing with sibling rivalry isn't being ignorant of some specific technique of child rearing; it's being overinvolved in their children's lives. Enmeshment, not poor parenting skills, is the problem.

Remember that families are comprised of subsystems with boundaries to protect them from excessive interference. Unless the boundary around a subsystem is clear, the members of that unit won't learn to function effectively.

Without a clear boundary between generations, the parents' executive functioning is impaired. If everyone is the same, no one is in charge. Children must be taught to respect their parents. But parents must also respect their children. Parents who try too hard to *teach* their children to get along violate the boundary around the sibling relationship and cheat the children of the opportunity to *learn* to get along.

By the time our children have grown up and left home, most of us are experts on how to raise kids. We may not know much about children when we begin, but we learn a lot, mostly through trial and error. Trial-and-error learning, as you probably know, works through reinforcement. We try several approaches and keep those that work, and drop those that don't. This is the same way white rats learn to negotiate laboratory mazes; they keep going until they find the cheese. If one alley doesn't have cheese at the end of it, the rat will try another one. The difference between human beings and rats is that we have more complex brains. For this reason, we pursue some paths for years, even though there's no cheese. Maybe next time.

In family life, people are sometimes rewarded for making mistakes. Consider the following familiar scene. A harassed mother arrives at the supermarket check-out line and her small son reaches for a candy bar. The mother tells him it's too close to dinner to have candy, and the little darling starts to wail. Now she's mad. "If you think I'm going to buy you a treat when you make such a fuss, you have another thing coming, young man!" This only escalates the tantrum, and the boy shrieks louder and louder. Finally, exasperated and embarrassed, the mother gives in, saying, "All right, if you quiet down *right now*, you can have a cookie."

Obviously, this mother is teaching her child to demand what he wants; she's reinforcing his temper tantrums. Less obvious, but equally important, is that her own behavior is also being reinforced: giving in leads to peace and quiet. Behaviorists call this *reciprocal reinforcement*, and it's one of the major ways we maintain spirals of undesirable behavior.

I deliberately chose to introduce the concept of reciprocal reinforcement using the example of temper tantrums, because almost everybody knows that it isn't a good idea to give in to temper tantrums. When it comes to fighting between siblings, we aren't so clear. Parents, especially enmeshed parents, interfere too much. Unfortunately, this interference leads to reinforcement. The problem is that sometimes we get reinforced for interrupting a problem, without solving it. Here's a typical example.

Just as the family is about to sit down for a holiday dinner, the children start arguing over who's going to sit where. "I'm going to sit next to Daddy." "No, I'm sitting here." "No, me!" At this point, their mother interrupts. "If you're going to fight, go up to your rooms." The argument subsides, to be resumed later. They always are.

The best thing for parents to do is stay out of the children's arguments. Let them settle it.

❖

Most parents suffer from an illusion of control. We think we can mold our children, protect them, shape them, that we can get them to do whatever we want—what's best for them. When they're little, we *can* control them to a large extent. Using bribes and threats, we bend them to our wills. Some parents never let go. Most of us, however, slowly learn to draw the line between what's theirs and what's ours. We let them pick out the color of a new shirt, we let them choose the pictures to hang on their walls, we may even let them name the family cat. But when they fight, we get upset and step in, offering solutions that only make things worse. We tell them to "be nice," "share," "take turns"—and if we're really brave, "fight fair." As long as parents attempt to control their children's battles, they prevent them from developing their own competence.

In order to respect the boundary around the sibling subsystem, it helps to clarify what belongs in their relationship with each other and what concerns their relationship with their parents. What time they go to bed, who goes to bed first, whether or not the parents will tolerate yelling in the living room while they're trying to read—these things necessarily involve the children's relationship with the parents. Who called who what on the playground, who gets to sit in the front seat of the car this time, and the well-known Who Started It—these things are their business. Parents should stay out of it. Let them learn to negotiate with each other.

The sibling group is a laboratory in which the children learn—or don't learn—how to get along. Some children learn only how to fight in the presence of an over-active referee.

"Yes, but what if they start screaming and yelling and cursing?" They will. If they expect their parents to intervene, they know that no matter what they do they'll be safe. If they come to rely on parental interference, they can escalate their arguments with impunity. They know they won't get hurt or be held accountable, because they know mom or dad will step in. Once adults start interfering, kids will always try to involve them. They'll run to their parents with their complaints—"Kerry hit me!"—and they'll never learn to work out their own rules for negotiating as long as parents keep doing it for them.

If children start to argue or come to their parents with complaints about each other, the best thing the parents can do is to express faith in their ability to work things out, and leave the room.

"Mommy, Mommy, Tommy came in my room and took my flashlight, and now he won't give it back."

"I did not! That was *my* flashlight; yours is in the basement."

"See? I told you. Make him give it back."

"I'm sure you two can work this out. I'm going to finish cooking supper."

One of the worst mistakes parents make is trying to decide "who started it." For one thing it's almost impossible to figure out who started it. When did "it" start? When Jessie called C. J. a "dick head" or when C. J. came uninvited into Jessie's room? Older siblings have an uncanny ability to torment younger ones in ways that are invisible to parents. It must be genetic. They all know how to give that special look. You know, that sneering glance of mockery, flashed faster than a human parent can see. *I know*, I was a little brother. (As far as I know, younger siblings don't do anything to provoke the older ones. At least nothing I can remember.)

Another mistake is to hold one accountable rather than hold all of them accountable. Even if a parent *could* figure out who started it, that's not the point. If a parent must step in, he or she should punish the entire subsystem. That way they'll learn that they're all in it together, and they'll have an incentive to learn to work things out. If parents pick out one kid as the bad guy, they're teaching children not to work things out with each other, but to find a way to appear innocent to adults.

❖

Enmeshed parents also tend to blur the boundaries between their children. They try to be fair, and in the process, they treat unique individuals as though they were the same.

Sometimes a parent who's been traveling will happen to see a perfect gift for one of the children. It might be a souvenir T-shirt for the oldest boy or a poster for the youngest girl. Most parents then feel that they have to find something of equal worth for the other children. This may mean a long, anxious search through gift shops at the airport, or, just as often, deciding not to buy the serendipitously discovered present for the one child.

Forget about being fair. Rather than trying to give equal measured amounts, parents should give to each child according to individual needs. If a parent buys a present for one child and not the others, he or she should explain to them that they saw this one and thought it was perfect; next time, they may find just the right present for them. Children will accept this; they don't mind taking turns. It's only grown-ups who worry about giving every child a gift if one gets one.

Trying to give "equally" to children actually encourages rivalry—"Hey, Sara's piece is bigger than mine!"—and it may blur the distinction between the children. Parents should recognize the difference between older and younger children by giving older ones more privileges—larger allowances, later bedtimes, more latitude in the neighborhood—and giving younger ones additional support and leeway. In the following examples, my point isn't to tell parents what rules to make for their children, but merely to illustrate differentiating between siblings.

It's Friday night and the family is watching television, when "NYPD Blue" comes on. Mother tells Derek [age eleven]: "This show is not for you. You'll have to go upstairs and read." Derek protests: "What about Amy [age fourteen]? How come she gets to watch?" "Because she's older, that's why."

Michael [age eleven] wants to know, "How come you always help Raymond [age eight] with his homework, and you tell me to figure it out myself?" "Because he's only eight, that's why."

With some chores, parents can't win. If mother lets Eleanor [age fourteen] use the snowblower to plow the driveway, she may hear complaints from Teddy [age nine], "I want to do it, too"—*and* Eleanor, "Why do I have to do all the work?"

Once you realize that the children are different (some are older, some are younger) and have different needs (one may need extra help with school work; another may require more, or less, structured activity), answering these questions becomes easier.

What should a parent say if one of the children asks, "Who do you love best?" Most parents answer: "I love you both the same." This rarely satisfies the child. A child who asks such a question is expressing feelings of self-doubt and asking for reassurance. Help the child put into words what's bothering him or her—"What makes you ask that, honey?"—and then explain what's special about him or her. "I couldn't love you any more. You're my special boy, with that wonderful smile of yours and your friendly way with people. You're terrific."

❖

Some enmeshed parents try to control not only their children's relationships with each other but also those with their friends. "How come you're not friends with Katie? She plays the piano and she gets good grades."

Parents care about their children and want the best for them, including the best friends. Parents think it's important that their kids play with certain children and wish they would avoid others. So, they try to arrange their children's social lives for them. The result of this well-intentioned interference is that when we disapprove of our children's choices, they feel we are disapproving of *them*. Moreover, trying to make your children play with other children usually has a paradoxical effect. By blurring the boundary between parents and children, parents intensify the children's relationship with their parents, not with their friends.

It's not what we say to them ("You should make more friends." "Would you like me to call Cheri's mother and ask her to bring Cheri over?") but what we do and who we are that has the greatest effect on whether or not our children make friends.

Children without friends usually have parents without friends. This is because children follow their parents' example, and because parents with no friends of their own are more likely to intrude into their children's lives. Instead of separating themselves from their children and developing their own friendships, some parents can't stop worrying about their children, and worrying for them. They coach and coax, and usually get the opposite of what they want.

Parents should accept the fact that their children are different—from each other and from their parents—and that they have their own preferences. Parents may not like or approve of all their children's friends, but they should respect the children's right to choose and their right to fight their own battles.

❖

I once treated a family who called because fifteen-year-old Jamal was depressed. It seemed that he didn't have any friends and he was lonely. His mother responded by trying to make friends for him and by trying to get the neighborhood kids to stop teasing him. Jamal had complained to his mother that as a new kid in the neighborhood, he got teased a lot at the bus stop. But he was horrified when his mother came to the corner in the morning and told the other kids to stop picking on him. All she accomplished was giving them more ammunition. Now, in addition to calling Jamal a wimp and a nerd, the kids called him "mamma's boy." We can't fight these battles for our kids, nor do they want us to. Listen to their complaints. Sympathize, but don't interfere.

❖

By now I think the message is clear. Just as it's essential for parents to create a hierarchical boundary that sets them apart from their children in order to carry out such executive functions as decision-making and discipline, this same boundary is essential to allow the children room to work out their own relationships with each other and with their friends.

Because they love their children and want everything to work out, parents are tempted to intercede in the children's lives in countless ways, often crossing the boundary between what is the parents' responsibility and what is the children's business. When enmeshment occurs, parents need to do less, not more.

There is, however, one potential problem with this analysis. In talking about the problems of enmeshment, I may seem to be dumping on mothers, favorite targets of psychological analyses. Mothers willingly accept the blame. They're used to being criticized and used to taking responsibility. Enmeshment is *not* something mothers do. It's a *family* pattern. Mothers don't become overinvolved in their children's lives because they're intrusive and controlling. They become overinvolved with the kids to the extent that fathers are underinvolved.

## Disengagement

Stewart reached for Heather's hand and held it tightly as they walked down the aisle—past displays of pastel sweaters, designer jeans, and then a long row of color televisions, all tuned to the same game show—on their way to the bicycle section. It was a long time since he'd shopped in Sears, and he was struck by how big the store had gotten and how it had changed from the store of practical, serviceable goods he remembered to a glittering array of the fashionable and entertaining—keeping pace with the times. When they got to the bicycles, there were a lot more to choose from than he had anticipated. There were three-speed commuter bikes, ten- and twelve-speed tourers and racers, dirt bikes, freestyle bikes with knobby wheels for doing spins and tricks, and something called a "mountain bike," which was a more rugged version of the ten-speed. And the prices! Stewart had thought he'd be able to buy something nice for under a hundred dollars, but the prices seemed to start there and go up.

This was to be Heather's first new bike. She had finally outgrown the one she'd inherited from Jason, and Stewart wanted to be the one who bought her this special present.

"This is a special day," he told her. "You're getting to be a big girl. Mommy and I are very proud of you. You deserve your own bicycle." He was excited, proud of Heather and happy to be able to show it.

Heather was excited, too, but she held it in. In return for this special treatment, she tried to be what she thought her daddy wanted—appreciative but not too eager, hopeful but not too demanding. After they had seen several bikes, Stewart asked her which one she liked best. Heather said they were all nice, but Stewart could see that her eyes kept drifting over to a lavender and white street-style bike. Stewart had seen one like it before. Heather's friend B. J. had one, only hers was red and a little smaller. B. J.'s father was a vice president at Marine Midland Bank. The bike Heather had her eye on had coaster brakes and hand brakes; it also had a removable white wicker basket and a price tag of $149, well over the limit Stewart had set.

"You really like that one, don't you sweetheart?"

"Yes . . . but they're all nice, Daddy."

Stewart put his arms around this sweet child of his and held her tight. "Daddy loves you very much, Heather," and then, to the salesman: "We'll take that one," pointing to the lavender and white.

"Oh, thank you, Daddy! Thank you, thank you, thank you!"

With the salesman's help, Stewart put the new bike in the trunk of his car. When they were settled in the front seat, Stewart asked Heather where she'd like to go for supper. That was the plan, first look for a bicycle and then go out to supper. It was Stewart's favorite way to spend time with the kids.

Heather said she didn't care where they ate, maybe Chinese—which she knew he liked, and he knew she didn't.

"Honey, maybe you'd like to skip supper and go straight home so you can ride your new bike. I could call up and order a pizza."

"Oh no, Daddy, I want to have supper with you."

Halfway to the Golden Dragon, Stewart said, "Let's go home, sweetheart; I bet you'd really like to ride that bike."

"Yes, I really would," came the eager reply.

In Stewart's family, if you wanted a glass of water, you said "No, thank you" three times. Then, having proved that you were no bother, it was okay to say "Yes, if it's no trouble." Like father like daughter.

The minute they wrestled the bike out of the trunk, Heather hopped on and sped off down the block, eager to find B. J. Stewart watched her peddle off, happy for her, happy with her, happy to have given her this moment.

Half an hour later Jason burst in the door, shouting "Goddamn baby!" Heather, two steps behind, was in tears. "Daddy, Jason won't let me put my bike in the garage."

Now what? Stewart didn't mind the swearing so much (although Sharon didn't permit it), but why did they have to drag him into their fights? Why couldn't they just play and enjoy themselves? Why did they always find something to fight about? Goddammit!

"Heather took my spot. I always put my bike between your car and Mommy's, and Heather stole my space."

"There wasn't any room. Besides, you don't own it."

Stewart didn't want to hear any more of this. He was annoyed that they still expected their parents to settle their arguments. He didn't intend to intervene, and so he wasn't about to listen. "I'm sorry, but you two will have to settle this yourselves. Now go away and leave me alone."

Jason and Heather knew when their father meant business and so they left the room. But they didn't settle anything. There was nothing to settle. It was over. There was room for both bikes. What wasn't over was their upset.

What were they feeling? Stewart didn't have the slightest idea. He didn't think about it. The main thing was that they learn not to depend on anyone else to solve their problems, that they learn to work things out independently. That was the main thing. Wasn't it?

Jason was upset because Heather was always getting into his stuff. Ever since she was old enough to crawl into his room, she'd been getting in the way. And he couldn't do anything about it. Mom and Dad were always protecting her, telling him to share.

Heather was upset because Jason called her a baby in front of B. J. He *always* made fun of her. She didn't come to Daddy to ask him to make Jason move his bike, she told him that herself. But it's hard to act grown-up with a brother who knows how to torture you and make you cry in front of your friends.

Both kids went to their rooms and slammed their doors. Separately, they shared the same feelings. Both were angry and frustrated, and both felt cut off from understanding and sympathy. Heather picked up a book and tried to forget about how misunderstood she felt. Jason pulled his blanket over his head and went over the whole thing again in his mind, brooding about how misunderstood he felt.

❖

A clear boundary between parents and the sibling subsystem means maintaining enough distance to allow the children to develop their own competence at settling disputes. Unless the boundary is inappropriately rigid, it also means permitting the children access to their parents to get comforted when they're upset.

When Jason and Heather ran up to their rooms after the fight about the bikes, what were they feeling? Stewart didn't know, and the truth is that the children didn't really know either.

Although we usually speak of feelings as though they were clear and specific, they don't start out that way. Young children's feelings are inchoate, vague. Small children know little more than that they feel pleasure or pain. It takes time, and parents who help by understanding, for children to differentiate between feeling angry and feeling depressed, between excitement and nervousness, or between fear and guilt. You may know people who grow to adulthood unable to make these distinctions—the woman who only feels (is aware of) feeling bad when she's attacked, or the man who instantly transforms hurt into anger.

Parents don't *teach* children what they're feeling. They help them discover what they're feeling, by listening and showing understanding. This lets the children know that their feelings—even "bad" feelings—are natural, and it helps them differentiate chaotic affects into articulated emotions. (This is, by the way, one of the reasons we read novels: because the novelist helps to articulate what we have felt in our own lives.) The understanding that an upset child gets from an empathic parent takes the sting out of unhappy feelings. Unless this happens, siblings may continue to harbor resentments and jealousies toward each other, which fester and grow all out of proportion.

When children argue with each other, their parents should try to stay out of it. But when one of them comes to a parent crying or complaining, that parent should listen sympathetically and let the child know he or she understands. This is easier to do once the parent realizes that he or she isn't going to settle the argument.

When I first started teaching, one of the hardest things for me was listening to students who came in upset after an exam because they got a low grade. "Dr.

Nichols, you gave me a C, and that means I won't get a fellowship." I found these discussions extremely unpleasant and I tried to avoid them. Then I realized that I was confusing two things in my mind: the students' upset and my responsibility for it. Once I decided that my exams were fair and that I wasn't going to change any grades (unless my arithmetic was wrong), it became much easier for me to listen and show my sympathy. "Gee, I'm sorry you got a C. That's a shame. Does it really mean that you won't be able to get a fellowship?" It was implied, but rarely necessary to say, "That's the grade you earned, and I'm not going to change it."

When siblings come to their parents complaining about the other one's pestering or teasing, what do parents usually say? "She didn't mean it." "Just ignore him." "Shut up and leave me alone." As far as solving the problem, some of these suggestions may appear more or less useful. But the "problem" when kids come to their parents is really two problems: working out the disagreement and the child's upset feelings. Most parental responses carry the message *Don't feel that way.*

Parents and therapists should acknowledge children's unhappy feelings about their siblings. This is another example of the enormous importance of empathy. Separate feeling from action. Leave the action to them; help them understand their feelings, and let them know you understand and accept what they're feeling. "You hate it when she does that, don't you?" "Sometimes you wish she would disappear, don't you?" "He knows just what to do to make you mad, doesn't he? And he can do it in such a way that Daddy and I can't even see it—by making mean faces when we aren't looking."

These empathic comments actually help resolve the feelings. Once spoken, and heard, unhappy feelings lose some of their sting. Unspoken, they fester.

When we listen to what children are feeling and let them know we understand, we're inoculating them against shame. Children who aren't allowed to talk about "bad" feelings grow up ashamed of their feelings, and of themselves.

## Brotherhood and Sisterhood

"I'd like my children to be friends someday." These words are spoken with longing and regret.

Behind the deadlines that preoccupy us, and the work that consumes us, lurks loneliness. When we slow down, it catches up. We wish we could be closer . . . to our partners and friends, to our parents, and often, to our brothers and sisters. Parents want more for their children. They don't want them to be lonely. They want them to be friends.

They can be. Only their parents can't make them. Parents can only avoid putting obstacles in their way, and hope for the best.

When the flames of ambition and desire begin to cool, we long for more intimate relationships. One place we turn to is family. We begin to think about our brothers and sisters with fondness and longing. As they get older, siblings turn more to each other. Brothers and sisters help each other out with their own children, trading cribs and hints. And maybe more—closeness and caring. Our conversations may be about today, but they're enriched by recollections of a shared past. Where there is a residue of misunderstanding, we may have an urge to reconcile and reclaim the love we once knew. How successful we are at making connections depends to a large extent on seeds of intimacy sown a long time ago.

Parents can help make it possible for their children to be friends by offering them access without intrusion. Unlike Stewart, they can try to understand and sympathize with their feelings. Parents can make themselves available so that there is less need for their children to compete for their attention.

Sibling competition may be as much a function of access to caring adults as of the inherent rivalry of children. If a family is, like the Salazars, almost a single-parent family, then competition for attention is needlessly intensified.

Sharon's mistake was the opposite of Stewart's. Like a lot of people, she confused intimacy with harmony. As long as the myth of normal family life as placid and cheerful holds sway over the imagination, parents fret needlessly about their children's quarrels. Their fighting and bickering may obscure how much they love and need each other. They may fight to keep from getting too close, or to mask their dependency on each other, or to define their separate identities—or just because they get mad. A relationship with no room for anger is like a dance without touching, gyration without contact.

Fighting is part of intimacy. The sanitized vision of brothers and sisters always playing together cooperatively—"nicely"—without jealousy or anger and without working out these feelings between them, is a desiccated version of intimacy. Kinship without conflict is kinship without passion.

If we teach children to keep the lid on their conflict, to hide the truth of their feelings, we're preparing them for cowardly and constrained adult relationships, lived out within a truncated range of emotion. Blocking children's quarrels prepares them for a future of conflict avoidance and a lasting difficulty sustaining and resolving disagreements.

Sibling relationships are for life, ebbing and flowing, but always there. There are, however, many strains on this bond. Too often, siblings put their relationship with each other second to all others. Many of us are cut off from our brothers and sisters if our boyfriends and girlfriends, lovers and spouses, don't get along with them. For this reason, brotherhood and sisterhood may recede into the background in our twenties and thirties. When the chips are down, as for example in a family crisis, siblings come together. But how close they come may be limited by a history of third parties coming between them.

The greatest contribution parents can make to the sibling bond is the absence of interference. Let them work out their own relationship. Don't compel them to "play nice," or even try to make them play together at all. Let them play if they want; let them fight when they must.

# 11

## LOSS OF INNOCENCE

It was Sunday morning, a little before noon. Outside, the day was pearly white, the soft light from the sky reflected back by the first snowfall of the season. The clean, dry, granular snow clung to the branches of the long-needle pines and the stubby fingers of the spruce. The snowfall that lasted all through the night was over now, though when the wind stirred the trees, little clumps of white drifted to the ground, making it seem that the storm wasn't quite over.

Stewart and Sharon sat in the living room reading the *New York Times*. From his position on the couch, Stewart could see the remains of brunch in the dining room.

Stewart was reading the book review section, hoping to find a new novel that would be fun to read, hoping not to find any "important" literary biographies that he'd *have* to read. Sharon was leafing through the travel section. He glanced over to see which island in the sun she was dreaming about.

Sharon tossed the travel section on top of the growing pile of papers on the floor and walked over to the window. She stood there looking out at the snow. He was ten feet away from her, but he felt the distance. Something he couldn't put his finger on. Neither of them spoke. There is a kind of silence that is almost as loud as a shout. Stewart heard it. It was all around them, thick and hard.

There was nothing to indicate that she hadn't forgiven him for the affair. But he didn't know. She didn't say. He didn't ask.

What he did know was that he felt a chill every time infidelity cropped up in a movie or television program. Did she, sitting next to him, feel the same? She must.

The aftermath of infidelity was like a divorce; they divided the spoils. Sharon got the humiliation, the betrayal, and the self-doubt. She consoled herself with her innocence, but worried about the future. Stewart got the guilt, the shame, and the memory of the most thrilling sex he'd ever known.

They stayed together, but now there was a wall between them. Before, they didn't always talk much, but they *could* talk. Now, it seemed they couldn't. Sharon started going to bed later than Stewart and staying asleep until after he was up and dressed. All to avoid him? It wasn't obvious; he couldn't be sure. And if so, why did she stay with him? Was it love or need?

Stewart tried not to think about the affair itself. *Affair*—he hated that word, but he didn't know what else to call it. It was too painful. From time to time he'd think: *If only I knew then what I know now, I could have prevented all this grief.* Then, often as not, his mind betrayed him. Yes, *but, what about that incredible passion?* His ruminations felt like a shameful version of the old saw: "Is it better to have loved and lost, or never to have loved at all?"

❖

Six months earlier Stewart would have said that for him being unfaithful was impossible. He couldn't imagine it, and didn't. He was embarrassed when his friends made comments about female students. They talked about graduate students, even undergraduates, using crude expressions that made Stewart flinch. This one had "a nice ass," that one had "big tits." Driving back through campus with his regular lunch companions, Stewart was annoyed at all the sexual cracks, which became especially frequent in the springtime, season of renewal, season of halter tops.

One time, when they stopped on the way back from lunch at Colson's News and Variety, Pete and Don opened up a copy of *Penthouse* and said, "Hey Stewart, look at the boobs on this one!" He looked, but felt humiliated. How could they do this in public? Maybe they didn't find these slutty-looking women as disturbingly fascinating as he did. When he looked, he did so in secret, full of shame.

It was late spring when the new secretary was hired. Her name was Angela. She wasn't exactly pretty—her nose was crooked and she was tall enough to be self-conscious about it. But she had a good figure, which she made no attempt to downplay. Her previous job had been in a downtown law office and she continued to dress stylishly, even though she was now in a very different milieu. She wore slinky dresses in rich colors and silk blouses with straight skirts, and a little more makeup than anyone else in the office.

Pete and Don made the expected cracks about the new secretary—"I wonder how *she* got the job"—but Stewart sensed that Angela was too flashy for them. Not for him. He couldn't keep his eyes off her.

Despite the attraction Stewart felt for the new secretary, he kept his distance. Whenever it was necessary to ask her to type an exam or look up a student's folder, he was brief and businesslike. He probably seemed aloof. The truth is, he was intimidated by her sexuality. But after she'd been there about a month, all of that changed.

One Monday morning, Stewart noticed that Angela looked depressed. She kept busy at her desk, but everything took her twice as long as usual, and her smile was gone. Stewart could tell she was unhappy about something, but he was too shy to say anything.

The next day was the same. Angela looked miserable. Finally, late in the afternoon, Stewart came over to her desk and asked what was wrong. "Nothing," she said, "I just have a touch of the flu." Oh, so that was it.

The following day was Wednesday, the day Stewart stayed late to teach his graduate seminar, Contemporary American Fiction. He liked this course because it gave him a chance to reread the authors he loved. Saul Bellow, of course, and Ann Tyler and Toni Morrison, and his favorite, Philip Roth. He enjoyed explaining why he thought Philip Roth was a much better writer than the overrated John Updike. He liked the course but hated staying so late. It made the day too long.

At lunchtime Stewart was sitting in his office with the door closed, eating a tuna fish sandwich and escaping with the latest Dick Francis thriller. It was just getting interesting when he heard a knock at the door. Now what?

"Come in," he said, trying to sound polite.

The door opened and in walked Angela. "Do you have a minute?"

"Of course," Stewart said. "Sit down."

Angela's eyes met Stewart's for a moment, but then she looked down. Her nearness was exciting. Stewart struggled uneasily with his feelings.

"I hate to bother you, but I don't know who else to talk to. You're so different from the other people around here . . . more sincere. . . . You were so nice to ask about how I was feeling, and . . . well, my boyfriend moved out—and I don't even really understand why. He said something about not wanting to get too serious, but we'd been living together for over a year. It's not like I asked him to marry me or anything. . . . I just feel awful." At that she started crying softly.

"Gee, that's lousy," Stewart said. He was no longer intimidated. Instead of an attractive woman, Angela now seemed like an unhappy girl. He felt on more familiar ground.

Stewart listened sympathetically as Angela described how she met her boyfriend; how at first she hadn't wanted to go out with him but had eventually been won over, and then gradually came to feel that they were committed to each other. Now he was gone, and she was alone.

Stewart felt sorry for her, and angry at the man who had dumped her. He guessed the guy must have found someone else and just wasn't honest enough to say so. Otherwise, why move out? This he kept to himself.

After a few minutes, Angela wiped her eyes and blew her nose. "I don't know why I'm boring you with all this," she said. "I know how busy you are."

"Nonsense. I'm glad you felt you could talk to me. Please, feel free—any time."

"Well, thanks, Dr. Salazar."

"'Stewart,' please," he urged.

"Okay—Stewart—thanks for listening."

Stewart stood up as Angela rose to leave. He became aware again of how attractive she was, and he was uneasy standing there. She said good-bye and Stewart took inventory of his feelings. Now that she'd broken the ice, he felt more at ease with her. Sure, she was attractive, but she wasn't at all stuck-up. He didn't think he'd be uncomfortable around her anymore.

As it turned out, Stewart and Angela became friends. It began by him inviting her to walk across campus to get a cup of coffee. Once or twice, he invited her out to lunch. Mostly they talked about what was happening with her boyfriend. She made attempts to get back together, but it didn't work out. Stewart was comfortable playing the same avuncular role he adopted with his students.

One Friday afternoon, suffering from a late-summer attack of spring fever, Stewart asked Angela to go out for a drink. "Let's go someplace swanky," he said, and so they went downtown to the bar at the Hilton. Stewart was nervous, like a kid playing hooky, but after a couple of gin and tonics he started to loosen up. Angela asked him how he got to be an English professor, and Stewart started talking about how he'd always loved books and wanted to be a writer, but how, in college, he felt that he didn't have the talent and so decided to go into teaching. As he talked, Stewart found himself really opening up. It had been a long time.

Angela seemed genuinely interested and asked all the right questions. Stewart reveled in the attention. Sharon couldn't remember what he told her yesterday.

When Angela excused herself to go to the bathroom, Stewart looked around the bar. This was unfamiliar territory. The room was crowded with sleek young men and women, aggressively pursuing the serious business of being friendly. They looked like predators and prey, circling. The singles scene. Stewart began to feel uneasy. He didn't belong here. The he noticed the time and realized he was late. His heart was thumping when he called Sharon to say he'd gotten held up and would be home in forty-five minutes.

"Stewart . . . is anything wrong?"

Could she hear his heart beating? "No, nothing. What makes you ask?"

"I don't know, you sound kind of funny."

"I guess I'm tired, that's all."

"Well, you come on home and I'll fix you a drink, and then we'll have a nice supper."

Stewart drove Angela back to where her car was parked on campus and then went home. Inside the house he felt relieved. Safe and secure.

❖

After that, Stewart started avoiding Angela. He didn't trust his feelings. Oh, he said hello and was perfectly friendly, but he didn't think he should be going out to lunch or having a drink with her. Instead, he put his energy into finishing his book on F. Scott Fitzgerald. He'd written the first half with such enthusiasm, then got bogged down. Now, he got back to it and found that he had a lot to say.

About a month later, on a Tuesday afternoon, the department had a wine and cheese party for one of Don's students who had successfully defended her dissertation. Stewart hated these things. The faculty stood around like ministers at a church social, while the students clustered around like worshipful parishioners, eager for an audience, hoping to break down the usual barriers—and, who knows, perhaps receive a blessing. Stewart went late and left early. Two glasses of wine and a couple of brief conversations, then back to his office to work on his book.

Angela intercepted him on the way out. "You're not leaving already?" she asked breathily.

"Yes, I'm afraid so. I've got a lot to do."

"Too bad," she said, "I'll miss you."

Later, absorbed in his writing, Stewart didn't realize how late it had grown. It was 6:45 and everyone had gone home. He was just finishing up when there was a knock at the door. Before he could answer, in walked Angela, and with her the heady aroma of wine and expensive perfume. She was wearing a yellow silk blouse and a black leather skirt. She seemed edgy. Stewart's heart quickened and his breathing grew labored. Between the two of them there arose a sudden agitation, a breathlessness that was almost painful.

"Dr. Salazar—Stewart—I want to go to bed with you."

Stewart couldn't breathe. Shocked, unable to think, he answered on instinct. "Oh, Angela, that's very flattering. But I'm married . . . happily married."

"I don't care. It doesn't matter."

"I can't. Really, I can't."

Angela started to cry. Stewart's mind raced. She seemed so unhappy. Why on earth had she developed a crush on *him*? He wanted to comfort her; he wanted to hold her. Gingerly, he put his arm around her shoulder. "Don't cry, *please*."

She move into his arms and pushed against him. Stewart was beyond logic. All he could think of was how badly he wanted her. He slid his hand from her shoulder to the front of her blouse. She wasn't wearing a bra. Angela reached down and fumbled with the buttons, opening her blouse for him, but not bothering to take it off.

Stewart felt like a teenager, hot enough to melt. Still, he knew he should stop, so he pulled away. "We have to stop this," he said.

Angela just stood there, her blouse open but still hanging on her shoulders. Her eyes were lidded, her mouth was open, and her lips were wet. She was breathing heavily. Stewart was shaking, uncontrollably aroused. He couldn't keep away from her. Angela reached down and hiked up her skirt. Stewart slid both hands around behind her. She moaned as he pulled her toward him.

Stewart couldn't stop, but he couldn't go on. He didn't know what to do. Angela decided for him.

When it was over, Angela smoothed down her skirt and buttoned her blouse. "I'd better go," she said. "Okay," Stewart replied. Those were the only words they exchanged.

Stewart slept badly that night. His stomach was knotted so painfully that he had to keep his knees bent. His intestines felt like a living thing on fire, writhing and burning. Lying there, trying to sleep, trying not to think, his mind attacked him. *What if I get syphilis or herpes? How could I ever tell Sharon?* He had to find out.

He got up early, and as soon as he reached his office, he locked the door and called Dr. Weis. On the second ring, he banged down the phone. Better play it safe, he thought. So, he picked the name of an internist out of the Yellow Pages. He told the nurse who answered the phone that he was afraid he might have contracted VD and wanted to get a blood test as soon as possible. They were able to take him that afternoon. After drawing out what seemed like a lot of very dark red blood into a tube, the nurse told him they'd call tomorrow.

Another sleepless night. The next day, when the call came from the doctor's office, Stewart was immensely relieved. He'd been foolish, he'd been weak—but he'd been lucky, given a second chance. Now all he had to do was make sure there would be no recurrence.

Angela wasn't at work all that week. She'd said something about taking personal leave to go on some interviews for another job downtown, but Stewart wasn't sure. The following Monday Angela was back at work, and Stewart told her that he needed to talk to her. Could he buy her a cup of coffee that afternoon?

When it came time to go for coffee, Stewart was too nervous to sit, so they went for a long walk. Even though they walked very slowly across the open campus, Stewart's heart was speeding and he couldn't catch his breath. He told Angela that he'd made a terrible mistake. He was sorry. It could never happen again.

Angela didn't say much. She seemed nervous, too. She did say she understood, and, anyway, she had decided to try again as a legal secretary. The work was less interesting, but the pay was so much better. She'd be leaving in two weeks.

For the remaining two weeks, Stewart avoided Angela. Then she was gone. So. That was the end of it.

## To Tell or Not to Tell, That Is the Question

As H. L. Mencken once said, "For every complex question, there usually turns out to be a simple answer. And it's usually wrong."

Most people are way ahead of me on this particular complex question. They *know* you should keep an affair to yourself. The vast majority of men and women in Shere Hite's reports on sexuality felt—even aside from being afraid of their partner's reaction—that it's "more civilized, more polite, simply to keep their extra relationships secret and save their spouse's feelings."[1] Others believe, with equal conviction, that you should bring it out into the open. Frank Pittman, one of family therapy's wisest voices, believes that unless affairs are brought out into the open, they remain a secret source of poison to the relationship.[2]

I don't know. What I do know are some of the ramifications of confessing or remaining silent.

An unfaithful spouse who decides to end an affair—to choose the marriage and fidelity—may feel that it's dangerous and unnecessary to burden the partner with a confession. Dangerous because the betrayed partner may become enraged and demand a divorce; unnecessary because one person's mistake shouldn't be the cause of another's grief.

Infidelity is as much about lying as it is about sexuality. Choosing to remain silent is choosing to handle the problem yourself. It is a vote for silence and suppression.

Confession tests the strength of a relationship. It may produce a crisis that brings the couple closer together, creating an opportunity to close the distance that

---

[1]Shere Hite, *Women and Love*. New York: Knopf, 1987, p. 409.

[2]Frank Pittman, *Turning Points: Treating Families in Transition and Crisis*. New York: Norton, 1987.

made the affair possible in the first place. Those who try to avoid this crisis succeed in perpetuating the distance, reinforcing the wall between partners with guilt and secrecy. A permanent secret may stand as a permanent barrier, fixing a limit to intimacy and honesty in the relationship. It's a lie that makes possible future lies.

Make no mistake, confessing infidelity is almost certain to ignite a firestorm of emotions. This fiery confrontation may, however, make it possible to forge a stronger bond by uncovering and addressing problems in the relationship.

For most people the question of whether or not to confess an affair resolves itself. In the throes of guilt and ambivalence, they manage to get found out. Some of these discoveries may be completely accidental (it *is* hard to commit the perfect crime), but it's often difficult to imagine how the guilty party could be *so* careless, unless he or she somehow couldn't bear the burden of guilty secretiveness. I've heard some remarkable examples of blundering self-revelation from some otherwise very careful people.

There is, of course, the click of the phone hung up when the wrong person answers. Husbands leave love letters in pockets of clothes they give their wives to take to the cleaners. Absent-minded? How often do wives find $20 bills in their husbands' pockets? Some enterprising souls even leave love letters on top of their bureaus. I suppose that way there's less chance the writing will come out in the wash.

Once caught, some people have amazing excuses. My favorite was that of a businessman staying at a friend's house out of town. He was in the bathroom when—before he had a chance to defend himself—a friend of the friend's girlfriend burst in on him, seized his penis, and started committing an act involving oral contact with the male genitals.

❖

Stewart wanted to tell Sharon what had happened, but couldn't bring himself to. This was a turning point in the marriage—a chance for Stewart to risk more honesty, to face the music, and perhaps, to put the relationship on a more honest footing.

He felt as he had when he was a boy standing on a cliff over the lake. His friends were standing beside him. They jumped. He was terrified, equally afraid of diving in or turning around to walk back in shame. He stood, poised to jump, wanting more than anything to prove himself. But he couldn't. He was too scared. Now, Stewart the man could no more risk the disclosure standing between him and greater intimacy than Stewart the boy could prove his courage by taking that dizzying leap into space.

As the weeks passed, Stewart's anxiety slowly diminished. He still felt guilty, but less so. Yes, he was ashamed of what he'd done. But how many men in his position would have acted differently? At least he'd finally done the right thing.

Stewart was totally unprepared for Angela's call. He had no intention of ever seeing her again, yet when he heard her voice at the other end of the line a shiver ran through him. "I have to see you," she said, "it's important." Of course, he said no. "But I have something to tell you." Stewart's thoughts were in turmoil. He wanted to forget about this woman. Yet something in her tone made him afraid. If she got mad enough, she could tell Sharon and ruin his marriage. So, he agreed to find out what she wanted. She suggested meeting for a drink after work. "No, that's impossible," he said. Instead, he agreed to meet her for lunch downtown. "I'll only have a few minutes. Let's make it McDonald's."

Stewart arrived early. He ordered some food and sat down to wait at a booth in the corner.

Angela arrived right on time. She must be making more money, he thought. She was wearing an expensive-looking wool suit, dark brown, with a black satin blouse. She looked good.

Stewart took a sip of his milkshake but he was too nervous to eat. Her eyes caught and held his; her smile was warm and eager. He waited for her to say something. She waited for him to ask.

"What was it you had to tell me?"

Her voice was shaky. "I want to see you again. I think I'm in love with you."

"That's impossible! You don't even know me."

"Don't say that! I *do* know you and I think you're a wonderful man. I don't care if you're married, I want to see you again." As she spoke, her voice got a little loud, greatly adding to Stewart's discomfort.

Stewart's ears were ringing. He was visibly shaking. "Is there someplace more private we can talk?"

They went to Angela's apartment. Vaguely, Stewart knew they were going to do more than talk. But his thoughts were far from clear. Maybe they could just fool around a little.

This time was like before, only this time there was no stopping. When they'd finished, Angela excused herself to go to the bathroom. She returned a couple of minutes later wearing nothing but a pair of satiny red panties. By now Stewart was ready to leave.

"Can I get you something to drink?" Angela asked.

Stewart's throat was dry and so he agreed to have a Pepsi before he left. As he was finishing the soda, Angela slid next to him. "Is there anything special you like?" she whispered in his ear.

Stewart couldn't believe it. No one had ever said anything remotely that exciting to him. His mind went immediately to a scene of a striptease in a pornographic movie.

Stewart had never seen anything so erotic, so wanton. He didn't say so, though. He said only, "I like to watch you undress." Even that, he thought, was too much. That meant there would be another time.

There *was* another time, and another. Stewart felt no tenderness for Angela. It was pure desire. She was of no real importance to him. Just a human being—a human being who deserved what every human being deserves, a little understanding and respect. But Stewart didn't think about that. If he had, he might not have allowed himself to feel such desire.

He tried to bring that same desire, teased out of hiding by his unrestrained passion with Angela, back home into his own bedroom. But Sharon was put off. "What makes you think I feel like making love after spending the whole day working and the whole night picking up after you and the kids?"

Stewart was hurt, and angry. *The hell with her*, he thought. So, he plotted his infidelity with the self-righteousness of an injured party.

Stewart's anger at Sharon gave him an excuse to put off ending the affair for a few more weeks, but he knew it had to stop. This time when he told Angela it was over, he was more definite. There was no doubt in his mind and none in his voice. She became unreasonable, said she loved him, and then, weeping, told him he was a bastard. Stewart was firm. It was over.

That night the phone rang at 11:00. Sharon picked it up but heard only a click. Stewart was panicky, but the phone didn't ring again, and that was the last he ever saw of Angela. A month later he overheard one of the secretaries mention that Angela had moved back to the Midwest.

The following night Stewart and Sharon were sitting in the living room watching *Annie Hall* on television. He'd been a fool to disturb the simplicity and good sense of familiar routine. He'd run a terrible risk, but domesticity had triumphed. Custom crooned its soothing rhythm, and Stewart felt secure again. Diane Keaton phoned Woody Allen to come over and catch a spider in her bathroom. She was terrified of spiders, and her call gave Allen the chance to be her protector. Then a commercial came on, and Sharon asked him, "Are you having an affair?"

Stewart froze. He couldn't say yes, but he couldn't say no. Just an instant of hesitation, and that was that. Sharon became hysterical, sobbing and wailing and cursing all at the same time.

## All Hell Breaks Loose

We've seen how afraid Stewart was of confrontation. For him the first few minutes following Sharon's accusation were a time of unspeakable anxiety. He tried to lie but it was futile. And so he unburdened himself. It was the wrenching confession of a heart laid bare. He told Sharon everything, or nearly everything. Never had he been so afraid, never had he felt so craven. His worst fear was that Sharon would leave him. He would lose her and the children. How little he knew her.

There comes a point in moments of crisis when you know you're going to make it. The car starts to skid at high speed on an icy road, but you narrowly miss crashing and drift toward the safety of a soft embankment. Or you're caught in a small boat in a storm, and you *know* in your bones that you are about to capsize. But then the storm begins to subside, and you realize that you will not drown. Stewart told Sharon what happened, assured her that it was over, burst into tears, and pleaded for forgiveness.

Sharon lashed out like a wounded animal, shrieking, screaming, demanding to know what happened, how it happened, why it happened. If she didn't bend, the marriage would break. When Stewart could no longer bear his torment, he asked her if she wanted a divorce. "No," she said. "I don't want a divorce." At that moment, Stewart knew he would not drown.

Over the next few days, the storm gradually subsided. Both Sharon and Stewart lived every moment with the knowledge that something dreadful had happened to their relationship, but they knew the marriage was going to survive. And although neither one of them would have said so, there were moments when it felt as though the something dreadful had happened to both of them—that they were in this crisis together, and they were surviving it together. Stewart needed very badly to feel this way. Looking back, he knew he was in the wrong, and so now he had that bitterness to swallow as well. Still, somehow he felt relieved, no longer having to bear the burden of his guilty secret. He still had his marriage, his home, his security.

Sharon tried to put away her feeling that Stewart had done this to her, and she did—for a few days at a time. Then all the hurt and bitterness would storm up inside her, until she felt she was drowning in her own private anguish. There was at these moments no love. Her heart was tormented with grief and rage—ugly, awful emotions that crowded out hope and happiness.

So, how does the certainty that your husband was sleeping with another woman feel? Not wretched—worse. Sharon knew what Stewart had done, but she couldn't get her mind around it. She could no more let the image of him naked with another woman into her mind than she could have eaten a rotting fish. It was sickening. Eventually, when she could no longer contain her feelings, she would lash out again at Stewart.

❖

Extramarital affairs are epidemic in our society. Researchers estimate that between 50 and 60 percent of American husbands and 45 to 55 percent of wives become extramaritally involved by the age of forty. When you consider that in many couples only one spouse is unfaithful, this means that the number of families affected may be three out of four.

Despite the high incidence of infidelity, few people think it will happen to them. We take monogamy for granted—as though it were the norm.

Some would say that one reason for the fundamental instability of couples is the differences between male and female proclivities. If so, what happens when both members of the couple are male or are female?

Most of the research indicates that extra-relationship sex is not only more common in gay male couples[3, 4] but also more accepted.[5] Since the AIDS epidemic has cast a pall over the gay community, the unrestrained sexual freedom of the seventies is no longer prevalent. More recent AIDS-era research suggests that coupled

---

[3]Blumstein, P., and Schwartz, P., *American Couples: Money, Work, Sex*. New York, William Morrow, 1983.

[4]Weinberg, G., and Williams, C., *Male Homosexuals: Their Problems and Adaptations*. New York: Penguin, 1975.

[5]McWhirter, D., and Mattison, A., *The Male Couple: How Relationships Develop*. Englewood Cliffs, NJ: Prentice-Hall, 1984.

gay men may be more likely to be monogamous than previously, even though most admit to at least one "slip" during the tenure of their relationship.[6]

Apparently sexual infidelity doesn't necessarily threaten a gay male relationship, and therefore clinicians should not assume, without asking, that such couples are monogamous. Some experts on gay relationships believe that, although it may not be for heterosexual couples, nonexclusivity is a viable option for gay couples. However, if a gay couple wishes to be monogamous, infidelity may have the same destructive impact that it typically does in heterosexual couples.

Because there has been less research on the sexual behavior of lesbian couples, it isn't possible to cite comparable data. However, it would probably be a mistake to assume that lesbian couples are anything like their gay male counterparts when it comes to prevalence and tolerance of non-exclusivity in their sexual relationships.

❖

The aftermath of an affair is one of the most wrenching and painful crises a couple can face. The whole family is rocked, and its structure is undermined by the shock of betrayal.

What can be done until the immediate crisis passes? Hang on. Once the secret is out, expect all hell to break loose—within and between both partners. But know this: Infidelity is a common problem, and one that can be resolved gradually. Those involved—the guilty, defensive adulterer and the wronged, angry victim—may be so nearly overwhelmed with painful feelings that they entertain a variety of desperate courses of action. It's not uncommon to imagine murder, suicide, or flight.

There is no need for immediate action. Wait until the storm passes.

❖

At this most difficult of times, Stewart and Sharon could have used a therapist, not merely to bear up under their upheaval, but perhaps even to turn it to constructive advantage.

The emotional turmoil that's so hard to endure shakes up the system, unfreezing old patterns and making it possible to create new ones. A marriage jolted by an affair can be put back together again; the distance that made the affair possible in the first place can be closed. But two very difficult things must be accomplished: The couple must be able to talk about their feelings, and they must be able to negotiate changes in the relationship.

Stewart and Sharon made all the usual mistakes. Sharon had trouble bearing her hurt and so showed Stewart only her anger. Too much denunciation feels like excessive punishment and may set the stage for future affairs. Even if it doesn't, it drives a wedge between the partners.

Sharon tried to tell Stewart how awful she felt. He tried to listen. His eyes, with tragic intensity, would meet hers for a second, but she always went too far. He would turn abruptly, slam his private door on her, and walk away, feeling like a whipped dog.

[6]Berger, R., "Men together: Understanding the gay couple." *Journal of Homosexuality* (1990) *19*(3): 31–49.

Instead of hearing her, instead of sensing the hurt behind her recriminations, Stewart felt only the peevish shame of the persecuted. And so he never even considered taking the next step, which would have been talking about the dissatisfactions that led to his infidelity and then asking for some changes in the relationship. He hardly even thought about it.

Empathy, at this painful time, works wonders. But neither Stewart nor Sharon could imagine how the other felt. Their own private suffering was too awful and too absorbing. There was no room in their hearts for understanding.

## "Why, Why, Why?"

One of the most unproductive questions people ask about affairs is, "Why?" Deceived partners ask endless questions: What happened? When? Where? How often? Why, why, why? They tenaciously press for details, hoping to undo the feeling of vulnerability to the unknown and unpredictable. This is a game without end; and it's fruitless.

Once the secret is out, the unfaithful partner should be fairly candid about what happened. More lying, at this point, is intolerable. The betrayed partner, on the other hand, is ill-advised to ask for a blow-by-blow account of all that happened. The real motive for these questions is to find a way to still the unbearable doubt and confusion. It's better to talk about these fears directly than to try to put them to rest by asking for endless details. Relentless inquiry about the particulars makes the unfaithful mate feel like a criminal getting the third-degree and is likely to provoke half-truths and outright lies. Let there be an end to lies.

It isn't details that are needed at this point, but finding a way to address two kinds of hurt. The first hurt is a loss, like a death—the death of innocence, the loss of trust. Dealing with this loss is like dealing with any other. The healthy course is to feel the feelings—the pain and the anger—and then to go through a period of mourning.

The innocent, injured party will not be able to put aside her or his feelings of hurt and betrayal. Repression doesn't work. The betrayed partner will need to remember and feel all the bad feelings. However, that person should be aware that his or her mate will be able to listen to only so much of this. It's hard to listen to recriminations when you feel guilty. Every time you bring it up, he or she feels attacked.

When the ugly images come up, they need to be faced; when the awful feelings arise, they need to be felt. Some of this can be done in the context of couples therapy. But not too much. The guilty partner has a limited capacity to hear about these feelings without becoming defensive. The deceived partner may need to talk to someone privately.

If you tell a friend or a therapist that you feel hurt and betrayed, that person can listen sympathetically. If you tell someone who feels responsible, that person may tell you: "It's time to put this behind us." The reason unfaithful mates can't tolerate too much criticism is that it makes them burn with shame.

In addition to feeling betrayed, the deceived partner suffers a second kind of hurt, a wounded pride and a damaged self-esteem. *What's wrong with me?*

Some people don't ask this painful question; it hurts too much even to allow it into consciousness. These people keep their self-doubt buried beneath a smoke screen of rage and blame. But for most people whose partners have an affair this is the hardest part of all—feeling rejected, and feeling that the reason must be their own inadequacy.

At a deep level, we're all insecure, though we work to forget how vulnerable we are. Infidelity jolts the memory. On the other hand, is a partner's unfaithfulness really a confirmation that there's something wrong with you? As a therapist, I've sometimes asked people who feel that way, "Who elected your partner The Great Arbiter of Human Worth? If you lined up in a row all the people who really know you well, would they say you're unlovable? If they knew about the affair, would they say it must have been your fault?"

❖

Then there is a different kind of why—not the obsessive search for reassurance, but an honest exploration of the reasons for the affair.

If there is an affair, there must be something wrong, right? Therapists can do a real disservice by presuming that they know why people have affairs: "There must have been something missing in the relationship." As opposed, for example, to those relationships from which nothing is missing? As though things being less than ideal explains infidelity—and, not incidentally, indicts the betrayed?

As a family therapist, more interested in the future than the past, I find it less useful to worry about the motivation for an affair than to look at the relationship for the reasons it wasn't prevented and the potential for possible recurrences. Often the adulterer—such an ugly word—is the weaker partner, the one who's unhappy but not honest enough to say anything about it. Affairs are like mutinous rebellions against a mate who is perceived as a controlling and depriving parent.

The likelihood of an affair is a product of three things: opportunity, the strength of desire, and the power of defenses. The magnitude of unsatisfied desire is related to the fulfillment found in the couple and also to the fulfillment found, or not found, in other avenues of satisfaction. Although some people pursue sex outside a committed relationship because their personal standards permit it, more of these people are found in popular fiction than in real life. Far more common than the calculated adulterer is the person unprepared to defend against unanticipated temptation.

Discussing the whys and wherefores of infidelity is complicated by the fact that affairs take so many different forms, from one-night stands to chronic philandering; from purely erotic dalliances to passionate romances. There are compulsive conquest seekers, partners in open marriage, homosexual liaisons in heterosexual marriages, and relative innocents (free of experience if not responsibility) like Stewart. I have emphasized the example of Stewart's unpremeditated, clandestine affair not because it's the only kind, but because it may be the most common.

Among the many motives for infidelity are anger, frustration, rebellion, boredom, jealousy, revenge, curiosity, need for acceptance, and of course, sexual desire.

We look for two sets of needs to be gratified by our partners: sexual and emotional. Over the years there is much disappointment. The soul-searing, dizzying kind of love can last forever—if, like Romeo and Juliet, the lovers die at the height of passion. In real life, romantic love fades. Some people can't accept that.

At the time he met Angela, Stewart was a prime but unsuspecting candidate for an affair. He and Sharon had drifted further and further apart. He was frustrated and angry about the lack of sex in their relationship. His own frustration and sense of inadequacy were compounded by anxieties and self-doubts about his career— anxieties and self-doubts that festered within him. Finally, although like Jimmy Carter he had lusted after women in his heart, he never imagined acting on his fantasies. He certainly never imagined having to say no to a woman who made the first move.

"Eve tempted him?" Sure, and he let himself be tempted, not only by sex, but also by the need for affirmation. The nature of a couple's bond may be more important in determining not what happens, but what happens afterward. Triggered by sexual desire—which, once ignited, became a fire out of control—Stewart's affair was fueled briefly by hostility toward Sharon. Most affairs are sustained as much by resentment as anything else.

In *Women and Love,* Shere Hite points to a similar motive as the prime reason married women have affairs. Most married women, according to Hite, are emotionally alienated from husbands who are unable to give them what they most desire, intimate connection. It's this emotional hunger that drives women into the arms of other men.

Hite concludes: "Having an affair can put new love and humanity into one's world, enabling one to go on living." In other words, the affair "props up an inadequate marriage,"[7] as though the relationship were a thing that existed outside the control of the person who is unhappy.

I've treated several married women who had sustained extramarital affairs, and all of them expressed similar motives. They felt stifled and stagnant in their marriages. The affairs made them feel more alive and appreciated. This is precisely the motivation Shere Hite is talking about. She claims that the needs of women in our culture aren't met in marriage, and it's therefore understandable for women to have affairs. That may be, but in the cases I treated there was some confusion about where the problem lay.

Where is the problem: in the relationship or in the person? All of the unfaithfully married women I've treated began their affairs in their thirties or early forties. All were unhappy with their lives. They'd been in a rut and were in the process of finding themselves. Some discovered, or rediscovered, dormant artistic talents; others found new life through exercise and sports. It was at this time in their lives, this time of emerging from a cocoon of self-denial and drudgery, that each of these women met her lover. The men were art teachers, writing coaches, karate instructors, and others involved in some newly discovered activity. And like most partners in affairs, they were opposite sorts of people to the women's mates—not

[7]Hite, *Women and Love,* p. 409.

better, different. The lovers were part of the process of renewal, but were the affairs cause or effect?

Most of these affairs were partly the result of a personal reawakening. Perhaps that same energy could have been applied to revitalize those stagnant marriages.

It's said that an affair can revive a moribund relationship, reawakening one partner's sexual desire and creating a crisis that brings up dormant conflict. Sounds good, but it's equally likely for an affair to keep a bad relationship going or destroy a good one. Affairs are still the most widely accepted justification for divorce.

The stories in Shere Hite's book of married women's unhappy lives are remarkable—remarkable for the recurring theme of loneliness and emotional distance, but remarkable, too, for the lack of appreciation that couplehood is a relationship between two people and that both partners might have a role in their problems. And remarkable as well when unfaithful wives compare their feelings toward their lovers with their feelings toward their husbands. A woman in love is like a man in love. Temporarily insane.

It's crazy to compare a lover to a long-term partner. One woman in Hite's study remarked on how nice it was that her lover didn't care whether or not the ironing got done. So? Most of us felt the same kind of passionate love toward our sweethearts before we got married. If you must compare, compare that.

## Moving On

An affair is a product of drives and defenses in the individual and the balance of forces in the couple. An unfaithful partner may be trying to shore up sagging self-esteem, desperate for sex, compensating for career setbacks, looking for love, or just tired of looking after everyone else. As a family therapist, my approach to helping couples move on is to ask: "Why couldn't these dissatisfactions be dealt with in the couple?" The point isn't that we lose personal responsibility and initiative just because we're members of a couple, but that strengthening the partnership is often the best way to enrich the lives of its members.

Once an affair is over, it is productive to consider it a symptom of missing satisfaction in the relationship, and then to find ways for both partners to work together to achieve greater satisfaction.

From a family systems perspective, infidelity is related, as cause and effect, to disengagement. Disengagement makes affairs more likely, and more possible. Affairs aggravate disengagement, and the extent of disengagement affects the outcome.

Committed and in love, most couples start out very close.*

$$H \quad \vdots \quad W$$

*For purposes of illustration I will describe partners as husband (H) and wife (W), although obviously not all committed couples are married, or heterosexual.

In time, however, tension and conflict enter the relationship. Even the best relationship.

$$H \approx\!\!\approx\!\!\approx W$$

Despite their efforts to resolve these tensions, most couples begin to move further apart, increasing the boundary between them as a way of avoiding the pain of conflict. Perhaps both move apart. Or they may establish a distancer-pursuer pattern.

$$\longleftarrow H \quad | \quad W \longrightarrow \qquad \longleftarrow H \longleftarrow W$$

Over the years, the rigidity of this boundary increases the likelihood that competing relationships will become more intense. If the couple has children, the boundary between one or both parents and the children will be diffuse, and the boundary between one or both partners and outside interests will also be diffuse.

$$\text{Career} \; \vdots \; H \; | \; W \; \vdots \; \text{Children} \quad \text{or} \quad \text{Children} \; \vdots \; H \; | \; W \; \vdots \; \begin{array}{l} \text{Friends} \\ \text{Career} \end{array}$$

Among these "outside interests" are affairs.

$$\text{Lover} \; \vdots \; H \; | \; W \quad \text{or} \quad H \; | \; W \; \vdots \; \text{Lover}$$

From this perspective, the immediate goal is to redraw the boundary around the couple, and then move them closer together.

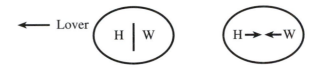

The first priority is damage control; keep the couple afloat by ending the affair. If the unfaithful person promises to end the affair but doesn't, the couple's relationship may turn into a game of "Who's lying and who's crazy?" The hardest thing to forgive is a faithless partner who promises to end an affair but is then discovered to have been lying, again. The betrayed mate feels doubly violated. If the one having the affair is openly unwilling to end it, it may be wise for the couple to separate. Often the spell of an affair is broken during a separation. Unfortunately, by then it may be too late.

Are separations sometimes a good idea? Maybe. In my practice, I used to refuse to treat couples if there was an ongoing affair or a separation. My position was that I couldn't help a couple work on their relationship when there was insufficient commitment or too much emotional energy invested elsewhere. Now I'm not so sure.

Drawing a boundary around the relationship involves strengthening the couple's commitment. "Commitment" is one of those much-used words that have taken on the status of clichés. If you're like me, you may start nodding off when someone talks about commitment. Nevertheless, commitment is one of the essential ingredients in a strong relationship.

Commitment is never more important, and never more difficult, than in the aftermath of an affair. It's the glue that holds the family together when not all of them feel like staying together.

Commitment is another name for the boundary around the couple that protects the relationship from outside interference. The same boundary—commitment—protects the relationship from dissolution during hard times. With insufficient commitment, there is little pressure to face each other, and little protection against dissolving the relationship if (when) hard times come again.

Note well: Moving disengaged partners closer means surfacing buried and avoided conflict. Couples don't distance themselves from each other without reason. The reason is conflict, and it must be addressed or the distance won't be closed.

Moving closer—breaking down a rigid boundary—requires speaking up and listening. Both partners must voice their resentments and negotiate unsatisfied needs if they are to feel like moving closer. And both must be open and receptive to their partner's feelings, complaints, and requests—if they want that person to feel like being close.

Most people are intuitively aware of the need to address unsettled old business before they can move on to a more stable and satisfying relationship. But most people have great difficulty avoiding the same pitfalls that drove them apart in the first place—blaming instead of asking for changes, and withdrawing in the face of attack instead of speaking up.

Communication involves talking *and* listening, but it's hard to do both at once. What passes for communication in many couples is both parties talking, either taking turns or competing for the same turn. This kind of spontaneous give-and-take may work when discussing relatively safe subjects, like movies and restaurants. It's almost impossible with emotionally charged topics—the gut issues of couplehood.

So, make sure the partners take turns. If they have trouble doing so, help them by meeting with them together but talking with them one at a time.

Finally, it's important to realize that every couple has limits on how much closeness it can sustain. In the aftermath of an affair, people who want to strengthen their relationship will need to move toward each other—sharing more of their hopes and expectations, as well as disappointments and resentments. But therapists should be careful not to impose utopian ideals of openness and intimacy. A good rule of thumb is to have modest expectations, take small steps, and be alert for signs of the anxiety that signals that someone's tolerance for intimacy has been exceeded.

❖

Bringing up, talking over, and getting through conflict is the most important step in opening up a rigid boundary between two people. However, in some couples, after the partners have cleared away unresolved conflict, little is left. Over the years the relationship has petrified—a living thing has turned to stone.

It may, therefore, also be necessary to work at creating a renewed vitality in the relationship. A therapist can help by encouraging partners to open themselves to the possibility of being interested once again in their mates. The greatest secret to finding interesting people is to be interested. Urge the partners to express their care, and love, and concern—even if they have to work at creating them. The couple will find each other's interest as refreshing as a sudden shower on a hot day.

Urge couples to find ways to spend more time together. This, too, may take some work—the shackles of habit don't just fall away under good intentions. Suggest that they make a list of their ten favorite activities. Then note when they last did these things. They may be in for a shock.

Have them compare lists. Scheduling time together to do those things they both like is the easiest place to start. Then have them consider taking turns sharing their individual interests. Maybe one likes outdoor activities, such as camping, canoeing, hiking, picnicking, stargazing, playing outdoor games, bicycling, walking, running, and swimming. The other one may prefer movies, restaurants, concerts, and dancing. Suggest that they try to strike a balance among doing things together just as a couple, doing things separately, and doing things as a whole family (if they have children). Strong couples balance time alone with time together.

❖

Stewart and Sharon got over the affair. Time passed, life went on. The marriage survived.

Stewart realized that he'd been bitter and angry about the lack of sex in the marriage. And so, when things calmed down, he was more insistent on getting Sharon to make love. But instead of trying to rekindle their friendship, Stewart waited for his chance to rush into passionate sex. That was his way, holding himself in until his self-control reached the breaking point, and then making a nervous, pushy assault.

At first, Stewart was on tenterhooks. He watched Sharon very carefully, looking for a sign that it was okay to make a sexual advance. That had always worked in the past. A month went by. Stewart grew more frustrated and more anxious, but because he didn't want to make the wrong move, he didn't make any move. He didn't hug Sharon, or hold her hand, or even kiss her good-bye. Exercising what he considered self-restraint, he gave the impression of being cold and uncaring.

Then one night the barrier between them seemed to melt. After a dinner with candlelight and wine at Luigi's, Sharon asked Stewart if he wanted to go to the movies. Surprised, he said sure. Sitting there in the dark, watching a prettier version of life flicker past on the screen, Stewart felt Sharon reach over and take his hand. After a few more minutes, he moved his hand to Sharon's lap, and she held it there with both of hers.

Later, when they were in bed, Sharon came over to curl up beside him. Stewart lay stiffly, wondering what to do. After a few minutes of holding himself back, he felt an upsurge of desire and pushed himself against her, hard and insistent.

Sharon had been ambivalent, uncertain. She wanted to end the cold war but needed time before opening herself completely again. Stewart misread her signals and pushed through her ambivalence. She let it happen. What else could she do? To turn him down now would only lead to more hurt and withdrawal.

The result was a repetition of what had happened on their wedding night. It had been late, very late, and they were both very tired. Nevertheless, Stewart felt they had to consummate the marriage. It was a bad idea. Sharon went along, but it was the beginning of trying to do what she didn't feel like doing, and it was the beginning of the end of her passion for Stewart. It was their wedding night. She did it. It wasn't very good. Compliance had been a mistake then; it was a mistake now.

Sharon felt used, turned off. After that, sex between them dropped off once more, and again Stewart started avoiding her. Guilty and angry, he pulled away, in the bedroom and in the relationship. Soon Sharon was again feeling emotionally deserted, and again she responded by pursuing and attacking. Stewart was no longer willing to hang his head and slink off, but he was no better able to listen. He just started fighting back.

The arguments were more frequent now, every few days. Angry shouting matches, touched off by a thousand things. Jason and Heather were older now. They heard everything. They hated it, each in their own way. Jason was angry. Heather was scared.

# 12

## DIVORCE, REMARRIAGE, AND STEPPARENTING

Late one night Heather awoke to the sound of her parents arguing. Their voices were loud and mean. She tried to shut out their angry words by pulling the covers over her head and mashing the pillow around her ears. But even though she couldn't make out what they were saying, she could still hear the noise. It seemed to go on forever.

Finally a door slammed and the shouting stopped. The only sound Heather could hear was her mother crying. *Maybe they'll get a divorce*, Heather thought. So many of her friends' parents were divorced.

❖

When we hear that someone is getting divorced, we often say, "I'm not surprised." But sometimes our reaction is, "Them?"

One friend of mine has never said a word of complaint about his wife. He never talks about his marriage at all. The only thing I know is that they do very little together. How happy they are, or even content, I have no idea.

I know another couple who fight all the time. Going out to dinner with them inevitably means listening to their sniping and griping. It's been that way for twenty years. Maybe they're just one of those couples who do most of their fighting in public, where the presence of witnesses keeps them from taking the gloves off. The truth is, no one but the participants ever really knows what a relationship is like.

❖

They met at the University of Wisconsin. Ed was a freshman; Kathleen was studying to be a physical therapist. She was a green-eyed girl who glanced up from a cup of coffee in the student union to find a ruddy, handsome boy staring at her.

She looked away. But he came right over and struck up a conversation. That's how it started.

He saw her as buoyant and energetic. "She looked very Irish—I felt comfortable. We both had liberal political values, though personally we were very conservative."

Kathleen thought Ed was very smart. And he was sensitive, more gentle than most of the boys she knew. But he was strong, too. "He seemed sure of himself, and very outgoing. He certainly knew how to have a good time. I guess I liked that because I was so shy."

Their courtship was a stormy one. According to Ed, "Sometimes we had a great time. But at the big events—parties, dances—we'd have problems. Big fights. If I paid attention to anyone but her, she'd feel rejected and withdraw, and that would spoil everything."

Once on a skiing weekend with friends, Kathleen thought Ed was flirting with his roommate's date. So she went to her room and wouldn't come out to join the party by the fire. She felt he wasn't paying enough attention to her. He thought she was being a big baby. They had their worst fight ever. "I should have known then," Ed told me, "that we weren't right for each other."

Many unhappily married people look back to conflicts that cropped up when they were dating as warning signs they should have heeded. But powerful yearnings overrule a lot of doubts.

Sometimes things were wonderful. Ed recalled a formal dance at the Palmer House in Chicago. Kathleen was visiting her folks in Green Bay and a big snowstorm hit. "I thought the weekend was off. But she drove down in her father's pickup truck. All that way! And she looked sensational. She wore a black strapless gown. God, she looked just like Ann-Margret."

Ed didn't hesitate when I asked him when he decided to get married. "I always wanted to get married and have a family. It was never a decision. It was just a matter of time."

When Kathleen visited Ed in the fall, they had another of their fights. By now Ed was sick of it. When she left, he thought, *Good riddance.* Neither of them called or wrote. Then, on Valentine's Day, Kathleen sent Ed a red terry cloth bathrobe with a hood. It opened his heart. In an excess of loneliness, Ed drove up to see her, and it all started again.

"We talked about getting married," Kathleen remembered, "but the big question was where to live." That question, however, and all it involved was pushed aside by the need to plan the wedding.

It was a big wedding, lots of family. Both of them were happy. And yet here, too, there was a moment. Ed was upstairs in the hotel with his best man, getting dressed to leave for the honeymoon. Looking off into the trees in the distance, his eyes grew watery. Why, he didn't know. He was happy and sad at the same time. "Hey, bridegroom," his best man said, "you look like you're gonna cry." They both laughed at the idea.

Two months after the wedding Kathleen was pregnant. When is the best time to have a baby? I don't think there's any formula, but this was probably too soon.

Before the couple had a chance to work out their own relationship, they had another adjustment—and another distraction.

Ed fell in love with the baby right away. "Those were the days when they didn't let fathers in the delivery room. I remember going to the nursery and seeing all those babies. And then her. She was right up front, with her cute little pink face, all smiles. In front of her was a sign: 'Girl O'Brien.' She was mine."

That year was a good one. They kept busy, doing something every weekend—trips to Chicago, going to plays at local colleges—and they stayed very involved with their families. Kathleen said, "We added excitement and other people to our relationship."

Would Ed and Kathleen have been able to forge a stronger bond if they'd built a stronger boundary around their relationship? I don't know, but without it there was less of a chance.

Often after the worst moments in their marriage, Ed and Kathleen experienced a sudden release from their torment as they forgot themselves in some new venture. The baby, their hectic social life—later there would be other things. "We had so many distractions, we didn't think about our relationship," said Kathleen. Ed remembered this as a time of feeling fulfilled, happy. Most of his memories, however, were of the baby.

The next distraction was moving to New Haven, where Ed went to graduate school. Only it was more of a distraction for him than for Kathleen.

Ed was in his late twenties, living in the stimulating atmosphere of a great university, surrounded by interesting people. As he put it, "I was in my glory." Kathleen felt left out. She began to resent being treated as "Ed's wife." The marriage went from bad to worse. Kathleen got depressed and began seeing a psychologist. The psychologist insisted that Ed come too, but he refused. "She's the one who's miserable," he said. "Let her go and get herself straightened out." This touched off one of their worst fights. Afterward, Kathleen said she was thinking of moving out.

Ed was stunned. He had taken her more or less for granted while he got on with his career, but losing her was unthinkable.

Considering how he had blinded himself to problems in the relationship and how little either of them got out of it, I thought this was an odd reaction. Perhaps the heart of the matter was that to Ed the idea of being a whole person was tied to being married and having a family. It wasn't so much Kathleen he was afraid of losing, it was being married.

❖

Often it's in therapists' offices that abstractions about marriage and divorce become real and immediate. Some people already have one foot out the door—even though that may not become apparent until after a show of trying to work things out. But when it comes to the hardest decision most people will ever make, it's more common to look for guidance. That's a nice way of saying they find someone to relieve them of the awful burden of making up their own minds.

What separates therapists from advice-givers is the ability to pull back and not take sides. The time to practice this skill is when one person tells you a story about how another person mistreated them. When it comes to powerful and provocative decisions, like whether to leave an unhappy relationship, it's hard to resist the pressure to help people resolve their ambivalence.

When people ask what they should do, it's easy to say, "I don't know. You'll have to figure that out for yourself." But it's hard to remain truly neutral if you aren't aware of your own biases. Pretending you don't have them only allows them to work in the dark.

Another thing to watch out for is clients who induct you with projective identification. To my lasting shame, I remember a woman who consulted me after she'd had a brief affair. She was depressed and wracked with guilt. "I am a vile and disgusting person," she told me. She was just getting warmed up. After a couple of sessions of this, I finally said, "Do you think you're the first person who's ever had an affair?" That's about all I said, but she took it as permission to take love where she found it. So she left her husband for the new man in her life, and they lived happily ever after, for about six months. After that she was a single mother.

It's no good saying that my statement was an innocent one. It apparently conveyed an attitude about something I had neither thought out nor had any personal experience with.

With or without a therapist's influence, when things get bad enough and people think they're prepared to deal with the consequences, they get divorced. When that happens, some people make a lot of mistakes. Divorce isn't something most people have much practice at.

❖

Because Ed refused to go to therapy with Kathleen, much of the advice she got concerned how to make herself happier, rather than how the two of them could improve their marriage. Few therapists ever take direct opposition to a marriage, but when one partner goes alone there's a danger that his or her dissatisfaction will become magnified. Individual therapists say, "Be honest. Be true to yourself."

Since Kathleen had raised the threat, Ed had to confront the possibility of divorce in his own mind. When he did so, he had to face his own dissatisfaction. So he turned to the coping mechanism he had always relied on: self-improvement. He started working out in the gym, to make himself stronger.

Then something shifted. Now he wanted out. But he couldn't find a way to tell Kathleen. Finally, he told her in an awkward, roundabout way. She cried. She was confused, unsure of what was right. Finally, she conceded that maybe he was right. Ed was unaccountably upset. That wasn't what he wanted to hear. Though he hadn't known it, he was hoping for a declaration of reassurance.

That same week, Kathleen found out she was pregnant again. When she told Ed, it was the first time she'd ever seen him so happy. That discouraged her. She didn't really want another baby, and besides, his reaction made it clear that it wasn't her he cared about, only the baby.

Kathleen had a miscarriage in the third month. The doctor told them there was no way it would have ever gone full term. "It just wasn't meant to be."

Once again they got sidetracked. Ed finished graduate school, and they started making plans to move to Madison, Wisconsin, where he got a job in the state government. Talk of moving and houses brought them together. Some couples can talk about a lot of things—children, jobs, friends, politics, whatever. Others get into arguments about any one of these things. The number of subjects two people can discuss without becoming reactive is one measure of the strength of their relationship. Kathleen and Ed could talk about houses and furniture.

For a time they were content. But then the same old things started happening. Ed's job consumed him. Kathleen talked more and more about moving out. She kept complaining about being saddled with a house and child, and she had trouble finding a job she felt satisfied in. She blamed the marriage for holding her back.

Kathleen went to a lawyer; then they went together. "Get yourself an attorney," Kathleen's lawyer told Ed. "I don't want a divorce," was his answer. "I'm sorry, but your wife does," she said. At first they agreed she would leave in order to reestablish herself professionally and find the freedom to move ahead with her life. But then Kathleen changed her mind. Two years went by. Two years of hostility and indifference.

Then Ed got a chance to spend a month in Ireland. There was no question of Kathleen's going, they were so alienated. Being on his own was a relief. Now he could think. There's so little thinking in families, normally such a jumble of need and conflict. In Ireland Ed fell in love with the timelessness of the landscape, and he began to think about his marriage in a more detached way.

When he came home he saw a lawyer and sued for divorce. Kathleen wanted to tell Meagan, now twelve. Ed wanted to put it off as long as possible. "Wait till we know what the arrangements will be." Finally he agreed to tell her. Meagan knew, of course, about all the tension. But she never guessed her parents would ever actually split up.

Ed fumbled for words. Meagan sat silently, her back to him, fiddling with one of her stuffed animals. He tried to keep from crying. She asked only one question, "When?" Then she said she didn't want to talk about it any more, and went down to watch cartoons. He followed her. "How about if I make us some popcorn?" "Good idea."

Months went by before they could get a court date. It was an agonizingly slow process.

The trial was ugly. Each of them had to say hateful things—lies, too—as if the truth weren't bad enough.

The judge was Catholic and very conservative. He called Meagan into his chambers and said, "Who do you want to live with?" Is there a more cruel question to ask a child? She said either one, but she wanted to stay in her house.

Then the judge said to Kathleen and Ed, "You two should be ashamed. You have a wonderful daughter. Why couldn't you work out your differences?" It was stupid and mean thing to say, but it was what they were feeling, too. "After considering all things, I'm going to award joint custody; but Meagan shall reside in the home with her father."

Ed felt a rush of relief. Kathleen didn't flinch. That night, Meagan stood at the top of the stairs and watched her mother pack. After she was gone the house looked empty.

❖

Divorce is like a death. There is a profound loss, a wrenching upheaval, and a need to remake one's life. But unlike death, divorce carries with it a sense of personal failure. The death of a mate is a brutal loss, but one that's surgically clean, clear-cut, and final; it carries no stigma. In divorce, the family is severed by a blunt instrument. Nearly everyone gets bloodied in the process.

## Families in Transition

Let there be no mistake, divorce is a wrenching, painful process. Unfortunately, the common perception that divorce means the end of the family only makes things worse. Divorce isn't an ending, it's a transition.

For husbands and wives and children, divorce is a loss and a liberation. For the family, it's a transformation from an old pattern to a new one. The family system has to maintain some subsystems, shed others, and develop new ones.

Much of the trouble in divorce is due to a blurring of the distinction between marital and parental subsystems. "Ex" and "former" refer to the marital relationship, not the parental one. Boundaries between divorcing couples must be strengthened to facilitate the individuation of the partners, boundaries between parents and children must be kept open enough to allow contact, and new relationships will require further complex boundary-making.

To begin with, it may be useful to realize that there are actually two processes in the divorce transition: separation and reorganization.

## Uncoupling

In the process of separation, almost everyone goes through periods during which they can't seem to manage. Their feelings are a jumble of griefs. At times, everyone involved will be confused—unsure of how they feel, unsure of what the other person intends to do, unsure of how to respond, and unsure of where all this is heading.

It may help to think of separation as divided into three phases: deciding to separate, physically separating, and restructuring the family to stabilize it after the separation.

The decision to separate often seems to be made primarily by one person. At least it seems that way.

❖

Glenda was a twenty-four-year-old graduate student who quickly outgrew her husband. It was easy to see that they were a poor match. Jack was handsome and had a good heart but was poorly educated and interested mainly in having a nice house and a family. Glenda was a creative intellectual whose talent and interests soon took her a long way from the lower-middle-class neighborhood where she'd met Jack. Within two years after they were married, Glenda had grown entirely dissatisfied with her husband, but somehow couldn't do anything about it, directly. Having dinner at Glenda's house meant getting a well-prepared meal but also listening to the hosts squabble. I'm not sure which was worse, Jack's inane conversation or Glenda's cruel, cutting remarks.

At the time, I was sympathetic to Glenda. Jack *was* boring. Glenda was lonely, she felt neglected; as time went on, she acted out her fury toward her husband. She stayed out late two or three nights a week, she was blatantly insulting to Jack in front of company, and when he complained in private, she laughed at him. After about six months of Glenda's calculated abuse, Jack announced that he wanted a divorce. Friends weren't surprised to see the couple break up—but they were surprised that it was "Jack's decision."

❖

Mitchell had a midlife crisis at thirty-seven. He was unhappy, and he blamed his marriage. When they came to therapy, he asked his wife to make some changes. He wanted to have more fun, get outdoors, go sailing, play tennis—enjoy life. What's more, he wanted Audrey to do all these things with him.

Audrey agreed to spend more time together and do more of the active things Mitchell liked. Still, Mitchell wasn't sure he was happy, and he felt that Audrey wasn't as expressive with him as he wanted.

While Audrey was sympathetic to Mitchell's unhappiness, she was annoyed that he put it all on her. However, she didn't think this was a good time to express her dissatisfaction with all his demands.

Because things weren't quite right, Mitchell moved out to think things over. To help him think, he went into individual therapy. As a result of his thinking and consulting, Mitchell decided that he wanted to be happy and keep his wife. He told her this and gave her a list of demands, ways she would have to change to make the marriage more satisfactory.

At first Audrey thought the separation was her fault: She had failed to keep her husband happy. After a while, she realized that wasn't true; they had never been terribly happy. Audrey would have liked to save the marriage, but she saw Mitchell's demands as putting all the responsibility on her. She didn't want a relationship where all the change would be unilateral, so she told her husband, "No, if that's what you want, I want out." A week later, they were separated. Who left whom?

❖

Uncoupling begins as a private decision. One person broods over hurts and mulls over the possibilities of what to do about them. By keeping these dissatisfactions to himself or herself, the unhappy partner initiates a breach. Silence protects the ability to think things through, but deprives the partner of the chance to understand—and the opportunity to respond.

At some point, the partner who's more actively dissatisfied gives up hoping for change and begins to view the relationship as unsalvageable. He or she now accentuates the negative, reversing the earlier process of idealization. Dissatisfaction is often magnified by seeing alternatives that look better—other relationships that seem happier, the lure of an affair, or the freedom of the single life. (The joys of single life are often especially clear to married people.)

Thinking about leaving is a crisis that triggers anxiety, and whenever anxiety rises in a relationship people tend to triangle in third parties.

I remember one young couple who came to see me about a marital problem. When I asked what the problem was, the man said he was in love with someone else and he was leaving. He wasn't kidding; he got up and left! He didn't have a marital problem, he had a separation problem—a problem he handled by leaving his wife in my hands, so that he could wash his.

When a couple is moving from decision making to physical separation, it's a good idea to talk to a lawyer. But lawyers can be part of the problem instead of part of the solution. In structural terms, there should be a clear boundary between the partners and their lawyers. (*Yes*, two lawyers.) Ask around for the names of experienced matrimonial lawyers. (But unless you're looking for a bloodbath, avoid lawyers with nicknames of predatory animals.)

❖

Becoming partners is a process in which two individuals restructure their lives into a unit: The Couple. Friends invite The Couple over for dinner; the IRS taxes The Couple; The Couple accumulates belongings; mail comes addressed to The Couple. Separation is a reversal of this process, in which members of a couple gradually redefine themselves as individuals, disentangling their belongings and identities.

Before the separation, things may not have been pleasant, but they were predictable. Uncoupling shatters these routines.

Separated partners feel rootless, without established roles to guide them. If you're separated, do you go to your office Christmas party alone? If the school requests a conference, do you tell your partner? If your friends know that you're separated, do they invite one or both—or neither—of you to a dinner party?

One man was surprised that his family understood and accepted his divorce. He was equally surprised to discover how his friends deserted him. "No-fault" applies only to the legal process; it's not a concept congenial to families and friends.

I've heard many separated people say bitterly, "Now you find out who your real friends are." Well, real friends may be just as confused as the separating partners. Encourage partners to tell their friends how they feel and to ask for whatever support they want.

❖

Once the decision to part has been made, physical separation requires a restructuring of the family. When a parent leaves, three subsystems are radically altered: the couple, the parental unit, and each parent's relationship with the children. The most functional structure at this time consists of a clear boundary between the couple while maintaining the parental subsystem as a problem-solving unit.

Suppose we look at what happens to a family when a husband leaves his wife:*

```
    H     W            H  /  W
    F     M            F     M
 - - - - - - -      - - - - - - -
    Children            Children
```

The fact that husband and father, like wife and mother, are the same person makes this adjustment easier to diagram than to achieve.

In a good marriage there's a boundary between the couple as partners and the couple as parents. In a failing marriage, however, when the couple's relationship ceases to meet the needs of both partners, it may decrease in importance or become so enmeshed with the parental subsystem that this boundary is eroded. When these distinctions become blurred, it's difficult for separating partners to recognize where their relationship ends and their obligations as parents begin. Boundaries must be clarified.

When the possibility (real or imagined) of reconciliation is present, reorganization is tentative. Separation requires a less rigid boundary than divorce. If a husband leaves, his family must readjust; if he returns, these changes must be reversed. If he was disengaged, his separation and reentry may solidify the coalition between mother and children. If instead of reconciliation the separation leads to divorce, structural changes can be stabilized. Separation is disorganizing; divorce is reorganizing.

## Reorganizing

After a divorce people need to let go and get on with their lives. This takes psychological work and a reorganization of the family system. Emotional acceptance requires that the lost love be mourned, which can take as long as a year. No one but those who've gone through it know how terrible divorce is. A therapist can

---

*Once again, I will illustrate the process of separation in terms of "husbands" and "wives." Obviously, these aren't the only possibilities.

be helpful by empathizing with what the individuals are going through—not trying to cheer them up with rosy promises or talk them out of feeling that they "shouldn't be" feeling as bad as they do. Try to remember that mourning is a healing process; don't attempt to subvert it.

The interval of grieving doesn't start, though, until the reality of the loss is accepted. I've seen many sad cases of depressed partners who prolonged their suffering because they couldn't accept that the relationship was over.

In cases where one partner seems to be clinging to unrealistic hope of reconciliation, arranging a conjoint meeting can be useful. The partner who wants out, but is reluctant to say so directly (because he or she can't face the mate's grief and anger) will usually be more honest in a therapist's office.

This is the time to let go of bitterness and blame. One way to help someone get perspective on their bitterness is to ask them who in their family was a bitter person. In other words, help them get over thinking that bitterness is something inflicted on them and realize that it may be partly that, but also partly a result of a family legacy of feeling like a victim.

Once they give up the bitterness that's been consuming them, people are liable to feel empty and lost. Rootlessness is hard to bear. It may help to realize that these feelings are part of the process of uncoupling from old dependencies and becoming one's own person again. If divorce is a destruction of order, it's also an optimistic reaching for authenticity.

❖

Viewing the postdivorce family as a reorganized system helps us recognize the importance of clarifying boundaries and establishing clear and separate roles for subsystems. Each parent and his or her children form one subsystem. There will be two households but only one family system. Regardless of what type of custody is awarded, two things are essential for the welfare of children: a stable and predictable arrangement and access to both parents.

Although joint custody is becoming popular, it's still more common for one parent to have guardianship. The custodial parent and the children are often called a "single-parent family," but this isn't strictly accurate.

Let's look for a moment at the structure of this unit.

Custodial Parent
- - - - - - - - - -
Children

This diagram is as incomplete as the following one is for an intact nuclear family.

Mother
- - - - - - - -
Children

Obviously, the father is left out. Whether he's involved or disengaged, he still belongs in the picture. If he's disengaged, that may suggest the need for changes—namely, getting him more involved with his wife and children.

A single parent and his or her children have similar structural needs; namely, that there should be a clear boundary between parent and children, and the parent should develop sustaining involvements outside the relationship with the children—with friends, family, probably a job, and perhaps a boyfriend or girlfriend.

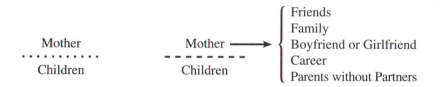

Loss of access to the noncustodial parent (usually the father) is associated with problems in children's adjustment to divorce, while loss of access to the children is associated with problems for fathers. Mothers with sole custody report more depression from the overwhelming burden of taking care of the children without help. To prevent—or minimize—these problems, divorcing parents should remain civil enough to coordinate whatever version of shared parenting they chose.

The parental subsystem after divorce is a limited partnership. A clear boundary is best. Some people ask, "Can't we be friends?" There's nothing wrong with being friendly; remaining entangled is another matter. Enmeshment may take one of two forms: either the partners try to preserve their intimacy or they continue battling.

If parents fight after they're divorced, older children may withdraw from both of them. Younger children choose sides. Most kids long for a natural relationship with both parents. Parents shouldn't create loyalty conflicts for their kids by criticizing the other parent.

Permissiveness often becomes a special problem for divorced parents as children learn to exploit inconsistencies between households. Parents may be demoralized. It's difficult to assert parental authority when you're confused and lonely, especially if you depend on your children for companionship. If each household is clear about rules and roles, children can switch back and forth comfortably. Some parents allow guilt over what's happened to make them give in or make speeches when the children say, "*Daddy* lets us watch whatever we want on TV." Clarity, not symmetry, is important for the children's adjustment.

Because they tend to think of themselves as visitors, noncustodial fathers often feel pressure to entertain their children ("Uncle Dad"). A father can arrange special activities for his visits—roller skating, movies, expensive suppers—but he can't program meaningful conversation. He may console himself with the notion of "quality time," but there's no substitute for being there.

Guilt and distance combine to make noncustodial parents doubt their authority. Some are prone to sermonize. Seeing less of the children, they have fewer opportunities for discussions and often try to cram everything in with heartfelt lessons about life. Many noncustodial parents are insecure and wonder if their children will hate them for the rest of their lives. This makes them overly sensitive, and over reactive, as the following example illustrates.

❖

Barry was divorced for two years and living with Jeanette. Every other weekend Barry drove 245 miles to pick up his children and take them to his apartment for the weekend. Both he and Jeanette worried about the children's feelings and were ever alert for signs of insecurity. One Saturday night Jeanette told Markie, age eight, that it was time for his bath. When Markie started to fuss, Jeanette told him sternly that it was time for his bath, whether he felt like it or not. Markie ran upstairs crying. Barry went into Markie's room and, after finding out what the problem was, comforted his son by saying that he shouldn't worry, "Jeanette and Daddy love you." ("What's love got to do with it?") From downstairs, Jeanette could hear Barry talking to Markie and she felt excluded, so she went upstairs and began a lengthy—and unnecessary—explanation of what had happened.

Hearing this story, I felt sorry for all three of them—all that anxiety. If I were in a similar position, I hope I could remember to continue to treat children as children (let them complain if they want, but expect them to obey) and not worry that they would stop loving me if I spoke firmly to them.

❖

There is little evidence that the rise in divorce rates indicates disillusionment with marriage. Eighty percent of divorced adults remarry within three years, opening new possibilities, but also a host of hard problems.

## Blending

Before they can get on with the complicated business of developing a new structure, with new rules and new traditions, stepfamilies must deal with unfinished business from the past. Stepfamilies are born of loss—death or divorce. Homes are disrupted, schools and friends left behind. Children are often hurt and angry. They need assurance about their well-being and time to mourn their losses.

Children do a lot of scary thinking. They've seen their parents stop loving each other. For a child, that can be like seeing the earth open up beneath your feet. Children of divorce are at high risk to develop problems with intimacy—making and sustaining close relationships. It isn't seeing the parents break up that's the worst thing, it's the fear of being abandoned.

The most important thing for remarried parents to keep in mind is the need for structure. Children need security and predictability. They need to know where they're going to be next week, at Thanksgiving and Christmas, and during the summer.

To develop and maintain a clear structure, it's important for the children's parents to work together as a team. Otherwise, they're liable to triangle in the children or new partners. New partners usually know how much emotional energy is used up carrying on a vendetta with "the ex"—although if they're insecure they may be relieved to perpetuate the ex as a villain, a repository for unresolved bad feelings, and a scapegoat for future conflict.

Kids hate it when one divorced parent refers archly to the other as "*your* father" or "*your* mother." To them, it's still "Mom" or "Dad." Similarly, it isn't fair to expect them to call a stepparent—a stranger—Mom or Dad. First names are easier. Children shouldn't be pushed into instant love with their stepparents. Where is it written that stepparents and children will love each other?

## "You're Not My Mother!"

The most difficult role in a remarried family is likely to be that of stepmother. Any child can tell you what word modifies *stepmother*. *Wicked*. Custodial fathers often try to turn over the care of the children to their stepmother. After all, mothers take care of children, right?

When children complain that a stepparent isn't their real parent, they're right. What works best is for the biological parent to be in charge of his or her own children. He or she is the only one with the moral authority to discipline. The stepparent should begin as an assistant parent and given time to ease into a more fully sharing role.

Support goes both ways, though. Although the biological parent remains primarily in charge, he or she should teach the children to respect the rights of the stepparent.

In one family I treated, the father assumed full responsibility for the discipline of his two children from a previous marriage. What brought the family to therapy was the stepmother's complaints that the children were rude and disrespectful to her. Not being in the role of disciplinarian, she wasn't sure what to do. My advice was simple: I suggested that the father tell his children, "This is my wife; you will treat her respectfully, or you will answer to me." That seemed to work.

The best way to develop a relationship with someone is to spend time alone with that person. However, it's best not to push. Initially, the child's time alone with the stepparent should be brief and casual—perhaps a walk to the store, going to a movie, or playing a game together. Look at it from the child's point of view. Suppose your parent falls in love with someone new. Suddenly you're competing for your parent's time and affection with a stranger. How would that make you feel?

### *"It's Got to Work This Time"*

Having "failed" once, remarried parents often feel a tremendous pressure to create a happy family the second time around. What may seem equally obvious—that the new couple needs time alone together—is, unfortunately, easily forgotten in the pressures of dealing with the children.

❖

One of my cases was a couple married after the man was divorced for the second time. He was consumed with guilt over the possible harm his divorces might do his children and consequently was acutely concerned about their needs. His wife, married for the first time, was equally aware of the children's sensitivities, and eager to be accepted by them. Both partners were so worried about the children that they were reluctant to exclude them from any of their activities. The result was a kind of driven stuck-togetherness. The children didn't have time to be children, and the couple didn't have time to be alone. Until they were able to use therapy to help them draw a boundary around their relationship, they were in danger of letting their fears—another traumatic dislocation of the children—become a self-fulfilling prophecy.

Children may be the most vulnerable members of the family, but it's important to remember that the life of the family depends on a strong couple bond.

❖

Sharon and Stewart didn't divorce. Oh, they thought about it, all right, but something held them together.

# 13

## SEX, DRUGS, AND ROCK 'N' ROLL: THE REBELLIOUS TEENAGER

Time is funny, isn't it? You're waiting in the airport on a rainy night for a delayed plane, and half an hour seems like forever. Then one day your birthday catches you by surprise. Suddenly, instead of eighteen, you're thirty or forty, wondering where all those years went.

❖

Sharon could hardly believe that Jason was sixteen. Not long ago he was a mischievous little elf; now all of a sudden he was a hulking adolescent. Almost overnight, it seemed, her little boy sprouted hair on his face, and his baby fat hardened into broad muscles. Heather, too, had changed. The once cheerful and slender little girl had become a moody teenager, unable to conceal—but not quite ready to accept—her developing curves.

Heather still spent a lot of time with her mother; they went shopping together and sometimes even exchanged clothes. Sharon liked to joke that they were "best friends." But Heather often lapsed into periods of gloomy self-absorption. She had her father's talent for withdrawal.

The change in Jason was even more dramatic. He'd grown from a willful little boy to a defiant young man. He fought Sharon over everything—clothes, chores, curfews, drinking, homework, grades—everything! Sharon was worn out, sick and tired of all the arguments. But she was afraid to relax her grip, afraid that Jason was too cocky to exercise good sense in the wide world of adolescent temptation and adult risks.

When the children were little, the house was large enough to provide islands of privacy. Now, Sharon felt that they had taken over and there was no room left for her. The four of them were like cats in the city, too crowded to stay out of each other's territories, with the inevitable results. Fur flew and there was plenty of shrieking caterwauls; but nothing ever got settled.

By the time Jason was thirteen, Sharon found that nothing she served for supper pleased him. He picked at his food. If she told him to eat, he complained that it was lousy.

The problem wasn't really food. Jason was challenging the rules that governed their relationship. He was getting to be more independent, more defiant. But Sharon still expected him to accept her choice of what to eat. She reacted to his defiance with a mix of resentment and anxiety that he wouldn't get the proper nourishment. When she intensified her efforts to make him eat a decent supper, he escalated his refusals to comply. In Jason's eyes the relationship should have become more one of equals; in Sharon's eyes, Jason was a big boy, but he was still *her* boy.

All parents go through this struggle with their children. The only things that vary are the personalities and dispositions of the parents, the temperaments and inclinations of the children, the relationship between siblings, the parents' different reactions to different children, the influence of the children's peers, and the parents' relationship with each other. That's all.

After Stewart's affair and the couple's abortive attempt to resurrect their intimacy, Stewart pulled further away from the family and Sharon tightened her grip on the children. Heather accommodated; Jason rebelled. He grew angrier every year, frightening Sharon with his defiance and recklessness. Some nights he stayed out until one or two in the morning. Once he didn't come back until dawn. They tried all the usual punishments—grounding, taking away his allowance, making him do extra work around the house—but nothing seemed to work. Besides, Sharon wasn't sure punishment was the answer. She began to think that something was wrong with Jason.

He was so changeable. One day he'd steal $10 from her purse and lie when she confronted him; the next day he'd come to her for a hug and tell her that he needed her to act more like a mother and not always be picking on him. Sharon was never sure who she'd be talking to when Jason walked into the room.

❖

A person is made up of many and diverse strivings, likes and dislikes, moods, wants, and fears. The search for a self—the famous "identity crisis"—comes from the effort, not to create something, but to find harmony and integration among these strivings, purposes, wishes, and ideals.

❖

Heather was going through the same struggle to discover who she would become, but she kept her questions about herself and doubts about her parents' values to herself. She was as quiet as Jason was obstreperous.

People often ask, how can two children from the same family be so different? The fact of the matter is, they aren't born into the same family. Jason was born into a young family, with a father preoccupied with his career and a mother eager to devote herself to her baby. Both parents were unprepared for the strain of caring for a demanding infant, and that strain divided them. Heather was born to a more experienced couple. Her mother was tired, less willing to do everything for the new baby. Her father was aware that he couldn't abandon his wife to all the burdens of child care, and so he helped out more.

Then, too, there were differences in temperament. Jason was fussy, Heather was placid. Even where such differences are slight, they aren't static. Instead, like so many complementarities of family life, these differences get polarized.

When the first child comes along, the parents create a niche for him. Jason was the "lively" child—demanding and assertive, but also energetic and forceful. Whatever Jason did that didn't fit this image wasn't acknowledged. Thus is formed a powerful persona that convinces a child: *I am this and nothing else.*

Sharon was willing to have an aggressive, outgoing son, but her own sense of femaleness dictated that Heather should be less demanding. Sharon didn't want her daughter to become another source of aggravation in her life, and didn't want her to grow up to be as defiant and ungrateful as her brother. Stewart was happy to have a vigorous son and an affectionate daughter. Jason was his frisky puppy, Heather was his cuddly kitten.

And, of course, children have a polarizing effect on each other. Jason, who was jealous of Heather's easy, affectionate ways, thought of her as a goody-goody, and stiffened his resolve to be tough. Watching his little sister cuddle up with Mommy made Jason embarrassed by his own dependency needs. Heather, the younger sibling, was even more profoundly affected by watching Jason's progress through childhood.

The older sibling's legacy is a morality play interpreted by the younger child. So frightening to Heather were Jason's fights with their parents that she made a secret vow always to be good. In the wake of her big brother's storminess, Heather would be calm. She controlled her passions to avoid fights, but overcontrol led to apathy and withdrawal. When she was little, she put on a mask of passivity; as she got older, the mask became a prison.

Adolescence can be a time to correct the narrow reality of a family—to discover and actualize dormant potentialities of the self—but for this to happen a child must venture far enough to be exposed to wider realities. Heather stayed pretty close to home.

Heather learned not to confide in her parents because she didn't want them to be hurt or disappointed. She tried to be what they wanted. But she felt inadequate because she couldn't meet what she thought were their expectations. Stewart made a point of telling her how smart she was, even when she brought home Bs and Cs on her report card, and Sharon reassured her that she was popular, even though Heather knew she wasn't. But being human, Sharon and Stewart had a subtle way of letting her know when they were disappointed, and Heather read these clues like a twelve-year-old Sherlock Holmes.

So exhausted by Jason's escapades were Sharon and Stewart that they took Heather for granted. She never seemed to get into any trouble, so everything must be okay. Beginning at about age eleven, she began to slip away from them, retreating more and more inside herself. By fourteen she would be a mystery to them.

Sometimes when she watched her father and mother arguing, Heather thought, *They* couldn't *be my real parents*. She didn't belong in this family, she must have been born into it by mistake. Her father didn't usually argue back; Mom just yelled at him, and he just sat there. He yelled plenty at her and Jason, but he generally didn't say much to Mom. Every once in a while, though, he'd lose it.

Mom would be nagging him about something or other, and he'd explode, screaming at her at the top of his lungs, calling her all sorts of names until she ran out of the room crying. Heather watched with scared eyes, afraid the storm might engulf her. They didn't see her, though—as if she weren't even there.

When this happened Heather would go to her room and close the door. She felt safe in her bedroom—her special place, her refuge. She'd carry Sally, the cat, up with her. They'd had Sally since she was a little white kitten. Now that she was older, she pretty much ignored the family. She hunted for mice and fought to keep other cats out of her yard at night, but during the day she just lay around. If she stretched twice in the same hour, it was a major event. Sally was supposed to be the family cat, but Heather knew different. Sally was *her* cat. Who else loved her so?

Heather would lie down on her bed and put Sally on her stomach. Gently, she stroked the soft, silky fur—she had to be very still or Sally would hop down and walk off, looking for someplace to sleep undisturbed. Heather petted her very slowly, very softly, hoping Sally would fall asleep, or at least stop twitching her tail, and condescend to stay. Heather didn't want to be alone.

❖

Things got worse between Jason and his parents. The angrier he got at them, the more he sought refuge in the great preoccupations of adolescence: sex, drugs, and rock 'n' roll.

Parents rarely know very much about their children's involvements with these things. They have their fears and suspicions, but as to what's really happening, they have only clues. Often these clues match what the children are most conflicted about, things they seem to want their parents to discover.

I was to get two sides of the story of Jason's wildness. To his parents, Jason seemed reckless, defiant, and self-destructive. They saw him fighting with an excess of spirit against their "few and sensible" rules. They were concerned that he might be experimenting with drugs, but they weren't sure. They also worried about his deteriorating performance in school. Their confusion about what they should and shouldn't try to control made it doubly hard for them to respond effectively. According to Jason, he was just doing what all the other kids did.

Sharon's version of events was pieced together from what she discovered and what Jason chose to defy her about. Once she began finding well-worn copies of *Playboy*, *Penthouse*, and even *Hustler*, in Jason's closet, her greatest concern was pornography. Stewart was less concerned. He said it was just a phase, don't worry.

Sharon was furious. She thought her son was ruining his life—and hers too. She yelled down for him to come upstairs, and when he finally clomped up to his room he was mortified to see what she had in her hand. But she was so mad, she couldn't see that. She screamed at him, scalding him with her vituperations. Jason couldn't stand it, and he stormed out of the house.

Jason didn't come home for dinner that night, and he didn't call. When he finally walked in the front door at 2 A.M., Sharon thought he looked drunk. "You've been drinking," she said, trying to sound more certain that she felt.

"So what?" was Jason's reply.

This was new. His denials were bad enough. But this was different. "So what?" was worse than a lie. It was scornful mockery of her authority as a parent.

Sharon's fury was choked off by a feeling of impotence. She managed to make "Go to you room!" sound angry and disgusted, but she was scared.

## That Awful, Awkward Age

Hell, with all its famous inconveniences, is only slightly more intimidating than raising a teenager. Most parents begin to notice a change in their children a little before they turn thirteen. The kids start to become sarcastic, they answer back, they begin to look more like adults, and they're more threatening.

I remember, for example, when my own daughter was twelve, she began taking a tone with me that I found hard to accept from my little girl. Once she was looking for her hairbrush and asked if I saw it in the living room. I couldn't find it, and said, "I don't know, honey, I don't think it's in here." She replied in a voice I was completely unused to, "Then where the hell is it!" I was speechless. It wasn't the "hell," it was that tone.

These early signs of "disrespect" and "defiance" are the hallmark of adolescence, and the parents' response is critical.

What most parents miss is the *circularity* of parent-child relationships. They see their dear, sweet children turning into sneering, ornery adolescents. What they overlook is their own failure to accept their children's growing autonomy. What's really ornery is their insistence on growing up.

Parents underestimate the mutuality of their interactions with their children because they overlook the systemic nature of the family. Teenagers and parents are, of course, separate individuals, but they are also part of a unit. Each member of this unit is torn by competing forces—one pulling in to preserve the stability of the family, another pushing out to establish the autonomy of the individual.

The individual is both a member of the family and a separate person. At various times of their lives, some individuals are more related to contexts outside the family than to the family. The following diagram depicts the Salazar family at the time Jason entered adolescence. You can see that some family members are more contained within the family than others.

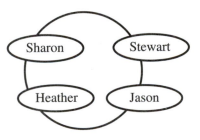

What the diagram suggests is what family members assume: that the family is static. Like Sharon and Stewart, the diagram overlooks the reality that the family unit is unstable. Jason is moving away.

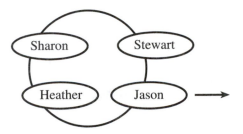

Jason pushes for autonomy, his parents pull for stability. Teenagers struggle against the family's constraints. Parents struggle to maintain family cohesion and enforce the family rules (the old rules, the ones that used to work). Together they are a family in transition. Conflict is almost certain because the parents want to slow the transition, while the teenager wants to speed it up.

❖

I once treated a family in which the presenting complaint was the sixteen-year-old daughter's "defiant" behavior. This defiance turned out to be almost laughable: She sometimes stayed out thirty minutes past her curfew, she had to be reminded to clean her room, and when she got mad at her parents, she walked out of the house and slammed the door!

This was a family with eight children. The three who were younger than sixteen were very close to their parents, and very obedient. The four older children were out of the house; none of them was on speaking terms with their parents.

The youngest of the oldest (nineteen) had recently been banished by her mother. Her crime? She married a boy she met at a church social. The mother liked the boy and approved of the marriage. Her only reservation was that she felt three months between the engagement and the wedding was too short. Her daughter insisted; she wanted a June wedding. Each of them dug in her heels, until, as had happened three times before in this family, the mother told her daughter that if she didn't obey, she'd have to get out.

If this example seems extreme, that may be because it is. The dynamic, however, is universal. A family structure that doesn't bend, eventually breaks.

❖

Adolescence is almost inevitably a difficult time for the whole family, but it needn't be as antagonistic and wounding as we've come to expect. It can be altogether more pleasurable, even exhilarating, for everyone in the family. The adolescent is a conduit to the world at large, bringing new styles, new attitudes, new information—even a new language—into the family. Adolescent children help keep their parents up-to-date; they keep their parents informed, and they keep them on their toes. Often, however, the infusion of new ideas is unsettling.

The adolescent becomes a critic—challenging parental beliefs, exposing hypocrisies, and undermining long-standing prejudices. Although it's possible for parents to accept and appreciate this challenge as good for their children and good for themselves, many parents are threatened and fight back. This often begins an escalating series of conflicts, which in many cases are never settled, only broken off when the children leave home. Too bad, because children need their parents. For all their opposition to their parents and breathless enthusiasm for the adventures of adulthood, adolescents still need their families.

Parents react to their children's adolescent passage in two ways. They're resentful, jealous, even competitive, but at the same time they feel joy and pride in their children's growing autonomy, their vigor, and their assertiveness. The secure parent will grasp the fact of having become a target for the child's self-assertion and will respond with tolerance and respect.

When an angry teenager demands to know *why* he has to be home by midnight, an understanding parent will ask him to express his point of view—*and* will listen to it. After hearing the child's opinion, the parent will rethink the rule—not necessarily change it, but not automatically insist on sticking to it—*rethink* it, taking into account the child's growing ability to make his or her own decisions but reserving the final decision for the executives of the family. This is a shift from a complementary position ("Because I'm your father, that's why!") to a more symmetrical position ("Because I worry about you when you're out. Why, what's your proposal?"). What's decided should make sense to teenagers, even if they don't like it.

Joy and pride are the mature, self-confident parents' responses to their children's growth and development. While these important responses are comparatively silent, especially when deep-rooted and genuine, they are nevertheless pervasive. They are an expression of the parents' relative self-sufficiency as individuals and relative cohesiveness as a couple. The lucky adolescent is the beneficiary of his or her parents' emotional maturity and marital stability. Parents who are secure as individuals and united as a team will welcome their children's adolescence, despite its anxieties and conflicts, as a new chapter in their lives.

How does a child who is the recipient of these wholesome responses experience adolescence? It's still a time of turmoil and confusion. But the child who's anchored in an accepting family faces this turmoil with a sounding board, a testing place, a home base. At the same time the adolescent is creating an individual identity, he or she also retains a sense of belonging—a family identity. A boy like Jason, on the verge of adulthood, is discovering what it means to be Jason, but he is still a Salazar.

❖

Families can err in either of two directions: by letting their children go too early and too easily, thus depriving them of support; or by holding on too tight, too long, and thus becoming a force against which to rebel. Clear boundaries give children room to explore, but provide contact for support and guidance.

Two guidelines to keep in mind are: (1) The limits of effective parental control end at the front doorstep. Since they can't enforce what their teenagers do away from home, parents ought not to squander their authority by trying. (2) While attempting to strike a balance between too much and too little control, parents should make every effort to minimize the extra stress they put on their children. Those children unlucky enough to be driven by ambitious, controlling parents find the perfect defiance in passive-aggressive nonperformance, and the perfect escape in drugs.

A pressured environment leads to pressure-releasing activities. For quiet, inward children like Heather, escape takes the form of passive, soothing pursuits—in her case, television, romance novels, and dreams, endless dreams. For lively, outgoing children like Jason, escape takes the form of drinking, partying, and staying out late.

What do kids do when they stay out so late? Most parents would love to know. If asked, teenagers usually say they're going over to so-and-so's house. Sometimes they do; sometimes they don't.

Sometimes a group of kids will get together to go to a specific event, such as a dance or a rock concert, but more often they simply arrange to meet and hang out at each other's houses or at the mall. Some kids cruise the malls, sample fast foods, and go to the movies. Others succumb to pressures and temptations to defy authority by shoplifting, taking drugs, and experimenting with sex. They make out in secluded corridors or in the parking lot. Many kids leave the mall and seek out places where they can be alone together. Relationships tend to be brief and nonbinding, one result of which is likely to be an increased number of sex partners.

There's so much variation among individual teenagers that it's hard to generalize about patterns of sexual behavior. Later we'll see, in the case of Jason, how some teenagers pair off to experiment with sex. Kids take drugs for the same reasons they engage in sex play (and sex serious)—to defy authority, to be cool, to satisfy their curiosity, and because it feels good.

The exposure to drugs can start at any age, but the pressure to experiment often begins as early as junior high school. If a kid doesn't feel good about himself, he can find someone to sell him something that will make him feel better, at least for a while. The main reason teenagers take drugs is to transcend their experience—to escape from stress and frustration and to liberate their imaginations. The motivation for getting high plays a part in determining the drug of choice, which can be anything from beer to cocaine. Often, however, the particular drug a kid plays around with is an accident of circumstances.

Most kids sample beer, some with their parents' approval. (Many parents believe that "If you can't lick 'em, join 'em.") Kids like Jason who are angry, unhappy, and unsupervised engage in orgies of beer consumption, regularly drinking themselves into a stupor, trying to prove their manliness. (Teenage girls drink beer, too, but they're less likely to do so to show off.) In warm weather, they sneak off into the woods; in cold weather, they find a house with no adults at home or, if there's a college nearby, a dormitory. They have "continuous keg parties"—opening the spigot of a keg of beer and guzzling nonstop until it's empty. Jason used to go to a college dormitory and sit around drinking beer and watching television with a group of alienated undergraduates, playing "Beer of Fortune": watching Vanna White turn letters while the spinning wheel determined who was the next person to have to chug down a quart of beer. Another variation, popular among high school kids, is "Love Boot" (meaning barf). The kids watch reruns of "The Love Boat," and each one is assigned a character. Every time that character appears on screen, the kid has to chug down a beer. The object is to be the last one to throw up. Cute, eh?

Despite well-publicized antidrug campaigns ("Just Say No," "D.A.R.E."), drugs still retain their appeal as a means of flaunting convention and authority. Even though today's kids are more aware of the dangers of drugs, they still think of themselves as somehow magically immune from harm. Taking drugs is wonderfully counterphobic.

Psychedelics, which fell out of favor in the seventies, are once again becoming popular. Kids use psychedelics because, if you stop to think about it, inducing visual hallucinations with drugs comes naturally to a group weaned on MTV and the bright lights and electronic bleating of video games. They take trips. Why "trips"? Because they're a means of transcending time and space, escaping rules and pressure. Some of this pressure is external (academic and social), some of it internal (self-doubt, questioning of authority, identity confusion, and the great soul-searching of adolescence).

## "How Worried Should I Be about My Teenager?"

The time to worry is when psychological impairment becomes persistent, predictable, and pervasive. Transient adjustment reactions rarely last more than three months. Usually the distress is obvious. There is decreased pleasure in all areas, antagonistic relationships with parents, poor grades in school, loneliness, and isolation. A child is in trouble if he or she doesn't have at least one close friend outside the family. Another ominous sign is the child who no longer has any plans or dreams for the future. Physical symptoms—such as persistent headaches, stomachaches, or trouble sleeping—are cause for alarm if they become relatively constant. Sometimes things look fine on the outside, but the child's inner experience is bleak. These children can't seem to get relief from persistent stress, or they rely on external means of feeling better. Abuse of food, alcohol, tobacco, drugs, or caffeine becomes a necessary crutch.

In the nineties, self-injury joined bulimia and anorexia as a prevalent, silent, and serious sign of adolescent unhappiness. It's hard at first to understand, but apparently cutting or burning their arms and legs helps some troubled teens cauterize the pain they feel inside. Afterward, tending to their own wounds, which many self-injurers do solicitously, is the final part of the experience. Thus the self-injurer assumes all the roles of an abusive relationship: the abuser, the victim, and the comforting presence who soothes her afterward.

Some parents go too far in erecting a boundary between themselves and their teenage children. Many of them are preoccupied with their own midlife worries. Parents who have, or take, too little time to supervise rely on "communication" with their children to keep them informed. Some children learn that as long as you tell your parents what they want to hear, you can do anything you want.

❖

Mrs. Seguin brought her fifteen-year-old son to see me after he'd been put on probation by the county's family court judge. Rick had been brought to court by the school for chronic truancy. This problem falls in the general category of misbehavior and can usually be resolved by monitoring and enforcing the child's school attendance. (Failure to do so may be a sign of disengagement.) The first place to look for problems is—at the triangular level—the parents' relationship with the school; just as two parents must work together to effectively enforce discipline, so must parents coordinate their efforts with the school, in the case of school problems, or with any other agency that may be involved with their children. The second place to look for trouble is in the boundary between parents and child. If the boundary is rigid, the parents may not know what their child is doing; if the boundary is diffuse, the parents may not be strict enough to enforce the rules.

Mrs. Seguin was too busy to be in touch with the school. That was easy to remedy. She was also too busy to supervise and discipline her son. In principle, that too is easy to remedy, but I was appalled to learn how long Rick had been doing whatever he pleased.

It wasn't hard to discover the reasons for Mrs. Seguin's laxity. Her husband moved out when Rick was three. After that she started drinking. The drinking got so bad that she ended up in an alcoholic rehabilitation center. Once she got her drinking under control, Mrs. Seguin went to work and Rick went to nursery school. He was a good boy, independent and so eager to please that he needed little discipline. So that's what he got. Mrs. Seguin got into the habit of letting Rick look after himself. This worked fine until he became old enough to make decisions contrary to adult expectations. In Rick's case, that started early.

When he moved to the middle school in seventh grade, Rick had trouble adjusting to the changes, especially the additional homework. About the same time, Mrs. Seguin's husband stopped making child-support payments and she became depressed. Just as her son was starting to skip classes and stay out late, she was too despondent to respond effectively.

Rick's defiance started getting out of hand. He stayed out until all hours and skipped school more and more frequently. He failed one grade and then another. Finally, the school principal concluded that Rick was in trouble, and he decided to take action. By this time, unfortunately, the problems had become entrenched. How do you help an overworked and depressed mother start taking control of a fifteen-year-old boy who's been doing things his own way for three years?

The simplest solution—setting and enforcing rules—had by now become almost impossible. Recapturing control once you've lost it requires enormous power. If the child over whom you have lost authority over is a teenager, regaining control may be impossible without the intercession of outside agencies, including the police and courts. Even then it isn't easy. Mrs. Seguin never really succeeded in taking charge of Rick. Eventually, he dropped out of school and took a job. She maintained their relationship by recognizing that she couldn't stop him from quitting school, and so when he told her his plans, she accepted them. Her hope was that someday he might return to school Under the circumstances it was probably the best she could do. It was a shame that she hadn't taken action earlier.

❖

Wise parents establish rules for teenagers and expect them to obey. When a rule is established, it's best to state it explicitly and give a reason: "Please have the car back by 10:30 because I worry about you out driving later than that, and I want to get to sleep." Expect obedience, but tolerate grumbling. Obedience means accepting the family hierarchy that puts parents in charge; grumbling is just a way of expressing feelings. Don't overreact.

Parents should be advised to recognize the boundaries of what they can control. They can make and enforce rules about what their children do in the house, including when to come home at night, but they can't enforce rules about what goes on outside the house. So they shouldn't try. Setting rules they can't enforce only erodes what authority they have left.

Remember that teenagers have the right to negotiate the rules. Discipline should now be explained and guidelines worked out between parents and youngsters. When kids are six, the parent is the unquestioned boss; at ten, it's time to start explaining decisions; at thirteen, the rules should be negotiated, but the parent should retain the prerogative to have the last word. At eighteen, parents should be available to discuss rules and problems, but recognize that now the child has the last word about his or her behavior. Parents should be as flexible as they can. The biggest mistake parents make is transforming their teenagers' experimentation into a struggle against the family.

## The Terrible Teens

When parents think of teenagers as defiant, they make two mistakes: they confuse autonomous striving with stubbornness, and they overlook the dialectics of their interaction.

Most teenagers are strong-willed, not oppositional. They struggle to achieve independence and self-determination—and they struggle however hard it takes. How far they carry that struggle, how extreme their behavior gets, is determined largely by how tenaciously parents resist in an effort to retain control.

A boy who can't win control over how to arrange his bedroom may seek to express himself by wearing an earring or perhaps by spiking his hair. If he can't win that battle, he may escalate further (refusing to come home at night or physically fighting with his parents) or resort to sneaky defiance (secret drinking, shoplifting, drug-taking).

Unfortunately, many parents don't see both sides of this interaction. They see only the teenager's "unreasonable" behavior; what *they* do themselves is perfectly reasonable. This myopia starts early.

The young child's achievement of a capacity for volitional action leads directly to a new kind of relationship with adults. Infants can do little more than cry when they want something; toddlers can choose to touch that shiny object that happens to be Mommy's crystal bowl, and they can run away when Daddy says, "Come here." It's a wonderful game! The child wants to exercise autonomy; adults feel obliged to exercise constraint and teach rules of conduct. Thus begins a complicated and close connection between the psychological development of autonomy and the child's relations with adult authority.

In the first real flush of autonomy, at about two years, when the child has acquired a certain degree of muscular development (and therefore a greater range of volitional activity and control), adults may begin to describe the child as "willful," "stubborn," or "difficult." This is a one-sided description—the product of adult prejudice. Two-year-olds don't contest adult authority. They simply want to do what they want to do. This isn't negativism; it's determination.

As the child grows, volitional control is gradually extended. If the parents are sensitive to the child's rights, will, and capacity, this shift can take place smoothly and without special difficulties. But this developmental interaction presents various possibilities for interference with the child's exercise of autonomy.

The problem need not be blamed on parental stubbornness and stupidity. Rather, the problem of willfulness and control can be understood in the context of family dynamics. As a result of enmeshment, parent-child relations become an arena for a contest of wills. When the parents exert—or attempt to exert—coercive authority, the result may be anxious obedience, a readiness to submit or surrender, or a reflexive and angry resistance to authority.

This brings us back to the Salazars: Heather's submission and Jason's rebellion.

# 14

# THE SALAZARS' FAMILY THERAPY

We can now return to the story of the Salazars' family therapy, having seen how their attempts to resolve their difficulties were limited by linear perspectives. The Salazars were stuck like Br'er Rabbit to the tar baby because each of them played out their parts in an interlocking pattern of self-defeating behavior.

In the first session, we heard Sharon complain about Jason's defiance and his "addiction" to pornography. Considering the harshness of her attacks, we might be tempted to consider Sharon a bitch—a mean-spirited, domineering personality. No, Sharon was not a bitch—or a shrew, or any of those unkind epithets we unthinkingly apply to mothers trapped in a pattern of enmeshment and disengagement.

We've seen what happened to this trusting and vulnerable young woman over the years. I hope we've seen it in a way that doesn't shift the blame from one person to another. For all his faults, Stewart did the best he could. That doesn't mean he was blameless, or that he couldn't change; it means only that his behavior, like Sharon's, was understandable.

We have seen Sharon and Stewart's marriage become impoverished and devitalized. Now it seemed dead, or almost dead. Sadly, these two people, once so much in love, had become increasingly separated by their private griefs, many of them inflicted unthinkingly on each other.

Of course, I didn't know all this about the Salazar family at the time of our second session. I did know that they were hurting, and that they were uncomfortable about participating in family therapy. In this, they were no different from most people. Knowing this, I resolved to go slowly, to let them know I understood their anxieties, and to avoid premature confrontations. Therapy, when it works, is a balancing act. The therapist offers empathy and understanding, accepting individual points of view and accommodating to the way the family is structured. Later, I would challenge the Salazars, saying, in effect, "What you're telling me isn't true; it's too narrow." I would challenge their definitions in order to expand their possibilities. Later.

The second session turned out to be much different from the first. The family pulled back from the open conflict of the first session. Sharon and Stewart struck a wordless bargain to avoid a repetition of their previous confrontation. This *conflict-avoidance* was a measure of the intensity of their anger *and* their skepticism about whether it could be resolved. Even Jason seemed to realize that it wasn't safe to be so antagonistic. (At home, family members can avoid conflict altogether or walk off when arguments heat up. In therapy the door is closed, at least for an hour.)

The second session confirmed the structural patterns I had seen in the first. Jason and his mother were enmeshed and his father was disengaged. It was easy to see.

Unfortunately, the easier a family's structure is to see, the harder it is to change. With the Salazars, I had already tried some of the usual moves to test their flexibility; I activated but did not dent their structural rigidities.

My plan was to separate Jason and his mother—to reinforce the boundary between them.

But I wouldn't be able to accomplish this in a vacuum. I would have to move Stewart closer to Jason, and closer to Sharon.

Heather was so quiet I wasn't sure how she fit in, but she seemed to be enmeshed with her mother.

I entered the third session resolved to block Sharon and Jason's unproductive quarreling and look for a pretext to encourage conversations between husband and wife, and father and son. I had my agenda; they had theirs.

❖

I could tell something was up as soon as they walked in. Jason was the first one into the room. He walked with none of his usual swagger and sat dejectedly in the chair nearest my desk. He avoided looking at his mother, but she glowered at him with such intensity that even though he was looking away, he was clearly preoccupied with her stare. Stewart, too, seemed upset. He sat next to his wife and tried to take her hand, but she jerked it away without bothering to look at him. Heather was the only one who showed no emotion. As usual, she was reading.

As soon as I shut the door and sat down, Sharon turned to Jason. "Do you want to tell the doctor what you've done now?"

Jason didn't answer. He just looked at his feet.

Sharon shifted to face me. "After we left here last time, I made him promise to get those filthy magazines out of the house—*and keep them out*. He assured me he would. I *thought* I could trust him. But yesterday afternoon I happened to be cleaning out his closet, and I found a whole box full of that smut. Now I don't know what to think. This boy is sick. And he's turning into a pathological liar. Would you allow a son of yours to bring that kind of filth into *your* house?

When I said nothing, she insisted, "Well, *would* you?"

"I don't know," I answered lamely.

"Well, *I* don't intend to tolerate it!" Then she turned back to Jason. "And that's not all. I told him that if he was going to live by his own rules he could just get out. Do you know what he did? He started yelling at me. He told me to stop picking on him, and he said that if I didn't shut my big mouth, I'd be sorry. This boy has no control over his temper. You have no idea what he's like.

"I went down to the kitchen, and he followed me, screaming, totally out of control. Then his father walked in and told Jason to quiet down and apologize. Jason told him to go to hell, and Stewart went crazy. He punched Jason right in the face and then the two of them started wrestling on the floor. I couldn't believe it. We're living in a mad house."

I tried to interrupt, but she wasn't about to be interrupted. Instead, she started in on Jason again. "You have *absolutely no respect* for me or your father. If you don't straighten out, and soon, you're going to find yourself out on the street."

Jason, his tough act beginning to wear thin, tried to ignore her. He gave me a look of exasperation and then swiveled around to face the window. Stewart was visibly pained, but he didn't seem to know what to do. Heather pretended to keep reading.

Here, played out in front of me, was the story of this family: the father's lack of participation, the daughter's withdrawal, the son's relatively normal experimentation, and the mother's fury. My immediate impulse was to take this woman on, to tell her not to be so hard on her son. But why was I feeling the pressure to do that?

Whenever a therapist feels the urge to assume an active function in a family—discipline the children, sympathize with a neglected partner, or counteract one parent's harshness—he or she should consider, who *should* be doing that? In this case, the answer was obvious: Stewart Salazar was unwilling to protect his son from his wife's attack because he didn't want her anger directed at him—he couldn't (wouldn't) risk the hot emotion necessary to close the distance between them.

Since I already knew he would have trouble facing his wife's fury, I decided to calm things down a bit. (Calming down a family crisis is simple—uncomplicated, not easy. Just give emotionally distraught family members a sympathetic ear and block the others from interrupting. Someone has to understand, not argue. What keeps the usual noisy conflict going is an escalating spiral of people repeating their own point of view, without bothering to listen to and acknowledge the others.) After they calmed down, I could get them to speak to each other. I would play a role in the family (mediator), but only temporarily.

I spent the next few minutes talking to Sharon, drawing her out and empathizing with her distress. It wasn't hard to do. The minute she was free of Jason's defiance and her sense of her husband's lack of sympathy, her anger began to melt. "He always" and "he never" changed to "I worry so much about him" and "I don't want anything to happen to him." The change was remarkable.

Now it was time to press Stewart to talk with his wife. He didn't share her harsh point of view about Jason's behavior, but by refusing to contest her opinion, he left the field to her. The point wasn't to get them to agree, but to close the distance between them—to break down the rigid boundary separating them, so they could become a team of parents and begin to rebuild their relationship as a couple.

"Your wife is worried about your son, and I don't think she feels she has your support." This was a weak-kneed invitation to dance. I would have to use more pressure to activate this reluctant partner. "As for you, I think you have a slightly different opinion about Jason's behavior, but you're afraid to express it. You seem to want to avoid argument at any cost. In this case, I'm afraid the cost is leaving a son without a father and leaving a wife without a husband. Unless you get more involved, I don't see anything changing in this family. In fact, I see things getting worse."

That did it. Stewart turned to his wife and began to tell her that she worried too much. "Jason's not really a bad boy. Why can't you give him a little more room to breathe?"

Sharon was stung by her husband's remarks, but her anger was tinged with sadness. "If I worry too much about the children, whose fault is that?" she said. "Who's never really been a parent, never really been a husband? I've had to do it all alone."

Back and forth they went, each one terribly vulnerable, each one showing it in a different way. Sharon covered a deep-seated feeling of helplessness with anger; Stewart was afraid of his anger and controlled it by pulling back. But now the pressure of my attention kept them at it. They talked about Jason, they talked about their relationship and, as they talked, the hurt came pouring out. He spoke of how much her criticism hurt him—if she wanted him to be more involved, why was she always finding fault with him? She spoke of her frustration at trying to get him to take an interest. "For years, I begged you to pay a little more attention to me, to give me some of your precious time. But no, you had to read this and write that. I think you spend so much time at work just to avoid me. I don't think you ever faced up to the fact that you're married."

I didn't want this to go too far in front of the children, but there is always the question of when to interrupt. To intervene right after Sharon had said Stewart was a lousy husband would punctuate the interaction on a negative note. I didn't want it to end that way.

So, I asked Sharon if she thought her husband heard her. "He heard," she said. "He's heard it before."

"I don't think so," I said. "I don't think he hears you when you come on that way. He clenches his ears the way some people clench their fists. I don't think he hears the hurt and loneliness—because I think you're afraid to let it show."

Sharon began to weep, softly at first, then harder. She didn't say anything. She didn't have to. Stewart sat there, looking helpless, touched but not knowing what to do. "It's sad the way you two have grown apart," I said. "I think she needs you." This time when Stewart took Sharon's hand she didn't pull away. It was time to stop.

For the next two sessions, I met with Sharon and Stewart alone. I asked about the history of their relationship. "What did you think when you first laid eyes on each other?" "When did you know you were in love?" "What did you hope marriage would be like?" These bittersweet questions opened up a lot of feeling.

It isn't just feelings, though, that such explorations can uncover. Asking about the history of a relationship gives people a chance to talk about their expectations in nonblaming ways. Instead of berating each other for not living up to unspoken desires, family members can begin to understand what each other expected, what they hoped for, and how they preferred to be seen before things turned sour.

Sharon and Stewart told me about their courtship, and the wedding; about the babies and the unbelievable strain; about how the babies grew into children, and how hard it was to keep up with them. They told me how their differences grew. Hopes and frustrations, disappointments—one damn thing after another. And the affair. The distance that ate away at their relationship, until they sometimes wondered if there was anything left. And now Jason.

They'd heard all this before, of course. Heard it? They lived it. But I was offering them something different from reviewing the facts, something different even from "talking things over." I was offering them the chance to be heard.

Therapists of all persuasions have tricks for teaching understanding, from training in "communication skills" to analytic interpretations. But the nag factor in all this teaching and preaching often outweighs the message. The best way to teach understanding is to show it.

For Sharon and Stewart, listening while I talked to the other one was like overhearing the conversation of strangers; the common element lay in being relieved of the obligation to respond. They each brought up a heartful of hurts and disappointments, feelings stored up over years of misunderstanding and neglect. Because they were talking to me instead of each other, these ancient griefs came out like appeals for understanding, not like attacks. As they heard each other's side, perhaps a little more clearly now, they began to see some of the reciprocity of their actions.

Sharon and Stewart were moving closer together, but I didn't want to do what so many therapists are tempted to do: uncover marital problems in a family with a difficult child, decide that the marriage is the *real* problem, and then devote all the time to the adults, assuming that the child's problems will automatically benefit from improvements in the parents' relationship.

Sharon and Stewart's problem wasn't just them as a couple. They had once managed being a couple reasonably well. Oh, they had problems, all right, but they might well have worked these out if they hadn't gotten sidetracked by a couple of little things—Jason and Heather. That transition from being a family of two to a family of three trips up a lot of people.

My sessions with Sharon and Stewart helped draw some of the heat away from mother and son, and put it back between husband and wife, where it belonged. With some of the heat off, Jason cooled down, some.

I knew I wanted to meet with Jason, but before that I played a gambit designed to put some distance between Sharon and Jason by moving Stewart into the space between them. I said that I thought Sharon had done more than her share of parenting (no argument) and that I thought she was tired. In fact, in my professional opinion (I love to say that), she was depressed. I paused to let the authoritative-sounding diagnosis sink in. It did. Sharon nodded; Stewart looked concerned.

"Jason *has* gotten out of control," I said (no need to lie about that), "but right now, I think Sharon needs a rest. Stewart, you need to assume more responsibility for the boy's discipline, and for that reason I want to meet with you and Jason for a couple of sessions to help you work on it."

I spent the next couple of sessions with father and son. Some of what we talked about was Jason's need to improve his behavior, some of it was just about the two of them, father and son, spending more time together. It's easier to work on a dormant relationship than an overheated one, and these two guys made quick progress toward getting closer.

It was fun seeing the two of them together, but I knew that I shouldn't do so for long. You can't pry an overinvolved parent away from a child without hooking him or her up somewhere else. Otherwise, he or she will spring back like a steel coil. I reconvened the whole family for a progress review, and was careful to downplay the improvement in Jason's behavior. One message I didn't want to give was that Stewart was doing a better job than Sharon. Then I said I wanted to have some sessions with Jason, "who's old enough to start taking some responsibility for his own actions."

I wanted to talk to Jason about the pornography—I assumed it was a harmless teenage thing, but I didn't know—and about drugs, about school, about girls, about a lot of things. By talking with him privately, I hoped to reinforce the boundary between him and his mother. Adolescent sex is a private experience, one that children shouldn't be expected to share with their parents.

But first of all I had to get him to talk. You don't just sit down with a teenager who thinks he's a bad-ass and say, "Okay, tell me all your problems."

❖

One way to form an alliance with recalcitrant adolescents is to offer them help getting something they want. That might be lenient treatment from a juvenile court judge or high school disciplinary board. But don't make this a one-way agreement. Tell the teenager, "You need to convince me that if I stick my neck out for you, you won't let me down."

Another way of joining with an adolescent's resistance is to work together to convince his or her parents that the teenager doesn't need any more therapy. Work with them to help them get their parents off their backs. I often tell these youngsters that there must be a good reason why they're angry—and that I'd like to hear their side of the story.

❖

At first Jason was stubbornly unresponsive. He showed up on time and suffered through the hour, but said little. I was, after all, an extension of his parents' authority (*he* certainly wasn't paying my fee), and he didn't want to expose himself. To show me his feelings would leave him open, and he didn't want to make himself any more vulnerable than he already felt. So I just waited, asking enough questions to keep him talking, not enough to turn our meetings into question-and-answer sessions.

Jason tested me by degrees, moving slowly from safe topics to less safe ones. He told me about school and some of the pressures there. He told me how he and his friends sneaked off to drink beer, and about the late nights when they got blasted. As he told me about "Beer of Fortune" and "Love Boot," he watched my eyes for signs of disapproval.

I did disapprove. I'm too old to think that kids drinking themselves into a stupor on a regular basis is harmless fun. But I tried not to show it. Instead of criticizing his excessive indulgence—which would have cast me in the role of the controlling, and therefore ignored, parent—I asked him more about his own experience, hoping to help him discover for himself the unhealthy consequences of his behavior. The closest I came to expressing my disapproval was asking him if some of his friends were still young enough to think that drinking made them hot stuff. It was a clumsy ploy, but I was lucky. Jason said, "Yeah, a lot of them do. I only drink to help me relax."

After a while, we got around to sex. We didn't exactly get around to it, I brought it up. Jason certainly wouldn't have. My asking signaled a shift in my stance, from purely receptive to probing. The easiest way to be a therapist is just to accept everything and always sympathize. This is a popular version of therapy: therapist as friend. It's an expensive friendship.

Jason told me that he had been sexually active for a long time. Recently he'd been seeing Kim, a girl ideally suited to aggravate his mother. Kim had been expelled from school for selling marijuana, and now she lived with grandparents who were unable to provide much supervision. Sharon had forbidden Jason from seeing Kim, and so the young lovers carried on in secret. Once or twice a week, Jason waited until his parents had gone to sleep and then climbed out his bedroom window, crawled across the roof, and dropped down to the ground. Then he got on his bicycle and pedaled the two miles to Kim's house, where he repeated the same procedure in reverse, climbing up to the roof, through the window, and into Kim's bedroom.

Tired of his everyday routine and full of hopeful expectations for pleasure and excitement, Jason planned a special weekend with Kim. Actually, it was Kim who suggested it. She was, despite her sex and being younger, the more daring of the two. She said, "Let's go away somewhere for the weekend and take a couple of hits of LSD." "Sure," Jason said. Though he had reservations, he kept them to himself.

Once he accepted the idea, it gave him a splendid chance to engage his imagination in a plot to outwit his mother. A week before Christmas, Jason mentioned casually to his mother that he might be going over to Kevin's house for the weekend after Christmas vacation.

When the eagerly awaited day finally came, Jason said, "Mom, I'm going over to Kevin's for the weekend, remember?"

"Do you have any homework?"

"Just a little chemistry; Kevin and I are going to work on that before we go to the movies."

"Have a good time."

Jason walked to Kevin's house and together they drove to meet Kim. Kevin took them out to the country and dropped them off near an abandoned barn he and Jason had discovered. It was a short walk, but because they had to wade through knee-high snow carrying armloads of food and blankets, it took several minutes. Once Jason forced open the door to the barn and they were inside, he felt a growing excitement. And a little scared.

They decided to eat first and then get high. So, they ate peanut butter and jelly sandwiches and Twinkies that Kim had brought, and then, while she smoked a joint, Jason ate half of one of the marijuana cookies his cousin had brought back from college. One thing he vowed he would never do was put smoke in his lungs— or a needle in his arm.

Being high was wonderful. He just lay back and thought about why people take drugs. It was simple, really: to feel happy and escape from worry. What's wrong with that?

Then each of them took a tab of LSD. Jason had tried it once before at a party. That time he'd been leery and had taken only half a tab. This time the effect was stronger. The kerosene lamp looked like a flickering tube of colored balloons, and the snow outside took on a kaleidoscopic array of shifting colors: blue-white, pink-white—the whole fucking world was gorgeous!

Jason began to think of himself as "Mad Max." When he told Kim, she said, "Ooh, I love Mel Gibson," and started kissing him. The rest of the weekend was like a wet dream.

Jason was an imaginative liar. Previously I'd had no reason to doubt his honesty. Now his stories were an undecipherable mix of truth and fiction. The hours on the phone talking to girls and his mother's nagging about it—that I believed. His trouble finding the nerve to ask "nice" girls to go out with him—that too I believed. But the number and extent of his conquests, and his minimizing his involvement with pornography, seemed, shall I say, unlikely.

When I asked him if he still hid erotic magazines in his room, he denied it emphatically. His self-righteous indignation gave him away. People lie with adamant denials. The truth is seldom invested with such heat. His lie, for surely that's what it was, put me in a spot. To challenge him directly would only provoke a stronger denial; what's more, it would set us at odds. He was quick to assign adults the role of jailor, and I didn't want the job. On the other hand, to act as though I wholeheartedly believed him would make me seem a fool, and it would begin an erosion of honesty between us. So I said, "Really? That's amazing," trying to walk a thin line between skepticism and distrust.

Jason responded to my almost imperceptible challenge by moving away from the subject. He changed topics, but in the process he came as close as he could to telling me that his sexual exploits were fantasy.

He told me about his fascination with science fiction. He spent hours reading fantastic and utopian visions of how things could be, losing himself in futuristic dreams. It was a good subject for us, because I knew nothing about science fiction. That allowed him to be the expert. He also taught me a little about rock and roll, explaining the differences between "heavy metal" and "speed metal" and "hard rock." Jason liked heavy metal thunder. He even liked some of the "older generation" musicians—the Grateful Dead and Jimi Hendrix. What mattered to Jason was that they were real.

Now that we'd reached this level of respect, I decided to explain to Jason the connection between his fights with his mother and his father's lack of involvement. I had mixed motives for teaching Jason about the family triangle. I wanted him to understand the hidden dynamic behind his war with his mother, but I would settle for his simply dropping the struggle as futile. If nothing else, I wanted to keep the peace in the family long enough for Jason to graduate from high school.

I explained how his mother fought with him as a stand-in for his father. I explained how his mother would continue every fight until she made him wrong and herself right. And I made him understand that by backing off, he would get more control and more freedom. Sometimes this meant avoiding her; but since that wasn't always possible, it also meant learning to say, "Yes, Mom, you're right."

Jason seemed to grasp the idea of the triangle. It made him feel less of an outcast. It made us coconspirators; together, we plotted to outwit his parents. And yet he couldn't seem to stop fighting with his mother. He would play it cool for a couple of days, and then he'd blow. His mother would tell him to get off the phone and he'd start yelling at her, calling her names, and refusing to back down. Stupid, stupid, stupid. I couldn't believe he was doing this. And then I thought, maybe he has to.

Why should anyone behave in a way so clearly calculated to antagonize his parents? Some of Jason's behavior seemed stupid, but surely it was purposeful, related somehow to enhancing his self-esteem. But how?

I didn't feel I should confront the irrationality of what he was doing. For some reason, the need to court antagonism fulfilled his expectations. His mother nagged at him and he yelled at her, provoking the inevitable blowup. It was pitifully predictable, like moths who fly at a bright light no matter how many of their fellows get burned in the process.

Jason was opposing me, too, although it took me a while to see it. He'd "forget" what we discussed and somehow "not get around" to apologizing. Things got worse at home, and I got mad.

He was doing with me what he did with everyone else—arousing antagonism—so he could play the only game he knew how to play. (Of course, *I* didn't deserve this. I was just trying to help—only manipulating him for his own good. Honest!)

Yes, I was angry, but I held my feelings in check. I tried to maintain my cool long enough to understand what he was feeling.

I pointed out that what he called "forgetting" must accomplish something indirectly that he couldn't do openly. I was thinking that he wouldn't let go of his fights with his mother. His response surprised me.

He was angry at *me*. He was responding to me not as I understood myself, but as he assumed I must be—someone who would only try to control him. "You're making *me* do everything. You're on her side!" His forgetting to apologize to his mother was a refusal to submit to my manipulations. Without words, he was saying to me, just as he said to his mother, *I will be manly toward you—the way I learned from my father.*

This was a turning point in our work together. Here was Jason's struggle for autonomy, not retold by his mother or even by himself, but right here between us.

Therapists love to attribute this kind of resistance to "transference," a wonderful concept that attributes conflict to unresolved feelings from the past—and modestly gives full credit to the patient. Jason was resisting me as though I were his mother. (Silly boy, I'm not your mother. I'm just acting like her.)

❖

Parents struggle with their teenagers to protect them from making mistakes and to preserve the parents' rights. Teenagers fight back to win the freedom to do what they want and what they think is right. The theme of this struggle is autonomy—which isn't the same thing as freedom. Autonomy means thinking for yourself, not acting without restraint.

❖

In the matter of wanting his freedom, the deeper truth is that Jason was divided against himself. He was at once attracted and frightened. He advanced on the world, he shrank from the world; he desired his liberty, he feared his liberty. It's a conflict within us all, and it's never resolved.

But Jason fought out the conflict with his parents, especially his mother. To her he assigned the role of speaking for his inhibitions and fears, and she readily took the part. It was a closed system. The mother must fight the son, and the son must fight not only his own fearful self, but the mother as well. No wonder they were on the ropes, those two, locked in pain and rage.

My sessions with Jason were cooling things off, draining some of his fury and providing him with an ally. Seeing a child alone can be a restructuring technique, solidifying the boundary between parents and child, and encouraging the child's exploration of the world outside the family. Or it can freeze the scapegoating process in place. Working with a child alone suggests that there is no need for his parents to change. Treating a child under these circumstances is like breaking a wild pony.

I was afraid the struggle for control was clouding the issue of differentiation. Differentiation—individuality—doesn't mean letting a child run wild, it means clarifying the separate identities of family members. I didn't want to help Jason win total freedom from his family any more than I wanted him to develop a false independence like his father. Stewart's apparent independence was a product of emotional distance. He could only think and act rationally when he was cut off from emotional contact. Up close, he became as fused as Jason. They *acted* in opposite ways—Stewart disengaged, Jason enmeshed—but underneath they had equal trouble thinking for themselves under the pressure of anxiety.

It was time to see the whole family again. I had two goals in mind: differentiation and boundary-making. The crucible for forging an independent identity is in one's relationship to one's parents. I wanted Jason to discover who he was and what he thought, in contrast to automatically opposing what his parents wanted. I also hoped to help Sharon and Stewart learn to set limits without undermining Jason's nascent sense of self. Parents shouldn't be afraid to take a stand, to tell teenagers, "This is what we believe, and this is what we want from you." Teenagers will accept and reject their parents' values selectively.

## Shifting Boundaries

Adolescence calls for a shift in the structural dynamics of the family. The boundary between parents and teens must be clear enough to allow the children freedom to experiment and room to grow toward independence. Adolescents should be allowed to move slightly away from the sibling unit and given increased autonomy and responsibility appropriate to their age. The underlying structure that supports the transition from parent–child to parent-young adult is a clear boundary.

```
      M      F                          M        F
   - - - - - - -    Becomes     - - - - - -|- - - - -
      Children                  Adolescent  |  Siblings
                                            |
```

One or both parents may resist changing in relationship to an adolescent child, because *this change is not made in isolation*. It requires a shift in the relationship between the parents. A parent like Sharon, whose partner is distant, may have trouble letting a teenage child grow up. And as we have seen, the disengaged parent may join in tacit coalition against the enmeshed parent.

Divorced couples have a particularly difficult time. The custodial parent may be more aware of the child's growing autonomy and need to experiment; the noncustodial parent may argue for stricter discipline because that's what always worked in the past—which is just where the noncustodial parent may be living. If the parents have remarried, the opinions of stepparents add to the complexity and intensity of conflicts.

Just as the enmeshed parent's struggle to let go is tied to the ability to take hold elsewhere, so too is the adolescent's boundary struggle really two struggles. Achieving autonomy inside the family is directly related to making contact outside the family.

The boundary between the generations must be clear enough to allow teenagers room to grow, but still open enough to maintain the dialogue between parent and child. Parents need to relax their control but not ignore their teenagers. Teenagers are still children. They need to be confirmed and supported. They need parents to listen to their troubles, their hopes and ambitions, and even some of their far-fetched plans. Kids come up with a lot of wild ideas in the process of trying on different identities. A child may express a certain preference not so much because of profound interest, but more as a way of testing whether his parents will tolerate any deviation from existing family values. If permission to deviate is given, the child's interest in any particular choice may be short-lived.

❖

In the heat of conflict with their children, parents are often so preoccupied with the issue at hand that they lose sight of the underlying theme of these discussions. What teenagers want, and need, is increased respect. Unfortunately, as long as parents insist on winning all the arguments, kids get no respect. In response, they either escalate the struggle, like Jason; go underground; or give up, like Heather.

Some parents are afraid that letting their children be right makes them wrong, afraid that letting their children win means they lose. In fact, just the opposite is true.

It isn't just what family members do that shapes their lives but also the constructions they put on each other's actions. As narrative therapists have taught us, the truth of experience isn't discovered, it's created. The antagonistic relationship that develops between parents and their adolescent offspring is fueled by *totalizing views* of each other. Both sides reduce each other to one set of frustrating responses. Thus parents who view their teenage children as "irresponsible"—as though this were the sum total of their being—are likely to be seen in return as "not really caring." Similarly, parents who totalize their children as "lazy," may be seen as "pushy and demanding." These closed narratives reduce and polarize the individuals involved.

What can a therapist do to break the grip of these totalizing views? Inquire about "exceptions"—those not-always-noticed times when "irresponsible" children volunteered to cook dinner or wrote a really thoughtful term paper. Times when "not really caring" parents drove the kids home from a concert or stayed up late to help them with their homework.

The cybernetic metaphor teaches us to see family members trapped in dysfunctional feedback loops—acting and reacting to each other in unhelpful ways. The narrative metaphor teaches us to look not only at how family members behave in relationship to each other but also at how they story their exchanges. It's their stories (being "irresponsible," being "picked on") that affect not only what they notice (lateness, scolding) but also how they interpret what they notice. As long as they focus on their children's misbehavior, parents will be concerned mainly with criticizing and controlling them. As long as they think of their parents primarily as hassling them, youngsters are likely to remain reactive and rebellious. Family members' responses to each other become invitations to do more of the same and support further hardening of problem stories.

As long as both sides of the generation gap remain fixed on polarized and critical views of each other, they may be too busy to think about their own desires and preferences. In unhappy families, people may be so busy *not* being what others want that they have no time to figure out how to be themselves.

❖

One Thursday, two days before our Saturday session, Stewart had a particularly tough day at the office. One of his weakest students was defending her doctoral dissertation, and Stewart had to endure the embarrassment of championing mediocrity in front of his colleagues and the chairman. After it was all over, he looked forward to going home.

What did he find when he got home? No dinner was on the stove. A note on the counter informed him that Heather was having dinner at Maria's house and Sharon was at a town council meeting. And Jason? Jason was sprawled out on the couch watching MTV, the remains of a TV dinner lying on the rug at his feet. He hadn't fed the cat, emptied the garbage, or started on his homework. Stewart just stood there, surveying the room, too tired to protest.

Jason could feel his father's eyes on him. He didn't turn around. Jason would like to have talked to his dad, but he didn't want to hear a lot of nagging about the mess in the room. Stewart wondered what was going on in Jason's life. But the father didn't ask, and the son didn't answer. Stewart just stood there, nursing his private burden of grief—another moment of self-pity to add to his collection.

## All Together Again, and Out

The Salazars still had unresolved problems, and I was tempted to drift into an extended and indefinite therapeutic relationship with them. Sharon was emotionally hungry? I would nourish her with understanding. Stewart was isolated from the family? I would help him stand up to Sharon's criticism and help him see past her complaints to her loneliness. I would lend him strength and help the two of them get closer. I would promote clear and open communication between the couple. Heather was shy and moody? I would reassure and encourage her. Jason prolonged the fight with his mother to avoid growing into young manhood? I would support him in developing his own interests and competence. Unlike Stewart, I would be available to him. Unlike Sharon, I would let him come to me when he wanted to talk. I would be their hero, offering them a magically protective relationship. They could adopt me; that way I'd always be around to help resolve differences, soothe hurt feelings, and make everything okay. (If you're going to argue against a particular position, you might as well make it seem ridiculous, right?)

Despite my broadside at the therapist as Pygmalion, therapists often become just that. With a therapist around to translate between generations, calm things down, settle arguments, and handle each crisis as it arises, who needs to change?

Although there was much that could be done in the Salazar family, I felt that my job was to help them get past the point at which they were stuck. They needed not just to resolve the immediate crisis, but also to readjust the rigid boundaries that had led to the problems with Jason. However, once I'd helped them achieve a more functional family structure, and taught them a little about the need for altering boundaries so that the family could grow with the children, I would shift the responsibility back where it belonged—to the family. I would get out, so they could get on with it.

I had begun the process of boundary-making that would demarcate the parents from the son, putting their emotional energy back between the two of them and freeing the boy to grow up. What remained was to solidify these changes and tie up a few loose ends.

One of the things I hoped to accomplish before terminating with the Salazars was getting Heather to open up. I still wasn't sure whether she was depressed or just shy. It might seem reasonable for me to see her alone for a few sessions to get to know her better and to assess whether her moodiness was a sign of serious depression. Although I had seen Jason separately, to reinforce his independence and to separate him from his mother, I didn't wish to pull Heather out of the family.

Two good reasons for seeing children individually are unmanageable arguments and unsharable secrets. Otherwise it's best to help parents deal with their own children. I wanted to see how Heather's parents dealt with the idea that their good girl might be unhappy and need them more, and I wanted to see if I could bring the siblings closer together.

Heather didn't want to be dragged in as part of the problem. She was biding her time until she could get out of this family, with all its messy conflict. If she could become more of an ally to Jason, their bond might give her strength in the adolescent world, at the same time it might help Jason let go of the fight with his mother. I didn't try to force them into an alliance—it's hard to force anyone over twelve into anything—but I did try to get them to talk together.

The hardest thing for Heather was telling her brother how angry she was at him for causing so much trouble. But she would have to get that off her chest before she could get in touch with any sympathetic feelings. When she denied that she was angry, I said, "I don't believe it." I was leaving her with two difficult alternatives: own up to her angry feelings at her brother and risk an argument, or stand up to me. She chose a middle course, saying, "Well, it's true," but without force or conviction.

It was then that I suggested to her parents that she was depressed, offering the evidence of her moodiness, her constant reading, and her refusal to engage in normal arguments. I was trying to put the ball in their court. They tried to throw it back. "What do you mean? She's doing well in school" (Stewart). "She seems happy . . . she never complains" (Sharon).

"Well, I don't know," I said. "Why don't you talk to her."

Not surprisingly, Sharon began. "What is this, honey? You heard what the doctor said. Are you unhappy?"

Heather, mortified by self-consciousness, mumbled something that sounded like "I'm okay. Leave me alone."

Before Sharon went any further, I took advantage of the moment to try a strategic ploy. "I know that you two (indicating Sharon and Heather) are pretty close. What worries me is that she's too depressed to talk to anyone else—her father, for example. When a kid gets depressed, she can fool her mother, but she probably can't express herself openly to anyone else."

All three of them set out to prove me wrong. Stewart pressed his daughter to talk about what was going on in her life. Heather tried hard to put her feelings into words, and Sharon stayed out of it.

Father and daughter talked for almost ten minutes, proving that it's easier to open a dormant relationship than to calm a stormy one. In the process of their conversation, I learned—we all learned—a lot about what was going on inside this quiet child.

Heather talked about how she hated her parents always fighting with Jason. She talked about how no one at school liked her, and she didn't blame them. And she went on to describe a rather obsessive dissatisfaction with herself. Nothing was right—not her looks or her personality; she was no good at sports; and she wasn't even true to her principles. As to why she ate so little, she said eating was disgusting. They slaughtered animals just so people like her could eat.

I was relieved to conclude that although she was certainly unhappy, Heather wasn't clinically depressed. She was moody and spent too much time alone with her thoughts, but she didn't show the warning signs of depression: chronic depressed mood, distorted negative thinking, *anhedonia* (*nothing* gives any pleasure), and slowed mental and physical functioning. Heather was an unhappy, brooding child, but she hadn't lost her ability to concentrate and didn't show the classic red flags: hopelessness and desperation. There being no need for me to take over, I watched to see how her parents would respond.

Sharon and Stewart weighed in like tag-team wrestlers to bolster Heather's feelings. At least they were together on this one. They told her they loved her and they pointed out all her good qualities. To Heather, this only sounded like "Cheer up, you have no reason to be unhappy." For once, though, she told them what was on her mind. She told them that they didn't really care about her, all they thought about was Jason. Good for her, she was finally standing up for herself, even if it was only for her right to be unhappy.

I was pleased. Things were headed in the right direction. On impulse I decided to push Stewart a little closer to Heather by giving him a homework assignment. It seemed to me that this extremely private man might make more changes on his own than with everyone present.

I said it was too bad that Heather was growing up without really getting to know her father, who was, after all, the primary man in a young woman's life. "I wonder," I said, hoping to pique his interest, "if you'd be willing to try a little experiment?" (*The Devil's Pact*: first get the commitment, then explain the details.)

"Sure, why not. I'm game."

I suggested he spend some time sharpening his writer's understanding of adolescent girls. He should talk further with Heather about what she liked about her life and what she wished were different. Then, I wanted him to write a short story about a shy teenage girl, based loosely on Heather. ("Loosely" because I wanted Stewart to engage his empathy for what a girl like Heather might be going through, and I felt that if I encouraged him to fictionalize the story, he would feel less compelled to gloss over the girl's unhappiness.)

When the family arrived for their session the following Saturday morning, Stewart said nothing about his story. In fact, he had talked with Heather on several occasions during the week, and had indeed written a short story about a teenage girl—a shy girl, something like Heather. He hadn't said anything because he was a little embarrassed. "Would you read it?" I asked him.

Stewart's story, "Sketches of Theresa," was remarkable, much of it obviously about Heather, some of it embellished but still pretty close to the mark.

"Theresa was a shy girl, so quiet on the outside that no one realized how sensitive she was. Her mind was vigorous, straightforward, and brave. Her spirit longed for adventure. Her body was on the verge of deep feeling. But she was afraid.

"Like most girls, Theresa was closer to her mother than to her father. She shared a lot with her mother, but there was much that she couldn't share. (At this, Heather flushed.) When she became a woman (Stewart's pretty way of describing menarche), she became increasingly self-absorbed. At first this was reflected in a growing preoccupation with her appearance. Theresa inspected her body, feature by feature, spending hour after hour in front of a full-length mirror, trying on everything in her closet. (Heather's face turned bright red.) She had lots of clothes, but none of them were just right. If only she had something new, something special, maybe that would give her the panache she wanted. Sometimes she even practiced smiling. The mirror smiled back, but it wasn't quite right. Gradually, she began to lose interest in her looks, and started wondering instead, *Who am I? What am I going to do?*

"Theresa wanted more than anything to be popular. She saw other girls flirting, obviously working at it, but she was embarrassed to follow their example. So she inhibited herself, holding back the one thing that might have made her popular, her natural friendly self. She cultivated an interesting persona but kept to herself. Her mother tried to help, taking Theresa shopping for new clothes, giving her tips on being friendly—how to let a boy know you're interested. But a mother doesn't have the power to make her children popular (Sharon shot Stewart a look, but she didn't say anything).

"Alone in her room, clouds of longing descended on Theresa, just as when a plane escapes the noisy lower world into the pure cloud bank of the silent altitudes. (Jason made a face at this flowery bit. I liked it.) Theresa wished for so much, especially the unattainable: flawless skin, to grow up overnight, to have more friends. Above all, she longed to be loved. Her longing for love was personified by a series of passing fancies: movie stars—"Yeah," Jason chimed in, "E.T. and the Aliens."

"Shut up!" Heather answered. Stewart went on: "movie stars, older boys, sometimes even young teachers who seemed kind."

That was all. The story ended inconclusively.

When Stewart finished, no one spoke a word. After a long silence, I asked, "How does it turn out for Theresa?"

"I don't know," Stewart said, his eyes full of tears.

Heather started to speak and then changed her mind. Instead, she came over to her father and put her arms around him. "I love you, Daddy." Stewart held her for a long minute.

Before anyone could break the spell, I announced that the session was over. But as they were leaving, I said one more thing. "Sharon, you've done a good job. Stewart is learning what it means to be a loving parent."

Next session, Sharon was back to business as usual with Jason. She'd gotten an unusually high phone bill, and when she checked into it, she found that someone had place three calls to one of those dial-a-porn numbers. "I didn't recognize the number—somewhere in California—so I called and got a recorded message of some woman talking about all the filthy things she wanted to do to me. Those idiots don't even bother to check to see who's calling."

Fine. I wanted one more chance to strengthen the boundary between Jason and his mother, while at the same time breaking down the one that kept Stewart on the periphery. I would have liked an easier issue, but you take what they give you. As far as Sharon was concerned, this business about the pornography was still serious, and still unfinished.

"This sounds serious," I said. "What do you two plan to do about it?"

Sharon turned to Jason. "Why do you do this to me? Why do you hate me so much?"

To my surprise, Stewart answered her. "Sharon, this is something most boys Jason's age go through. When I was his age, I used to sneak looks at the underwear ads in the Sears catalogue. Jason's going through the great sexual awakening. When you're that age, all you think about is sex."

If these two had been more equally matched, I'd have stayed out of it; but they weren't, and I didn't. "I think you're *both* right. The problem *is* serious (Sharon relaxed noticeably). But the problem isn't just pornography. Jason's problem is that he doesn't have enough of a social life to begin to channel these sexual feelings the way he'd like to.

"Stewart, can you say a little about how you felt about dating when you were Jason's age, and what your parents did that was helpful, and what they could have done to be more helpful."

Stewart described his shyness at Jason's age, his longing to ask girls out, and his fear of getting turned down. I added that I thought Jason's problem with pornography was circular. He was ashamed of himself after he looked at that stuff, but he soothed his shame by doing it more. "I think this boy needs you two. He needs you to help him feel better about himself, and he needs you to support his socializing any way you can."

This was too much for Sharon. "Why should I have to praise him? Nobody pats me on the head for taking care of this family."

I explained how I thought the family was trapped in an unhappy pattern. Acting badly gets noticed, acting positively (here, I looked at Heather) gets ignored. Finally, I said (pushing my luck), "If you're hurt because nobody shows any appreciation for all that you do, wouldn't it be better to say that to Stewart rather than passing on the same treatment to the kids?"

That I was able to be so direct with them was a sign that they'd become much more open. In the few sessions that remained, I said less and less, pleased that the family was now handling their own problems with minimal input from me. Stewart and Sharon talked increasingly together about how to respond to the kids, and although Stewart generally went along with Sharon, he'd occasionally disagree. I helped them work out a little gimmick for renegotiating family rules to accommodate to the children's increasing need for independence. I suggested that they let the kids write down what they thought the rule for a particular situation should be, and then discuss the policy between themselves before getting back to them. It turned out that Jason and Heather were (usually) remarkably reasonable in their requests, and the structured talking-it-over sessions helped ensure Stewart's participation. My aim was to undercut parental overreaction without undermining parental authority.

The most remarkable changes occurred in Heather. I'll take all the credit for that. The fact that she was growing up was just a coincidence.

Sharon took the lead, using her bond with Heather to encourage Heather to get out of the house. The first thing she did was enroll the two of them in an aerobic dancing class. Then she concentrated on helping Heather find things to do with her friends on the weekend. At first, much of the impetus for this change came from Sharon, but after a while Heather became a self-starter, going to movies and basketball games and shopping with her friends.

Heather's first open arguments with her mother came over what to wear to school. Miniskirts were coming back in style and Heather wanted to wear them to school. "Not in this house, young lady! You're not going off to school looking like a little tramp as long as I'm your mother." I expected Heather to wilt, but she didn't. "Oh, Mom, don't be such a drip, all the girls wear them." Heather's fear of breaking the adolescent dress code was apparently stronger than her fear of standing up to her mother. Eventually, they compromised. Heather was allowed to wear the most conservative of her minis to school; the others were to be reserved for parties.

❖

Things were going along nicely. How would I know when my job was finished? Most therapists look for certain changes to let them know their work is done. I look for the changes but take my cue from the family. When things are going well at home, therapy sessions become boring. There isn't much to talk about. In short, families outgrow their need for a therapist. That's what happened with the Salazars. After three weeks in a row of desultory discussions of who was doing what—more like progress reports than problems—I suggested that maybe they had better things to do with their Saturday mornings and didn't need me any more.

Nobody said anything for a minute. They had gotten to depend on these sessions, each one of them for different reasons. Then Sharon said, "Well, if that's what you think."

I asked her what she thought. She thought things were going better, but then added, "I suppose we can always call if things get worse."

I said that I didn't think things would get worse, that Jason had outgrown his need to provoke his parents, that Stewart could continue to be more involved, and that Heather would continue venturing more and more outside the family. I couldn't help adding, "Maybe that will be hard for you, Sharon, letting Heather grow up. Maybe you'll find some way to try to keep her young, so that you still have a child to take care of."

Sharon didn't think so. That was that.

# 15

## LETTING GO

It was 7:30 on a Thursday morning. I like to get to the office early on Thursdays, drink a cup of coffee, and read over my case notes before the clinic staff meeting. This morning, however, was three weeks before Christmas and I was looking through my address book, trying to decide who to send cards to. Most of the names in my book are friends and colleagues, but when I got to the *S*s I came across *Sharon and Stewart Salazar*, put there in case of emergency. *It's been three years!* I thought. *I wonder how they're doing.*

Being a therapist is a funny business. People come into your life and you get to know them about as well as one person ever can know another one; then one day they outgrow their need for you and drop out of sight. Some therapists become friendly with their patients after treatment, but I prefer to maintain a certain professional distance. You never know when a patient might need you again. So, for me, no news is good news. Still, it's sad to lose sight of so many people over the years.

I decided to sent the Salazars a Christmas card—better make that Season's Greetings. On impulse, I added a postscript, asking them to give me a call to let me know how they were doing.

A week later, Sharon called. Everybody was fine. Jason was now a sophomore in college and would be home for the holidays in two weeks. Heather was in her senior year of high school, about to be inducted into the National Honor Society. Stewart's book on F. Scott Fitzgerald was out and he was already working on another one. Sharon thought it was about Philip Roth. "And me? I'm fine. I still have my job at the university, and I spend a lot of time with my friends."

I was glad to hear that Jason had gotten into college. Everything else sounded good, too, but I was curious to learn more, so I asked Sharon if they would like to come in for a follow-up session. "It would just be a progress report," I said, "as much for my benefit as yours." There would be no charge. "Sure," she said, "we'd be glad to come."

Sharon and Stewart showed up alone. Neither of the kids had wanted to come, and their parents decided to respect their wishes. I was disappointed to miss seeing Jason and Heather, but I figured this might give the grown-ups a chance to speak more openly.

We chatted briefly about the snow and the parking and the holidays. Then Sharon told me that she'd taken over Jason's bedroom for a sewing room. "When he came home from college, he was shocked to find that I'd repainted his room and packed away his old toys and sports equipment in the attic. Where his stereo used to be, now sits my sewing machine. When he saw it, Jason said, 'What's that?' I said, 'It must not be a bear; if it was a bear it would bite you.' He didn't think that was funny. Same old Jason."

Same old Jason, but this seemed like a different Sharon—calmer, more independent. Not only had she cleaned up The Shrine of Disorder, she'd even replaced some of the sacred relics. It seemed like a pretty clear sign that she was getting on with her life.

I wondered how they'd gotten from that turbulent time in their lives, when I'd seen them, to this more peaceful, apparently stable plateau. "What happened after you stopped seeing me? Jason was still in his junior year of high school, right?"

Jason settled down quite a bit after the family therapy sessions. He no longer seemed to go out of his way to defy his parents.

"That's good," I said. "You two must have been doing something right."

"I don't know," Sharon answered. "I think the change was mostly Jason. He was growing up, starting to realize that we weren't the enemy, and he started thinking more about his future. I don't think we did much different; the change was really his doing. In fact, I'd kind of given up on him. If he wanted to make a mess of his life, let him. But he surprised me by starting to straighten out."

"I think Sharon's right," Stewart said. "Things got better at home, but it wasn't anything special we did. One thing, though, was that I tried to spend a little more time at home that spring. So I was more aware of Jason's comings and goings, and I tried to be more involved in checking up on him."

"Yes, he did," Sharon agreed. "That is one thing; Stewart was around more, and when Jason did try to fight us over something, it was as likely to be with Stewart as with me."

So, I thought. This sounded like a significant shift—Sharon let go and Stewart became more involved—but they didn't think of the improvement in Jason's behavior as particularly their doing. It was him. It was Jason who had caused the problems in the first place, and it was Jason who was responsible for the improvement. So much for insight.

❖

The summer between his junior and senior years, Jason got a job pumping gas. He grew up a lot that summer. Although he'd never in his life been very responsible, somehow he managed to get to his job every day. Sometimes he'd stay out pretty late, but he always got himself to work. "I could hardly believe it was the same kid," Sharon said. "One weekend toward the end of the summer, Jason had agreed to mow the lawn. I reminded him on Sunday morning, and he said to stop bugging him, he'd do it. But that weekend came and went and so did the next one; he still hadn't touched the lawn. I remember being really annoyed and I said, 'How come you're so conscientious at your job and yet you can't be responsible in your own house?' He said, 'Aw, Ma, that's different. Mr. Wintle's my adult boss, you're my child boss. It's different.' "

When he went back to school in the fall, Jason got serious about his grades. He decided that he wanted to go to college, and he knew he'd have to bring his average up to get in. Before that, Jason just seemed to be in school to hang around with other kids. That year he seemed like a different person.

At the same time that Jason started straightening out, Heather became a little less agreeable. There were moments when Sharon thought, *Oh no, am I going to go through the same crap all over again with this one?* But Heather's rebellion—if you can call it that—was different.

Jason used to attack his parents personally, berating them about something they did, telling them they were stupid, unfair, wrong. Most of his comments were too rude to take seriously. Heather was different. Her anger was cynical, less direct. She was a silent, disapproving witness. For example, she would watch as her mother burned the milk in the clam chowder, making Sharon feel incompetent. Or she'd glance wordlessly at her father hurrying to have a drink before dinner. She read her parents' intentions and their weaknesses with uncanny and troubling accuracy. Her disparaging looks made them feel self-conscious—it was another kind of punishment teenagers inflict on their parents. Sharon and Stewart began to feel as though they were living with Ralph Nader.

It was an interesting paradox. Jason was letting go of the struggle that glued him to his mother, while his sister was generating antagonism as a prelude to propelling herself out of the nest. Jason's job had been to distract his parents from their conflict with each other. It was a job he never really volunteered for. Nevertheless, he filled the bill nicely. The three of them had been locked in an emotional triangle for years; now one leg of the triangle was going off to college. It seemed for a while that Heather might be taking over Jason's role.

Heather started getting ornery like her brother, but her anger took the form of social consciousness, and her relationship with her parents never really got bad.

❖

A child's leaving home can be a momentous time for families. I wondered how Sharon and Stewart had handled Jason's leaving. "How did you feel when Jason went off to college?" I asked.

They both answered at once: "Fine." "Awful." This was a surprise. Sharon felt "fine," Stewart felt "awful."

It's a large moment when you move out of your parents' house, leave the town you grew up in, and sail away from your childhood. It's a large moment, but it doesn't always sink in. Jason was standing on the steps of his dormitory—on the brink of his future—but as far as his parents could tell, he lacked the sentimental turn of mind to think of it that way. To Sharon and Stewart, he seemed to be thinking neither of the past, all that he was leaving behind, nor even of the present, this moment of leave-taking. He was thinking only about the immediate future. Would his roommate smoke cigarettes? How hard was college, really? Would it be difficult to meet girls? This large moment meant little to him. To his parents, it was enormous.

Sharon had invested eighteen years in her children, but she'd been so overburdened that Jason's leaving was a relief. She had anticipated the loss and prepared for it. Helping him fill out applications and driving him around to look at colleges, she'd thought about Jason's growing up and growing away, and thus dealt with the loss by degrees. She still had Heather to take care of, but that was more of a pleasure than a burden. She was ready for a new chapter in her life. She was tired of being a mother.

Stewart had worried with Sharon about whether Jason would get his act together and get into college, but he hadn't thought much about Jason's leaving. After they'd installed Jason in his dormitory room, Stewart had wanted to stay for a while, maybe see some of the campus. But Jason seemed anxious for them to leave. He didn't want his parents hanging around.

Driving home, Stewart was flooded with unexpected feeling. He remembered his small son toddling in to take him by the hand to supper: "It's foody-time, Dad." Was anything ever as dear to him as those baby-talk expressions? Stewart assumed that Sharon must also be feeling sad. "Our baby is all grown up, isn't he?" Her answer surprised him: "Yes, thank God."

Stewart told Sharon how empty it made him feel that Jason was leaving home. Alien emotions were washing through him and, uncharacteristically, he wanted to talk about it. Sharon was amazed at this outpouring of feeling. *Why now?* she wondered.

After a while they lapsed into silence. It's hard to talk when you're not on the same wavelength. Stewart turned on the radio and fiddled with the dial. Billie Holiday came on and he turned up the volume. Listening to the sweet suffering in the singer's voice was like putting a hot cloth over a sunburn—the heat of the cloth drew the heat out of the flesh. They played "God Bless the Child," "Lady Sings the Blues," and "The Man I Love." That voice—that rough, throaty croon. It went right through him. All steely soft, warm and sad all at once. When she sang about seeing her man, in all those old familiar places, Stewart was much moved. In the darkness, his face burned and his eyes filled with tears. A few minutes later, Sharon fell asleep and Stewart turned down the radio. Alone with his thoughts, he resolved to get closer to Jason and to take advantage of his remaining time at home with Heather.

❖

With Jason away, the house seemed suddenly empty. Heather was still around, of course, but she always seemed to blend in. One of the forms that Sharon's urge to reclaim her space took was fixing up the place. She enlisted Stewart's help in re-arranging Jason's room and went around the house looking for ways to make it more livable.

When Stewart was straightening up the den, he moved a bookcase away from the wall and found a plastic safety stopper in the electrical outlet. Suddenly he remembered the chubby, pink little babies crawling around on the floor. How he would love to hold those babies again. Too bad he hadn't taken more advantage of his opportunities when he had them. Just then he heard a knock at the door.

"Dad?" It was Heather.

"Oh, hi. Come on in."

"Dad, can I borrow the car? Mom gave me some money to buy clothes, but she said I'd have to ask you if I could take your car to the mall."

"Sure, honey, but sit down for a minute." Heather walked over to the stuffed chair in the corner and perched tentatively on the armrest. "How's it going?" Stewart asked.

"Fine, Dad. But really, I've got to go."

"Okay, sweetheart. Have a nice time." He watched her walk away, and then for some reason he couldn't have explained, he went to the window and stood looking out until the car pulled out of the driveway and disappeared up the street.

❖

Later that fall, Jason's college sent home a notice about Parents' Weekend. Stewart surprised Sharon by saying that he wanted to go. She hadn't expected that; he'd always been so negative about what he called "structured occasions." As it turned out, they couldn't go. Sharon's father had a heart attack, and Sharon and Stewart went down to see him in the hospital. There were a few anxious days, but Mr. Nathan proved to have strong recuperative powers and the crisis passed.

To make up for missing Parents' Weekend, Stewart decided that he would go by himself to visit Jason. It would be a chance to see the school and a chance to get to know his son.

When the day for Stewart's visit approached, he felt a boyish eagerness to return to college and to see Jason. It was the same kind of feeling he had once had on those rare occasions when he went fishing with his own father. Now Stewart felt the same sort of anxiousness about how to please his son as he'd felt about pleasing his father. Would Jason like to go into town for a fancy lunch? Would he mind if Stewart sat in on some classes with him?

Jason seemed happy to see his father. He showed Stewart around his dorm and then around campus. They chatted about school. Jason talked about how terrible the food was, how he had too much work and had to stay up all night to study for exams and write term papers—the usual freshman complaints. Stewart had heard the same gripes from his own students for years, but it felt good to be talking this openly with Jason. Jason seemed happy to be with his dad and to have his attention, but he didn't seem eager to introduce his father to his friends. It was as though he didn't want his two worlds to mix.

When Stewart suggested going into town to have a drink before dinner, Jason readily agreed. It was a recognition of his adult status that he was happy to accept. They went to the hotel where Stewart was spending the night, and after making reservations for dinner, father and son went into the bar—man to man.

Jason chatted idly about what he was doing and then switched subjects to talk about the football team. They were having a good season and they had a chance to win the conference title. Stewart felt put off. He wanted to hear more about what Jason was doing. He wanted to know about his social life, what courses he liked, what plans he had for the future. He also hoped that Jason would want to know what was going on in Stewart's life. No such luck.

Each time Stewart tried to turn the conversation to more personal subjects, Jason grew restless. Stewart made a few jokes—his most comfortable approach to affection—but that didn't seem to help either. Finally, Stewart said that he was proud of Jason and that he hoped the two of them could become friends. Jason said, "Sure, I'd like that too," but he seemed more embarrassed than pleased.

Stewart gave up trying to have a meaningful conversation and accepted Jason's wish to keep things light. Stewart decided that staying overnight would be a mistake, so he told Jason that he should be getting back home. He drove Jason back to his dorm and said good-night. He would have liked to hug his son, but he guessed that would only make Jason uncomfortable. So he contented himself with a handshake and set off for home.

The visit hadn't lived up to his expectations, but then, Stewart realized, maybe he was expecting too much. I was glad to hear that he hadn't gotten bitter.

❖

Jason's first two years at college followed a familiar form. The fall semester of his freshman year, everything was "terrible": too much work, lousy food, no social life. In November, Jason called home and said, "This place is weird. Maybe I'll transfer." By the second semester, he stopped talking about transferring. He joined the ski club, made some friends, and seemed to get used to studying. In his sophomore year, he moved out of the dormitory and shared a house with three other kids. By then he seemed much happier. He no longer called home as often, and when he did, he was as likely to be pleased about something as complaining.

The rest of the family changed too. The first semester Jason was away, Sharon and Stewart worried about his welfare. Would he be able to handle the studying? Would he make friends? Would he behave himself? Would he eat right? Gradually, they worried less. Jason seemed able to manage on his own.

Sharon commented that Stewart had more trouble adjusting to Jason's leaving than she did. "You were so melodramatic that night driving home after we first took him to school. Then, do you remember in the second year when we helped him move into that old house? The place was a mess. There was a bathtub sitting in the middle of the living room floor and an old blanket stuffed into the refrigerator. You thought it was such big deal. Everything worked out okay, though, didn't it?"

"I guess it did," Stewart agreed.

❖

Things had worked out. This wasn't exactly a fairy-tale ending, but maybe real life is more like living *reasonably* happily ever after.

Fathers and mothers may have trouble letting their children grow up—although as we've seen, the reasons have as much to do with the resistance of systems to change as with the private conflicts of individuals. Mothers don't necessarily suffer when the nest is emptied; in fact, many find it liberating. Today, when children leave home, it's often their fathers who feel the keenest loss. They realize how much they missed. It's a poignant discovery, because it's too late to do much about it.

Leaving home can be thought of as a personal accomplishment— a developmental milestone—but it's a transition for the whole family. Two of the family's subsystems—parent-child and husband-wife—are radically altered when the children leave home. Unless family members accommodate to the changes, the children may not make the successful transition to independent status.

## "It's the End of Our Family"

Leaving home is a reciprocal process of letting go and taking hold. To move out of childhood and into adulthood, a young person must make a start on love and work outside the family. Meanwhile, back at the ranch, boundaries must shift. Parenting isn't over when the children move out; it's different.

Some children have trouble leaving the nest. Some hang on, some arrange trouble—they can't face their own uncertainties, but if they get mad instead of sad, they can avoid the pain of separation. These abrupt and angry departures are often followed by setbacks and a return home. These kids have more growing up to do.

Away from home, unsupported by their families, some kids falter. When I worked at a college counseling center, I treated many students whose main problem seemed to be that they couldn't stand the pain of leaving home. Their symptoms varied; eating binges, drug abuse, and depression were common. Perhaps most common was "test anxiety." These students did well in classes but somehow got too nervous to pass their examinations. The standard treatment was to help the student learn to relax enough to survive the ordeal of exams. However, a significant number of students with "test anxiety" turned out not to *want* to pass their tests. The real problem was that they didn't want to be in school.

Some of the more confused students I treated dealt with their homesickness by entering religious cults. I remember one very disturbed young woman in particular. She couldn't stand being away from home, but couldn't admit this to herself. For a while she felt better as a member of "The Way Ministry." They conducted groups with titles like "Power for Abundant Living"—promising "the euphoric life." But this organization didn't really give her enough of the family feeling she wanted, so she responded to the voice of a mythical goddess who told her to smash her head against the radiator to drive out the devil (loneliness). She did so repeatedly and was admitted to the hospital. After she was treated medically and stabilized on medication, she was sent home—where she still is today.

Another young woman used to come to the infirmary every couple of weeks. She would fall down, break a leg, or somehow manage to get bruised enough to earn a bandage—the child's badge of hurt. Finally, she wound up in the counseling center. Not long afterward, she realized that she didn't want to be in college. She wanted to go home.

The most fascinating of these unhappy students was a young man whose first question to me was, "Do you believe in astral projection?" I said I didn't know much about it. He taught me. For three weeks, he explained various theories about how people can transport themselves through time and space. In the fourth week he told me how he came by all this interesting information. He himself was a frequent flyer. Two or three times a week he transported himself through time and space. Where did he go? Home, of course. Unfortunately, I made the mistake of questioning him too closely. I asked him if he imagined seeing the ground as he traveled, or did he just end up with a vision of his family? He answered politely— of course he saw the ground, he actually was traveling—but he must have sensed my skepticism, because I never saw him again.

Such cases, in which a person is unable to leave home, are exceptional. A more common occurrence is leaving in anger. This often leads to what Murray Bowen calls an *emotional cutoff*. The more intense the person's cutoff with the past, the more likely that person will re-create problems in future relationships. The person who runs away is as emotionally dependent as one who never leaves.

The hallmark of maturity is being able to leave home well. Ideally, this takes place when young adults manage to transform their relationships with their parents from parent-child to adult-adult. In practice, this means being independent— able to think for themselves, able to disagree without becoming emotionally reactive, able to agree without fear of losing their identity.

Less-than-ideal separations are a product of the young person's anxieties about leaving and the family's difficulty letting go. Many children who are worried and uncertain about their futures project their internal struggles onto their parents, and thus a war within themselves becomes a war between themselves and their parents. Some (like Heather) manufacture antagonism to push themselves out of the nest. Adolescent boys (like Jason) who make such a point of rejecting their mothers may be doing so in part to repudiate their maternal identification in order to shore up their masculinity. Pointing this out to parents can be extremely helpful in enabling them to see the developmental appropriateness of their teenagers' antagonism.

When the family needs a young person to remain involved at home, they prevent or undercut intimate relationships. The family boundary becomes impermeable—in Lyman Wynne's apt phrase, a *rubber fence*, which stretches, but not very far. A therapist can help by encouraging parents to express confidence in their children—"We trust your judgment"—and discouraging them from interfering too much.

# The Long Good-Bye

Saying good-bye is a big step, more difficult for many parents than they imagine. Thinking and talking about it ahead of time allows the loss to be absorbed in small doses. Psychoanalysts say that the ego deals best with potentially traumatic events by having time to prepare for them, so that defenses are in place. Family therapists say that the trauma of a child's leaving is an interpersonal event; share it.

When I left for college, each of my parents gave me one piece of parting advice. I remember what they said because neither of them was much given to making pronouncements. My mother, who is a very shy person, told me to be sure to make friends. My father, a workaholic, told me to remember that all work and no play is a good way to get ahead. I think I would rather have heard what they were feeling.

It is, of course, easier for parents to take pleasure in their children's autonomy if their own lives are full. A reciprocal rearrangement of boundaries is necessary: In order for the parents to be comfortable allowing their children greater distance, the parents must move closer to each other and to other interests outside the family. This boundary-making puts a certain amount of pressure on the marriage.

Even in a good marriage, the partners will feel a renewed strain and pressure when their children leave them alone together. This is a time of increased self-examination and an opportunity for redefining the marital relationship. Veteran partners may be better able to say what they want from each other than they were so many years ago when they were young and in love and afraid.

When families get stuck on the launching pad, therapists shouldn't assume that their job is to force the separation. If leaving home threatens a family's organization, the goal of therapy should be to facilitate a reorganization of the family to free the adolescent to leave. Try to get the parents to be supportive and encouraging, rather than overly helpful or critical.

# Boomerang Kids

If children are their parents' report cards, more and more parents are getting incompletes. According to the U.S. Bureau of the Census, 22 million young adults are now living under their parents' roof, an almost 50 percent increase since 1970. By the turn of the century more than half of all young adults aged twenty to twenty-four will be living at home.

There are a variety of reasons for this increasing return to the nest. The sexual revolution and consequent rising age of marriage means that, for many adult children, the most common rite of passage out of the family is postponed until their mid-twenties. Not only are marriages starting later, they are ending sooner. Divorce leaves many young adults emotionally battered and financially devastated. Where do you go when you're lonely and broke? For many young people, the answer is home. The economy has also contributed to the numbers of children who return to live with their parents. Education and housing costs are so high that many twenty-somethings can't afford not to live at home.

These are the generally accepted reasons for young adult children returning home. There may also be less tangible and less attractive reasons. Some families need children and can't function without them. Some parents are secretly relieved when they have children to worry about again. It keeps them from facing the emptiness in their own lives.

❖

One woman I know raised two daughters who were only marginally successful. They passed their courses in school, but just barely; they had friends, but not many. They left home, but always seemed to need money or to be driven somewhere. Both girls held a series of jobs, but none of them for very long. Their mother became depressed. She was, she felt, a failure as a parent.

Then one of the daughters took a turn for the worse. She lost her latest job, broke up with her boyfriend, and was evicted from her apartment owing three months rent. Her mother was upset, then angry. She felt sorry for her daughter's problems but didn't sympathize with her irresponsibility. Still, the girl needed a place to stay, so she moved back home. The mother's complaints didn't let up, but her depression did. Apparently, the daughter's failure and return home was necessary to stabilize the family.

In the midst of writing these cautionary remarks, I suddenly remembered something I'd completely forgotten. My brother, a successful business executive and family man whom I have always looked up to and admired, returned to live with our parents for a few months when he was in his mid-twenties. So, have I been too smug and too critical? Perhaps, but I remember that my brother returned home for a specific reason (he was changing jobs and going through a period with no income), for a specified period of time, and with a clear understanding between him and our parents about what was expected. I think the point is this: You can go home again—but you can't return to childhood.

## "Under Certain Conditions"

When adult children ask if they can move back home, parents would be well-advised to say, "Yes—under certain conditions." The ambiguity over who's in charge of what that occurs when the children reach adolescence is likely to be even greater when adult children return home. For this reason, it's important to negotiate agreements about what's expected, and to make these agreements as clear as possible.

Among the expectations that parents may want to spell out—before a child returns home—are: how much rent to expect, when and how it should be paid, what services will be expected of the child, and how transportation will be arranged. Perhaps the most important subject to discuss is how long the boomerang kid expects to stay. It isn't necessary to say exactly, but raising the issue makes it clear that the arrangement is limited.

Most kids are disappointed in themselves for having to return home. Having stumbled, they're apt to be acutely sensitive to any form of criticism, advice, or regulation. Above all, they need empathy. Leaving home isn't necessarily accomplished in one single step, at age eighteen. One-year-olds learning to walk stumble; two-year-olds learning to talk mispronounce words; young adults may accomplish their independence after one or two false starts.

One woman I know somehow managed to avoid getting embroiled in her adult children's problems—she listened but didn't become panicked or give unwanted advice. When I asked her how she managed this neat trick, she said, "Easy—I just pretend they're my friend's kids; that way I can be sympathetic without trying to control them."

Guilt makes it hard for some parents to refuse to pay the bills and clean up after their grown children. Parents are forever worrying that they didn't do enough. Perhaps if they'd been better parents, spent more time, given more, given less, the children would have become self-sufficient—would have turned out all right. Nuts! Few parents are perfect, but most do the best they can. Besides, suppose you weren't a perfect parent, will overindulging a twenty-three-year-old adolescent make up for that?

❖

When children return to the family after a false start into the world, we tend to think they were unable to take hold. Maybe they weren't ready to let go. Maybe they still need something from their parents.

A middle-aged patient of mine, a very wise woman who taught me a lot about being a parent under difficult circumstances, recently told the following story. Her daughter was a trial. Have you ever seen the test tracks of ruts and bumps they use to find out if cars and trucks can really take it? "Torture tests," they're called. This girl was a torture test for her parents. As a teenager she got into almost every kind of trouble you can imagine: drugs, promiscuous sex, stealing, vandalism, assault—you get the idea. She left home and returned several times between ages seventeen and twenty.

At times it seemed like the daughter would never grow up and straighten out, but when she got to be twenty-two she began to be relatively independent. She got and held her first job that lasted more than a month, she called home less often, and when she did call it wasn't always to present her parents with some crisis or other.

About six months into this stable period, the daughter called to tell her mother that she'd been fired from her job for telling the boss to go to hell. It was in the middle of the winter and she'd been planning for a long time to go to Florida for two weeks with her boyfriend. Should she find a new job and forget about the trip? Should she start a job and then tell them she was taking a vacation? Or should she just go, and then look for a job when she came back? Her mother said, "Honey, I can't tell you what to do. But it sounds like you really want to go. You've looked forward to this trip, and you've worked hard for it. So, if you go, you can get a job when you come back."

The daughter was thrilled. It was just what she wanted to hear. It's what she had always wanted to hear: Have fun, you deserve it.

Many parents are so busy telling their kids what they should do that they rarely hear what they so badly yearn to hear: that their parents love them, that they're proud of them, and that they should be good to themselves. If parents can arrange to tell their children that they're proud of them, that will help complete the relationship. "Complete" meaning make whole or consummate, not end it. It releases children from the frustrated longing that keeps them tied to their parents. Of course, some children make it hard to say these things. They screw up so often and create such headaches for their parents that it seems impossible to tell them that they love them and they're terrific. It's precisely the ones who screw up so much who probably need to hear this most.

❖

When other people make life difficult for us, we wish to God they'd change. If only they'd be a little more cooperative, we could relax and be nicer. If their children would straighten out and be responsible, then their parents could praise them. If our partners would be a little more considerate, then we'd be appreciative—and probably reciprocate. Stop waiting. Reach out.

# INDEX